Managing the Aftermath of Radical Corporate Change

Managing the Aftermath of Radical Corporate Change

Reengineering, Restructuring, and Reinvention

Eliezer Geisler

QUORUM BOOKS
Westport, Connecticut • London

658.406
G31m

Library of Congress Cataloging-in-Publication Data

Geisler, Eliezer, 1942–
    Managing the aftermath of radical corporate change :
reengineering, restructuring, and reinvention / Eliezer Geisler.
      p.   cm.
    Includes bibliographical references and index.
    ISBN 1–56720–150–4 (alk. paper)
    1. Organizational change. 2. Reengineering (Management)
  I. Title.
    HD58.8.G44   1997
  658.4′06—DC21   97–8852

British Library Cataloguing in Publication Data is available.

Copyright © 1997 by Eliezer Geisler

All rights resrved. No portion of this book may be
reproduced, by any process or technique, without the
express written consent of the publisher.

Library of Congress Catalog Card Number: 97–8852
ISBN: 1–56720–150–4

First published in 1997

Quorum Books, 88 Post Road West, Westport, CT 06881
An imprint of Greenwood Publishing Group, Inc.

Printed in the United States of America

∞™

The paper used in this book complies with the
Permanent Paper Standard issued by the National
Information Standards Organization (Z39.48–1984).

10 9 8 7 6 5 4 3 2 1

In loving memory of my mother, Mrs. Haya Geisler, who passed away during the preparation of this book, and is now forever in the company of angels.

CONTENTS

PREFACE

This book was born as a response to the need for a hands-on book on the aftermath of radical change for managers of reengineered corporations. My main purpose in writing this book is to help the manager to better understand the radical corporate changes that reengineering has caused. Since the early 1990s American work organizations have undergone radical transformations—under the umbrella of Business Process Reengineering—which have resulted in massive downsizing and a host of other side effects.

Much of what has been written recently by academics and consultants alike, has been directed at improving the reengineering intervention. I'll be using this term "intervention" throughout the book to describe the total phenomenon of reengineering. Some writers have looked at why certain aspects of reengineering have failed and others even offered some partial solution.

But the task has remained unaccomplished. American corporations have "downsized," "rightsized," redesigned their work processes, and improved dramatically their bottom lines in an economy that kept interest rates low and the stock market booming.

As I took a sabbatical from my academic position in early 1996 and went about my business of managerial consulting, I too often encountered large and midsize corporations in the period following the reengineering exercise or intervention. Many resembled a battlefield after a decisive battle. Some managers who still remained in their positions were increasing their productivity and resembled hyperactive beavers. Others just went about their work among the ruins of what used to be their departments, counting and mourning those terminated.

Everybody had questions, and almost nobody clearly understood why all this happened. More important, I was bombarded with questions such as: What now? How do we reorganize? lick the wounds? regroup?

The focus of this book is twofold: first, to describe and explain the consequences and aftermath of the reengineering intervention—the side effects on the organization and its managers; second, to advise executives at all levels of the organization of steps for cleaning up after the intervention and for restoring stability to the shattered organization.

With this book I wish to give the reader a valuable perspective on what happened in the organization and what to do in the aftermath of radical corporate change. The value added to the reader is a much better understanding of his or her corporate surroundings and possession of a workable framework to restore balance and promote stability.

This book is not a countermanifesto to reengineering. I support many of the premises and aims of Business Process Reengineering (BPR) as well as those of corporate transformation. My doctoral dissertation at Northwestern University was on organizational change and ways of monitoring it via the use of quantitative and archival measures of organizational transformations. I am familiar with the topic. My consulting experience has instilled in me aversion to stagnation and a keen support for change and improvement.

What this book does is assess the consequences and the damage from the BPR intervention and suggests ways and means to bring sanity back to the organization. This book is designed to help managers return their businesses to stability and balance *after* the intervention. This book brings value to the manager by helping in the design and execution of a program of recovery from the radical transformation. Everybody needs some help after they have been through a traumatic experience. This book offers a helping hand, sound advice, and a concise program.

Reestablishing balance, stability, and sanity is not, in itself, a condemnation of BPR and similar drastic corporate change. I'd rather consider this a clinical action that follows drastic intervention to cure a malignant situation. The intervention itself creates such powerful bad side effects and negative consequences that a comprehensive action is needed to restore balance and to counteract those side effects. The reader may consider this book as a prescription to restoring balance and reestablishing the course of a successful enterprise.

INTRODUCTION

In the past two hundred years business corporations have developed organizational structures and work processes that help them to achieve their business goals. In this century there has been a tremendous emphasis by academics and practitioners to gain better understanding of how these organizations function. In fact, business schools have academic departments devoted to the study of organizational behavior as a separate discipline.

What may be considered monumental progress has been gained in the past 50 years, in our incessant quest to make organizations more effective and work processes more productive and cost effective. The search for this mythical "holy grail" often has taken several forms and created fads—some enduring, many of a temporary nature.

FORMALISM AND BUREAUCRACY

The first of the original discoveries focused on the way complex organizations operate and what makes them productive, efficient, and resilient. Max Weber (1864-1920), a German socioeconomist, argued that organizations that have a very formal and rigid structure would be more resilient to changes in the environment and ultimately would also be more efficient.[1] His work gave impetus to studies of rationalism in building work organizations, and our improved understanding of how bureaucracies function in complex surroundings.[2] The roles that firms, rules, and hierarchical relations play in organizations were rapidly clarified.

TAYLORISM

The next target of our scholarly curiosity was work design and work processes. Early in this century, Frederick Taylor (1911) discovered "scientific management," which was the first manifesto for the design of business organizations.[3] He described it as a great revolution in the market attitudes of managers and employees alike. His ideas, which gave birth to modern industrial engineering, emphasized the enormous potential for increased productivity and work efficiency by the careful study of work processes and tasks. He called for the redesign of a task, based on minute steps and by making sure that work tasks were subject to specialization. Work can be redesigned to be more productive if analyzed and broken down to its component steps, and when done by specialized people assigned to a particular task in repetitive fashion.

HUMAN RELATIONS

Later in the century, after the Second World War, there was a countermovement that pointed to the "horrific" consequences from Weberism and Taylorism. Let's not be mistaken. The Taylor revolution was very successful. He implemented his ideas in steel mills and productivity skyrocketed. His revolution totally transformed manufacturing and gave birth to such sciences as ergonomics.

Yet the countermovement lamented the state of affairs that the scientific management legacy had generated, particularly its effects on people at work. Scholars and management consultants devoted their work to understanding the role that people play in the workplace. The discovery of this "human relations" movement was that work can be improved by improving work conditions for people and by understanding their motivation, drive, needs, and behavior. Among these scholars we have Douglas McGregor, Abraham Maslow, Warren Bennis, David McClelland, and scores of others. Their legacy was in catapulting the individual and the work group to a level of interest to management as having undeniable influence on the productivity and survival of the corporation.

TOTAL QUALITY MANAGEMENT

As competition became fierce and unrelenting, and American companies since the 1980s got a licking from European and Asian competitors, the knowledge accumulated in the management sciences became insufficient to explain the reversal in fortunes. American executives began looking for panaceas, longing for the one system or device which, when implemented in their company, would certainly contribute to dramatic improvements in competitive position and sustained performance.

Alas, the issue of quality emerged in the 1980s and was rapidly embraced by executives. Total Quality Management (TQM) became the hallmark of managerial thinking of the decade.[4] As with any program of change, TQM produced better products and promoted an obscure function in manufacturing (quality control) to a major executive dictum.

ZERO-BASED BUDGETING

Even before TQM, a system of revolutionary thinking was adopted by government agencies. In the 1970s the concept of zero-based budgeting (ZBB) gained acceptance and notoriety.[5] The idea behind this was that all programs must be reexamined from "scratch." Unless the program meets the needs of the agency and its objectives (perhaps reformulated), funding is eliminated. This meant that government programs had to be reassessed periodically, not only by their outputs, but also by their *raison d'etre*, if they still had a meaningful reason for continued funding. Unlike TQM, ZBB gained acceptance in corporate America, perhaps because it was originally designed for the government and other public entities, and had not been adapted to company usage. Yet ZBB's main theme of "starting anew" to evaluate the entire organization or activity had retained its hidden value. It reappeared under different forms in the management movements of the 1980s and 1990s.

REENGINEERING

This historical account may be interesting per se, but it is outlined here to clearly place the reengineering movement within the context of the continuous search for a better way to manage work organizations. Business Process Reengineering has not arisen from the vacuum of the original chaos to an orderly view of the world of work. BPR is the latest in a long series of proposed solutions and "revolutions" in business thinking. Michael Hammer, one of the creators of BPR, has written: "Business reengineering means putting aside much of the received wisdom of two hundred years of industrial management . . . . What matters in reengineering is how we want to organize work today, given the demands of today's markets and the power of today's technologies."[6]

The idea that we are at the brink of a new age—hence, in need of new organizational formats and solutions—has permeated the management literature in the late 1980s. In particular, there was the piercing and insistent view that advances in technologies, especially information and telecommunication technologies will soon revolutionize the way we manage work organizations. Not surprisingly, Peter Drucker brilliantly summarized these thoughts in an article in *Harvard Business Review* in January 1988.[7] He wrote some prophetic words as he explained the future impact of using modern information technology: "So far most computer users still use the new technology only to do faster what they have always done before, crunch conventional numbers. But as soon as a company takes the first tentative steps from data to information, its decision processes, management structure, and even the way its work gets done begin to be transformed. In fact, this is already happening, quite fast, in a number of companies throughout the world."[8]

Drucker foresaw the new business organization shifting from "command-and-control" to "information based," run by knowledge specialists. The management literature in the 1990s contains countless studies and models of such knowledge-based organizations. Moreover, there are many accounts of how organizations reinvented themselves.

David Kearns, chief executive officer (CEO) of Xerox, in 1992 told a breathtaking story of the reinvention of Xerox and its competitive stance against the Japanese.[9] Kearns explained:

Xerox pursued Total Quality Management because it was the right approach at the right time. And it paid dividends in spades. . . . But we may be missing the point. The key to American competitiveness is not to mimic others but to play to our own competitive strengths. . . . We believe we need to take a much broader view of organizational design. For we're convinced that architecture itself can be a remarkable source of competitive advantage.[10]

He also reiterated the importance of information technology in this redesign of his company.

Information technology enables companies to coordinate behavior without control through the hierarchy. It allows for autonomous units to be created that are linked together through information. It allows more "loon coupling" without running the risks of lost coordination and control. Hierarchy is load-bearing walls. Information technology is structured steel—a new way to frame a building.[11]

Two hundred years of knowledge accumulated in the managerial sciences cannot and should not be wiped out from decisions to restructure or reengineer. Nor should such knowledge be ignored in any program of organizational transformation. Like every other revolution, BPR claims to "obliterate" the past and build a brand new future. Yet reengineering is anchored in over a century of scholarly pursuit of better ways to organize and to manage work, workers, and work organizations.

This book is an ambitious attempt to give managers the tools to achieve three key objectives:

1. to clearly map the role that reengineering plays in their organization as a program for restructuring;
2. to clearly and comprehensively identify the aftermath of reengineering;
3. to effectively clean-up after the reengineering intervention.[12]

To do so, I have relied on a vast amount of knowledge in the management literature, and in my own experience in consulting and research. In addition, I have benefitted from the work of my students who collected data on cases of companies that implemented reengineering.

The main thesis of this book is that reengineering is one type of a change program of radical corporate transformation. Therefore, it will exhibit many of the strengths of change programs, as well as many of the fallacies, side effects, and negative consequences from them. The more dramatic and radical the intervention in the organization, the more its potential harmful consequences, regardless of the benefits it has achieved. Hence, the more we need to marshall our knowledge about changes, organizations, and corporate behavior —so that corrective actions may be undertaken to bring back balance and relative stability.

This is what this book is all about.

NOTES

1.   Max Weber, *Wirtschaft und Gesellschaft* (Tubingen: Mohr, 1956).

2.   Max Weber, *The Protestant Ethic and the Spirit of Capitalism*, translated by Talcott Parsons (New York: Scribner's, 1958).

3.   Frederick Taylor, "What Is Scientific Management?" in M. Matteson and J. Ivanevich (eds.), *Management Classics*, 3rd ed. (Plano, TX: Business Publications, 1986). This is an excerpt from the congressional testimony of Mr. Taylor, January 25, 1912.

4.   Thomas Peters and Robert Waterman, *In Search of Excellence: Lessons from America's Best-Run Companies* (New York: Harper & Row, 1982).

5.   Charles H. Levine and Irene Rubin (eds.), *Fiscal Stress and Public Policy* (Beverly Hills: Sage Publications, 1980).

6.   Michael Hammer and James Champy, *Reengineering the Corporation: A Manifesto for Business Revolution* (New York: Harper Business, 1993), p. 2.

7.   Peter Drucker, "The Coming of the New Organization," *Harvard Business Review*, January-February 1988, pp. 45-53.

8.   *Ibid.*, p. 76.

9.   David Kearns and David Nadler, *Prophets in the Dark: How Xerox Reinvented Itself and Beat Back the Japanese* (New York: Harper Business, 1992).

10.   *Ibid.*, pp. 295-296.

11.   *Ibid.*, p. 297.

12.   An excellent book on interventions is H. Boothroyd, *Articulate Intervention* (London: Taylor and Francis, 1978).

1

RADICAL ORGANIZATIONAL CHANGE

Change is endemic in our life and is an integral art of the normal existence of work organizations. As time passes and activities are executed, change occurs.

All companies and all executives are bombarded with the concept of change, with its importance, and with a variety of models for change. The current wisdom all around is that corporate or organizational change is essential and that those who fail to change or to institute and implement change in their organizations are doomed to fail. This conception has spilled over to politics and "change" is becoming a goal in itself, rather than a mechanism or a means to achieving a higher and more valued goal.

In the past decade American companies and their managers have been subjected to what I would call "change mania." Faced with increased competition from abroad, and with new technologies invading the workplace, managers were called to arms, and the battle cry was: "change or perish." As soon as everyone seemed to have agreed that change is essential and that "things cannot stay the same," the question became: *What should be changed and how?*

FOCUSED INTERVENTIONS

By and large, it was believed that the overall solution to the problems that American companies were facing since the early 1980s was change. At first, the solutions were models of focused interventions. What are "focused interventions"? They are change models directed at a specific function of the company, or at specific and predetermined portions of its work processes. The following examples will illustrate this point.

In 1985, Stroh's Beer Company closed its brewing facility in Detroit after 71 years of operation. Over 1,000 employees whose jobs were to be lost were guided by a very successful placement effort.[1] The brewing plant closure was an example of "downsizing" to obtain improved effectiveness from the rest of the company's brewing capacity in the other plants. This is a simple, yet effective, intervention directed at manufacturing capacity.

In 1996, AT&T, the giant telecommunications company, discharged 13% of its entire workforce. Of these, 7,400 were managers and 4,000 workers in operations and businesses that AT&T had planned to terminate or sell. These layoffs were also part of a downsizing process, as a planned change designed to reduce costs and to make the organization more flexible. The change process was based on the analysis by company managers of the minimum size of their individual workforce. Although there were some common criteria dictated by the corporation, the analyses were largely tied to the specific needs and assessment by the individual managers and leaders of the business units.

These two examples illustrate changes designed to improve efficiency and flexibility by instituting focused cuts in operations or people. Another type of such change is integration of functions. In 1996, Dun & Bradstreet Software recombined its sales units for mainframe software and client-server application into a single sales force. Doug McIntyre, the president of the company, justified this action by saying: "We are moving to a single team organized by customer instead of by product."[2] This action is a common tactic in organizing units (by function, product, client, or market). But any such shift is a structural change with its strengths and potential harmful consequences.

IBM had also opted to combine the operations of its personal computer (PC) service and support functions by creating a new business under the name Worldwide Customer Support and Services. The objective in this change was to reduce cost of support to IBM's largest customers and to make the business more efficient by cutting redundancies in service and support. The new unit is designed to be global in its reach and operations and relies on current information and telecommunication technology.

But focused changes are not only structural. In many instances they are directed at the implementation of a given technology to improve efficiency or to modify a work process. In the 1980s the emphasis in American companies was on changes in the manufacturing function. The introduction and implementation of new production technologies were followed by the movement to dramatically overhaul quality control. In the machine-tool industry, Noel Greis reported that when a change is introduced so that forming technology substitutes conventional cutting, the effects reverberate through the industry all the way back to the steel mills.[3] She describes such implementation of the new forming technology at Kinefac Corporation, which benefitted from the change by cutting costs and reducing waste. This example typifies the changes in manufacturing technology. In 1992 Donald Gerwin and Harvey Kolodny reviewed the use of computer-automated advanced manufacturing technology (AMT) and concluded that this change was introduced as a response to uncertainty and as a tool for improved competitiveness. Yet they also concluded that the AMT intervention also created uncertainty and other negative consequences.[4]

Focused interventions consist therefore of a variety of targeted change programs. They include the use of technology to improve work processes; making structural and organizational modifications; the redesign or restructuring of a process (for example, by eliminating steps or by combining resources); and adding a concept, viewpoint, or approach (such as focus on customers and service, or infusing quality control units, mechanisms, and procedures throughout the company). Focused interventions are change programs with varying degrees of radicalness and impacts on the company. By and large they are somewhat traumatic, at least in their effects on the units where they are applied. Repercussions to the rest of the organization usually also occur. For example, introduction of computer-aided design–computer-aided manufacturing (CAD-CAM) into manufacturing will impact such functions as sales, purchasing, and work processes in accounting and human resources. But, focused interventions are no more than limited change programs. They usually are born of a concise idea of what they are supposed to do and relatively clear knowledge as to what the outcomes would be when these programs are implemented in the company. Some focused interventions, such as Total Quality Management and downsizing are considered by some to be fads. Perhaps some are, and managers embrace them with fervor for a period of time only to discover some time later that they are not a cure nor "the" cure for what ails the company. The dictionary defines "fad" as "a practice or interest followed for a time with exaggerated zeal." What, therefore, have such "fads" accomplished?

The succession of focused interventions embraced and practiced by American managers in the last two decades have had two major contributions, regardless of whether their practice was exaggerated. First, these interventions have raised the level of awareness of managers and business educators to problems facing businesses and possible ways to resolve them. This is not a minor achievement. By focusing on a problem area and then attempting a solution through a change program, managers drew attention to the existence of problems. Moreover, they were able to implement, to test, and to improve various techniques for corporate analysis and problem solving. A learning process took place and many improvements were made possible. These change programs helped to generate an atmosphere of crisis, that things are not well, and that change is beneficial and may be the solution to the stagnation and the failure of American companies to compete globally.

Second, these focused interventions had a combined effect, over time, on the ability of American businesses to survive and to improve their comparative position vis-à-vis foreign companies. This effect is multifaceted. To the trained observer it appears that even before the appearance of reengineering in 1993 and the massive restructuring of the mid-1990s, American companies were pulling their weight and doing quite well internationally.

Of course, not every company was able to survive or to successfully compete in its industry. Failures are a part of business as are successes. Nevertheless, the overall effect of a string of focused interventions was the acceptance of change as an integral part of sound management. Indeed, some of the focused interventions (fads or just one-time experiments) led to in-depth radical changes in both the structure and processes of many companies. The TQM phenomenon that started with Thomas Peters and Robert Waterman[5] in 1982 has mushroomed into a host of change programs. These programs have substantial effects on how companies conceive and generate products and services, and the way these are brought into the marketplace.

To a large extent the legacy of the string of focused interventions to the art management was the legitimization of change (even radical and dramatic) as a rational way to resolve the problems of American business companies. Change programs are like surgery: they require a learned decision, they carry a certain risk, and they nearly always have side effects. In the past 20 years American business managers have learned to apply change even in cases where problems were not yet visible—as preventive surgery. Success of the business enterprise was not assured any more. Change became almost routine answers to on-going as well as potential crises and challenges. This led the way to facilitate the acceptance of reengineering as a radical solution and as a dramatic cure.

COMPREHENSIVE INTERVENTIONS

In addition to the combined effect of focused interventions, American companies have also resorted to comprehensive change programs. Imagine that you are visiting the battlefield of global competitiveness as a journalist covering the conflicts since the early 1990s. Why are some companies still standing and doing well while other companies have succumbed to the fighting? What instruments of war were used by the belligerents? What tactics and strategies did they utilize? Which were the winning ones? Why?

A successful company probably used a variety of instruments and several strategies and tactics. Adaptation to changing conditions and circumstances was probably a most important quality of the surviving victors.

STRATEGIC MANAGEMENT

In the 1980s the management literature emphasized the value of strategic management as a comprehensive tool for competitive companies.[6] This was combined with global thinking and redirecting American managers toward the global market-place.[7] Management scholars in the 1980s and even early 1990s admonished American executives for their shortsightedness and overreliance on short-term gains. The Japanese example of long-range planning and a decades-long time horizon was compared with quarterly earnings as the compass for American companies. "Strategic thinking" was proposed as a comprehensive change—limited to a global marketplace perspective which liberates the American managers from the shackles of provincialism.

Strategic thinking and its applications by senior management of American companies was a concept that called for a total evaluation of where the company is at present and where it is going, or being led by its managers. To do so, managers needed an analytical mechanism or tool which would be simple to apply, yet broad enough to execute comprehensive and radical changes in the business enterprise. A third criterion was that such a mechanism would be easily justifiable to shareholders and Wall Street analysts. Consulting firms such as McKinsey & Company and the Boston Consulting Group (BCG) had already developed matrixes that combined analyses of the company's strengths versus the state of the industry and the marketplace. The BCG Growth/Share Matrix was instrumental in categorizing companies as "stars," "cash cows," and "dogs." This type of analytical tool allowed both senior managers and Wall Street analysts to position a company roughly in a certain category and to observe and grossly measure and assess its growth.[8]

Yet the main contribution to the strategic management movement was the framework developed by Michael Porter, in which he proposed that there are five forces that impact the firm in a competitive environment.[9] As the firm navigates through these forces, he proposed some "generic strategies" that apply to specific aims and situations that a company might encounter. Porter's normative yet dynamic visualization of strategic choices had an immediate appeal, because his framework presented, in a simplistic manner, what every senior executive felt instinctively. Porter put it all together in an elegant yet powerful package.

CORE COMPETENCIES

In parallel to Porter's framework for strategic analysis and choice, C. K. Prahalad and G. Hamel introduced in 1990 the concept of "core competencies" of the firm.[10] This concept was hardly new, but they connected it to the strategic management framework. It thus became clear to senior managers that strategic choices depend on understanding the capabilities of the company, and on defining with some precision those capabilities or competencies that are critical to the business' success—or that are at the "core" of the business.

Conceptually, the path had been laid in the quest for a process that would distinguish between "core" (or critical, central, essential, etc.) and "noncore" capabilities, activities, and units in the firm. Those that are at the core of the business will thus remain, some will expand. Those that are not will be sold, decoupled, eliminated.

How, then, did strategic management and the concept of core competencies of the firm combine to become a comprehensive change program in American companies in the 1980s and early 1990s?

By the definition of its process, strategic management starts out with a thorough analysis of what type of business the company will pursue or be in the coming planning horizon. This requires an analysis similar to ZBB. The concept calls for questioning the premises upon which the current business is founded. Future developments and the future path of the company now depend on its ability to analyze its industry and its external environment, and to enlist its current and potential capabilities or competencies.

For example, a company that makes pressure resistant metal closures for bottles sells its product primarily to makers of baby food, ketchup, and other food, soft drinks, and cosmetics manufacturers and bottling facilities. In the late 1980s the company had learned that plastic would soon be replacing glass in various products and industries, including baby food, ketchup, and nail polish removers. This company's core competencies were in metal bending and cutting. It therefore developed a strategic plan to enter the plastics market. This strategy meant a top-to-bottom change in the company, well beyond focused changes in quality control or other functions. The new technology meant a total revamping of the company, its manufacturing, research and development (R&D), and sales. This was a "strategic" change as the company was abandoning the metal bending industry and moving into plastics and chemistry.

Strategic management and the concept of "core competencies" penetrated every function activity and unit of the American company. No corporate player was immune to the analysis of what one does and how this fits with the company's strategic plan and with the core competency of the business. Changes occurred at the corporate as well as the unit levels through acquisitions, mergers, buyouts, divestments, and other such actions that follow strategic decisions.

When these strategic choices were implemented, the firm's organization had to adapt to the changes. Whether it had to absorb a business just purchased, or do without a division diverted, or adapt to a merger, change was everywhere. In many instances changes occurred in structure, processes, and people, without a clear idea of why they were doing it, where it was going to take then, and what the consequences would be.

To many companies the outcome from strategic decisions was *radical change*, brought about by mergers, acquisitions, and other shuffling of the businesses which invariably created massive (and in many cases also dysfunctional) dislocations of resources and processes.

In a celebrated case of corporate change following an acquisition, Ray Vagelos, who in 1994 retired as CEO of Merck Pharmaceuticals, described his move to buy Medco Containment Services.[11] Vagelos suggested that he acquired the mail-order pharmacy and prescription-benefits-management company (PBM) for $6.6 billion in order to gain the capability of vastly improved information about the market, what doctors prescribe, and how this affects the sale of Merck's products. Vagelos applied a strategic choice to gain a more competitive position in his fragmented industry through improved access to customers and first glance at opportunities for innovative new products. This action led to increased vertical integration, the redesign of the marketing function, and an aggressive analysis of overlapping and redundant activities and units. The radical change in Merck, as in any other company undergoing strategic realignment, sent shock waves throughout the organization.

THE SEARCH FOR FLEXIBILITY

Since the mid-1980s, there has been an underlying theme in many of the pronouncements and publications which compose the conventional wisdom in management. This is the search for flexibility—a concept that is almost synonymous with competitiveness.

In the constant battle that companies encounter in the global marketplace, sustained performance and commercial success were presumed by many management scholars to be the logical outcome of corporate flexibility. The idea has its roots in the view that, in order to survive, organizations must adapt to changes in their environment. Such is a perspective that espouses the "natural selection" model of Charles Darwin, in which only the fittest survive. In the past decade, management scholars have also generated the "population ecology" view of organizations.[12] This view holds that organizational change is largely due to environmental selection, rather than to planned change through adaptation.[13] By looking at large populations or industries of hundreds of organizations, these scholars believe that they have a better grasp of the history of companies, thus getting a better handle over the way the selection process occurs in these populations.

In all of these conceptual frameworks the individual company goes through a life cycle of genesis, growth, maturity, decline, and failure. Some are able to delay the inevitable through mergers, acquisitions, *and* adaptation. The competitive environment forces the company to constantly adopt, and the best way to do so is to be flexible, agile, and in tune with changing conditions.

In the 1980s this view was manifested in flexible manufacturing systems (FMS), then to the entire corporation. Moreover, the combination of flexible systems and information technology generated the concept of the "virtual corporation," which is the ultimate in flexibility. Products and services don't depend on a structure nor on geography. They can be produced, managed, serviced anywhere in the world, while the existing corporate frame (whatever it might be) can easily be redesigned to meet environmental challenges. Like a chameleon it changes its form.[14]

The quest for flexibility can easily turn into a real nightmare for managers. There is a vast difference between managers who operate from their home, car, airplane, or the beach in a Caribbean island, and a "virtual" company. The manager today has others in the corporation—regardless of his or her physical location. Yet there is still a need for structure, people, buildings, apparatus, and all those things that make a corporation viable. Totally "ethereal" companies are a dream or a nightmare (it depends on your perspective). As I elaborate in Chapter 5 in this book, information technology is an enabling technology, but it cannot be a substitute for the physical world of a corporation.

When information technology became sophisticated and more ubiquitous in business organizations in the early 1990s, there was a universal belief that the "paperless office" is upon us. Alas, companies that manufacture and sell office furniture, particularly file cabinets, have prospered in the 1990s. Electronics is replacing some paper-based communications, but not to the extent that the corporation is becoming "paperless."

A similar logic applies to the quest for flexibility. The problem that managers face today is: how to manipulate structure, processes, and resources in order to become more flexible. The solution is not to totally "virtualize" the corporation, but to achieve goals such as getting closer to customers by effectively manipulating and, yes, "managing" the company's resources and competencies.

The point of this discussion about corporate change is that restoring the competitive edge and making the company successful is a doable task of management that doesn't overreact to what is happening in the world. Again, it doesn't mean to maintain a failed course or to ignore trends and changes in the environment. On the contrary, it means that change is inevitable and must be an integral part of successful managers of competitive companies. But change should be a program of transformation that doesn't overdo it by sometimes "throwing the baby out with the bath water." You don't get to the twenty-first century by managing a company with 1950s concepts, structures, ideas, and administrative technology. But you also don't embrace every screwball idea that comes along—simply because it heralds change and promises quick results.

WHERE WAS CORPORATE AMERICA IN 1993?

When reengineering entered the corporate scene in 1993, American companies had already been through the transformations that I mentioned in the previous section. Many had implemented focused and comprehensive change programs, and had achieved a certain degree of flexibility, renewed dynamism, and improved global competitiveness.

Now came the concept of Business Process Reengineering, which followed in the tracks of restructuring, mergers and acquisitions, downsizing, TQM, strategizing, and globalization. Overall, the American economy was indeed sluggish, but with low interest rates and an exciting political reality of the fall of communism and the opening of vast new markets in Russia, Eastern Europe, and the People's Republic of China.

Where was the crisis? Were American companies failing in dramatic proportions? Imports still outnumbered exports but at a declining rate. Automakers and heavy industry were slowly recuperating, and the economy was preparing for the move from military to civilian emphasis (at least in the planning stage). Indeed, the technology infusion into corporate culture was growing, with new and vastly improved software and computer networks that made many business functions easily automated. But from here to a crisis in management, the distance is enormous. The proponents of BPR claimed that companies were entering the twenty-first century with concepts and designs that were introduced over a hundred years ago. What about all the transformations that were occurring since the 1960s?

Let's take manufacturing, the first function to be totally rehauled. Compare a picture of a production plant in early 1903 with a plant in 1993. Flexible manufacturing systems, robotics, CAD, and CAM are the hallmarks of the new organization. There are very few people on the plant's floor, and those who do work there are highly trained professionals. Just in time (JIT) and TQM are imbedded in the structure and the processes of contemporary manufacturing. The production line of today's corporation is a far cry (in concept, structure, processes, and capabilities) from that of the days of Frederick Taylor and his "scientific management" associates.

Nevertheless, in 1993 corporate managers were more open to a radical change system such as BPR, simply because they had undergone so many other corporate transformations. It's kind of a catch-22. If the proponents of BPR had assumed that corporate America was still thinking in terms of the nineteenth century, how then could such managers be willing to adopt such a radical change program as BPR, which would catapult them into the twenty-first century?

NOTES

1. J. J. Fansem, "Easing the Pain," *Personnel Administrator*, February 1987, pp. 50-55.
2. Doug Bartholomew, "D&B Reunites Sales Force," *Information Week*, December 25, 1995, p. 20.
3. Noel Greis, "Technology Adoption, Product Design and Process Change: A Case Study in the Machine Tool Industry," *IEEE Transactions on Engineering Management*, August 1995, pp. 192-202.

4.   Donald Gerwin and Harvey Kolodny, *Management of Advanced Manufacturing Technology: Strategy, Organization and Innovation* (New York: John Wiley, 1992).

5.   Thomas Peters and Robert Waterman, *In Search of Excellence: Lessons from America's Best-Run Companies* (New York: Harper & Row, 1982).

6.   See, for example, Robert Burgelman, Modeoto Maidique, and Steven Wheelwright, *Strategic Management of Technology and Innovation*, 2nd ed. (Chicago: Irwin, 1996).

7.   See, for example, Kenichi Ohmae, *The Borderless World: Power and Strategy in the Interlinked Economy* (New York: HarperCollins, 1990).

8.   Basic readings in this area include: Charles Hafer and Dan Schendel, *Strategy Formulation: Analytical Concepts* (St. Paul: West Publishing Company, 1978); and William Glueck and Lawrence Jauch, *Business Policy and Strategic Management* (New York: McGraw Hill, 1984).

9.   Michael Porter, *Competitive Advantage* (New York: The Free Press, 1985).

10.   C. K. Prahalad and G. Hamel, "The Core Competence of the Corporation," *Harvard Business Review*, May-June 1990, pp. 79-93.

11.   Nancy Nichols, "Medicine, Management and Mergers: An Interview with Merck's P. Roy Vagelos," *Harvard Business Review*, November-December 1994, pp. 104-114.

12.   Illustrative publications are: Glenn Carroll and Michael Hannan (eds.), *Organizations in Industry: Strategy, Structure, and Selection* (New York: Oxford University Press, 1995); and Michael Hannan and John Freeman, *Organizational Ecology* (Cambridge, MA: Harvard University Press, 1989).

13.   This view of organization ecologists can be traced to the work of Paul Lawrence and Jay Lorsch in the 1960s, who pointed to structural changes such as differentiating the functions of a company as directly influenced by environmental conditions and pressures. See Paul Lawrence and Jay Lorsch, *Organizations and Environments* (Cambridge, MA: Harvard University Press, 1967).

14.   A basic text is William Davidow and Michael Malone, *The Virtual Corporation* (New York: Harper Business, 1992).

2

THE NEW WORLD OF BUSINESS

This chapter is about the new world of the American business enterprise, and the changes that have occurred in the past decade so as to dramatically transform the American corporation. Depending on who you ask, these changes were positive or negative—but they certainly left an enduring impact. The corporate scene of the mid-1990s is very different from that of the mid-1980s.

Describing the new world of business is an essential part of my argument in this book that reengineering was a costly mistake that brought about an impressive baggage of lateral damage. Reengineering did not happen in a vacuum, nor has the crisis in management (which I describe in the next chapter) evolved in calm waters of a stable environment. They happened in a scenario of continuous and dramatic changes in the world we live in, particularly in the world of business. What has changed in the past decade or so, and why, is crucial in understanding the role that reengineering played and its origins.

HOW THE ECONOMY CHANGED

In the few years since reengineering appeared on the American business scene in 1993, 8 million jobs were created. The inflation rate went down to 2.7 percent, unemployment maintained a 5.8 percent level (half the average level in Europe), and corporate growth fueled the strong growth in the economy, which in 1995 grew by 2.1 percent.[1] Corporate profits catapulted by 34% in this period, averaging 8.5% per year.

All indicators of the mid-1990s point to a much stronger business environment. Corporate spending on new equipment rose to 8% of the gross domestic product and despite a strong competitive climate from lower-cost manufacturing abroad, the capacity of American factories grew by over 4% in 1995, to a level almost 15% higher than in the 1980s. In early 1996, the industry's operating rate climbed to 82.9%.[2]

An economic boom and an industrial expansion are reflected in these indicators, from a trend that began in the mergers and acquisitions of the

1980s, when downsizing was heralded as a wonderful cure, and promises made of paybacks in the 1990s. What were the changes that occurred in the American economy and what were the main causes for these changes? Most economists and management scholars agree that there are three major phenomena that happened in the last ten years, directly affecting corporations and their workers. In Figure 2.1 I show the causes, their effects, and the subsequent dislocations and side effects that resulted from them.

The figure clearly shows the dichotomy between the good news to many industries and individual companies in contrast with the discomfort, dislocations, and lateral damage to organizations and workers. As one manager in a Fortune 200 company in the electrical and electronics industry commented to me recently; "If everything is so great, how come this company is experiencing such shock waves, and to me and my fellow managers the future looks very bleak."[3]

But the economy *did* change and these are *permanent* changes. In the ten years of the period 1985-1995, there were three main phenomena that changed corporate life forever: globalization of trade, information and telecommunications technology, and restructuring.

Globalization of Trade

In 1985-1995 the world has actually shrunk. Globalization of trade has progressed from the mere export-import relationship and the Multinational Corporations (MNCs) of the 1970s to an expansion of national markets and the inter-nationalization of national economies. First, markets and the locus of production are now international. Companies manufacture their products anywhere in the world, assemble them elsewhere, and market them everywhere. Allegiance to a country, state, or national boundaries is a thing of the past.

Second, these worldwide activities are fueled by a free flow of funds and investments. When you invest today in a mutual fund, you may be funding a production facility in India that makes goods for a French company that then sells back to your neighborhood store through another European wholesaler.

Several years ago my consulting company assisted a client in the purchase of industrial chemicals. The transaction was funded by investors from Saudi Arabia, transacted through a British bank, for a purchase of chemicals from a Dutch manufacturer, transported by a Japanese freighter ship, arranged by a German forwarder, sold to a Nigerian manufacturer, with consulting services from an American company. This example illustrates the intricate web of various companies and nationalities. Funds now flow to the more promising transactions—anywhere in the world.

Third, world trade has become much more standardized, as relations transcend national borders. All effort is directed toward removal of barriers to a swift flow of goods, services, and funding. Letters of credit and other financial instruments have become standardized.

Finally, there has been an emergence of trading blocs with even further removal of barriers, so that there is less of a need to resort to "free trade zones" that have sprung around the world in the 1960s and 1970s. Today, the flow is toward those countries, ports, and opportunities where the whole package of incentives, capabilities, skills, geography, and political stability (to cite just a few) promise a good business

Figure 2.1
What Happened in the Economy in 1985-1995

Phenomena of Change	Resulting Changes	Subsequent Dislocations/ Side Effects
Globalization • worldwide markets & production • international flow of funds • standardization in world trade • emergence of trading blocs & removal of trade barriers	*To the Economy* • innovation is up • exports are booming • real wages are up • standard of living is up • inequality in wages is up	• morale is down • loyalty affected • sense of loss & alienation
Information & Tele-communication Technologies • applications in many aspects of the business • networking and exchange of data-bases • rewriting the rules	*To Selected Indus-tries* • increased competition • change business or terminate • productivity is up • increasing product complexity	• uncertainty imploding • instability reigns • sense of chaos
Restructuring • downsizing • TQM • reengineering	*To the Company* • lay-off employees • restructure internally • higher profits • increased invest-ments internally	• declining performance

deal and a sound return on investment. All this, regardless of where in the world it is happening.

Information and Telecommunications Technology

The decade 1985-1995 has seen the diffusion of information and telecommunications technologies (ITT) and their infusion and rapid proliferation in business operations.

Proliferation was first in the form of extensive and user-friendly applications in many, if not most, aspects of the business. In the 1960s the major area of application for ITT was the "backroom" of the business, where accounts payable, receivables, and payroll were the main impactees of ITT. In the mid 1990s, almost all apects of the business, including the "front" of the business, such as sales and customer relations, have been converted by ITT.

Networking and exchange of databases are another component of the phenomenon of the proliferation of ITT in business applications. This includes networking with suppliers, customers, regulators, and even with competitors. The emergence of vast and manipulable databases allows businesses to access and to better utilize relevant information about their environment, and to do it faster, cheaper, and with more benefits than ever before. Add to this the impact of telecommunications by fax, computers, and cellular phones that essentially transform the company into an entity that is reachable anytime, anyplace, by anyone. The same applies to the company's employees at all levels.[4]

These changes are rewriting the rules of business and making transactions a function of ITT's capabilities. They also greatly facilitate the globalization of transactions and the shrinking of the physical world. While on the beach in Puerto Vallarta, Mexico, I was able recently to access my office phone and to transfer and exchange data with the office computer. In essence, I was running the business from a sandy beach, 2,000 miles away. These incidents are now more the rule than the exception.[5] Although we are not yet in the "virtual organization" mode all the time — and for every company and transaction—we nevertheless have achieved a state where physical presence is essentially irrelevant. Notwithstanding these futuristic attributes of ITT, the key effect on businesses remains the contribution of ITT to smoother and more efficient transaction processes and activities of the corporation, with many more options and capabilities to perform its tasks.

Restructuring

The restructuring of American corporations included at least three forms of intervention: downsizing, Total Quality Management, and Business Process Reengineering.

A. B. Shani and Yoram Mitki, two management scholars, have articulated the well-known fact that these forms of intervention have created confusion:

Many change programs, guided by one of the "umbrella orientations," have been launched by managers and consultants in diverse organizations. However, the increasing number of concepts, labels and managerial tools within each of the general orientations serves as a source of confusion. Furthermore, in many of the reported cases, while the espoused articulated purpose is one change orientation (Reengineering), a careful examination of the activities that took place reveals the use of another orientation (i.e., TQM or STS) or some combination.[6]

These authors have also suggested that there are similarities among these forms of change. They write:

We will examine four of the distinct *similarities* between the three orientations: all require a strategic decision that involves major financial and resource investment and commitment; all three focus on the entire system; they follow both a customer and an improvement focus; organizational learning is an integral part of the change process; and they all require transformation and/or modification of the organizational culture.[7]

The structuring of American companies was a powerful phenomenon that imposed a dramatic change in the business world of the mid-1990s. Together with globalization and the diffusion of ITT, restructuring has created a *different* business environment.

RESULTING CHANGES

Out of the phenomena of change, there have been many outcomes, which I have categorized in Figure 2.1 in three levels: the economy, the industry, and the individual company.

The Economy

The *total* effect of the three phenomena of change on the economy was relatively positive: innovation is up, exports are booming, real wages are up, and so is the *overall* standard of living. Yet, inequality in wages has also increased. It is clearly very difficult to assign a cause-and-effect link between each phenomenon of change and the resulting changes. Some economists, for example, have suggested that globalization of trade accounts for no more than 20% of layoffs and information technologies account for perhaps 15-20% of the rise in the standard of living. There is very little hard data to support any of these quantitative assessments. For example, innovation is up because investments in R&D have kept up with inflation, and corporate overall investment in R&D was maintained at an acceptable level, even when called upon to substitute corporate funding for diminishing federal support for R&D.

The Smith Kline Corporation is an $11 billion Anglo-American company, number 10 in the pharmaceuticals industry, with an R&D budget of about $1 billion. As reported in the press: "Smith Kline Beecham PLC (SB) closed a controversial $125 million deal in 1993 with Human Genome Sciences Inc. (HGS) in Rockville, MD, giving SB dibs on the largest database of human-genetic information in the world."[8] This is clearly a gamble since the joint effort has not yet produced a winning product. But the risk taken by the company is characteristic of the faith in the near future, and a wide corporate trust in the innovative capabilities of its R&D force.

Selected Industries

The effects of the three change phenomena on selected industries were generally positive. Industries that benefitted from these changes increased their world competitiveness, and saw their productivity go up. An excellent example (although somewhat specific to a nascent industry) is the growth of Internet-related software and service companies. In what some call the "War on the Worldwide Web," companies such as Netscape are a product of the 1990s. The company in 1996 had annual revenues of $80 million, with market valuation of about $5 billion. The meteoric rise of Netscape is due not only to the diffusion of ITT, but also to globalization, because an important component of its marketing has been large customers in Europe and Asia.

In other industries, such as transportation, energy, and consumer products, the overall changes caused by the phenomena of the 1985-1995 period had been radical turnabout in markets, products, services, and strategies. Some succeeded, many failed. Some low-cost airlines went out of business, whereas United, Delta, and American vastly expanded their webs to Europe and Asia.

Individual Companies

Internal restructuring, caused by globalization and the spread of ITT, occurred in many companies in addition to the major modes of intervention listed in Figure 2.1. All these change programs, minor as well as major undertakings, resulted in a higher profit, and increased investments internally in capital goods and in human development. At the same time these phenomena also resulted in layoffs, downsizing, and radical displacements in the workforce.

How much has each phenomenon contributed to each resulting change? Any attempt to provide a one-to-one causal link would be pure speculation. The spread of ITT has resulted in drastic modifications in the way many processes and activities are carried out—thus eliminating positions and specialties. ITT also directly influenced structural changes, by totally reformulating coordination, communication, and control processes. Globalization forced the installation of ISO-9000 quality control frameworks in many manufacturing companies.

Subsequent Dislocations/Side Effects

Many of the side effects listed in Figure 2.1 will also be discussed in the following chapter, as lateral damage caused by reengineering. This emphasizes the claim that all three phenomena are, in their collective effect, contributors to the subsequent side effects. As I consistently argue in this book, reengineering programs have accentuated the fragile environment created by the phenomena of change in the decade of 1985-1995. Business Process Reengineering was both a response to these phenomena and a major contributor to the negative consequences that they created, particularly in the individual companies where BPR was implemented.

The new world of business created an atmosphere of uncertainty and chaos, in the midst of higher productivity, higher profits, and a favorable economic bedrock of low inflation and robust growth. Inevitably, this led to a crisis in management.

NOTES

1. Michael Mandell, "Economic Anxiety," *Business Week*, March 11, 1996, pp. 5-57.

2. *Business Week*, April 1, 1996, p. 23.

3. *Business Week*, March 11, 1996, p. 50.

4. Peter Drucker, "The Coming of the New Organization," *Harvard Business Review*, January-February 1988, pp. 45-53.

5. For a description of these changes in a succinct way, see Eliezer Geisler, "Information and Telecommunication Technologies in the 1990s: Trends and Managerial Challenges," *International Journal of Technology Management*, Special Issue on the Strategic Management of Information and Telecommunication Technology, Vol. 7, Nos. 6/7/8, 1992, pp. 381-389.

6. A. B. Shani and Yoram Mitki, "Reengineering Total Quality Management and Sociotechnical Systems Approaches to Organizational Change: Towards an Eclectic Approach," *Journal of Quality Management*, 1(1), 1996, p. 132.

7. *Ibid.*, p. 136.

8. *Business Week*, March 4, 1996, p. 80.

3

THE CRISIS IN MANAGEMENT

As we rapidly approach the mythical milestone of the end of the twentieth century and the second millennium, there is an uneasy feeling in the business community. In my view, there is more than a feeling, we are facing a crisis. The crisis is not in the business enterprise, as has long been heralded by so many writers and business consultants. The crisis is also not in the quest for effectiveness, efficiency, and competitiveness. Since the early 1980s, American companies have improved their productivity and have greatly enhanced their competitive position in world markets.

The crisis is in corporate management. Indeed, as a consultant and educator I constantly encounter, interview, and converse with executives at various stages of their corporate careers. I've come to the conclusion that the crisis in management is rooted in at least four basic reasons: (1) stagnant business education, (2) bias toward analysis, (3) structural responses, and (4) inadequate solutions to change phenomena.

STAGNANT BUSINESS EDUCATION

Although confronted on a daily basis with an evolving business environment, managers are nevertheless educated by business schools in a stagnant and stationary manner. The business curriculum is founded on academic disciplines, with little integrative effort. The rationale is that managers need to absorb this fragmented, disciplinary knowledge and then incorporate these "boxes" or "cells" in their minds into a coherent and meaningful scenario of the business enterprise, their role in it, and the capabilities and options open to them. This incorporation is supported by experience and knowledge acquired from other sources. In a way, such incorporation is a selective process, through which the bright and skillful succeed, and the mediocre fail.

To make matters worse, business schools' curricula only lightly cover the world of such phenomena as change and its effect on the business enterprise. The topic is relegated a minor role in some management courses, with few schools venturing into creating an entire course on change. When taught at all, change is not taught as an interdisciplinary phenomenon that includes issues in finance, marketing, R&D, production, and human resources. Rather, it is usually taught as a topic in itself, in which students are exposed to the origins and characteristics of change, generally from a social sciences viewpoint.

When managers emerge from the business school or from an executive program later in their careers, they are exposed to, hence they utilize, a stagnant mode of thinking, reasoning, and decision making. The integration and incorporation of the curriculum is seldom completed, because managers are immediately engulfed by their daily routine and also because many lack the tools to create a lasting integration.

BIAS TOWARD ANALYSIS

Another reason that prevents many managers from a powerful and effective integration is that the curriculum is heavily biased toward analysis. Business students are taught analytical methods and tools, at the grave expense of synthesis. They emerge from their educational and training institutions with capabilities to analyze, dissect, and decide. Yet they largely lack the skills to synthesize situations and to create in their minds a comprehensive phenomenon out of the signals from their environment. In other words, managers make decisions in a robust manner on problems and situations that they fail to fully comprehend.

In a ten-year study I have conducted in 46 organizations, I explored the ability of managers to synthesize isolated indicators of change and to form a cohesive and meaningful picture of what was happening. The study offered even more interesting details since it investigated the ability of managers to create phenomena out of *archival* data and in *quantitative* form. The findings show that managers do have the innate ability to take very few (4-5) isolated quantitative pieces of data and to create in their minds a coherent and meaningful situation. However, these skills are not yet recognized by business educators nor are they fully exploited in the academic curriculum.[1]

The lack of a synthetic component of the business curriculum has contributed to the creation of managers who have analytical tasks yet who recognize the need for synthesis. So, despite their innate ability to perform such syntheses, managers increasingly turn to external consultants to provide them with such talent. Hence the growth of consulting companies and consultancy in general, which accompanied the dismantling of corporate staff which were supposed to have performed such functions.

It should be clearly understood that most problems and situations in the organization are broad, interdisciplinary, interfunctional, and comprehensive. They cut across units, expertise, turfs, and interests. This is true not only for the large corporation, also for the medium and even small company. Senior managers must therefore think and act synthetically. However, some Harvard Business School cases notwithstanding, the business education and training system is not geared to responding to this need.

STRUCTURAL RESPONSES

When senior managers finally act and respond to challenges and problems in the corporation, it is usually by instituting structural responses and solutions. These are normally recommended by management consultants.

What are the problems with structural solutions? First, they are difficult to implement, even when there is clearly a need for structural response to a well-identified problem. Structural responses include tampering with both the design of the corporation and some of its processes. Commonly used structural responses are increased or decreased formalization, centralization, or decentralization; creation of units such as groups or strategic business units (SBUs); and changing the control, communications, and coordination frameworks and their intensity. Tampering with these dimensions is always a difficult task because structural dimensions are well established and, to an extent, impervious to modifications. Any changes in them would require extra effort and the ability to inflict a surgical rather than a massive intervention so as to avoid side effects.

Second, the side effects created by the structural responses are many times massive and harmful. The current crisis in management is thus partly the result of the effects of structural responses where the company instituted the changes only to discover some time later that the solution had generated a tidal wave of side effects which now required immediate attention. With a lack of careful planning and little understanding of what is happening, managers turn to "fighting fires" in their effort to curb these side effects and to minimize their further snowballing into disaster.[2]

Third, the structural responses and some of their side effects have a long-term impact on the corporation, thus depriving senior managers of the flexibility they need in a volatile environment. Worse, when the response happens to be the wrong solution to the problem or situation, there are lingering effects and the structural response itself is now entrenched and difficult to remove or reverse. Since the mid-1970s, and in particular since the mid-1980s, we have seen many companies that have instituted such structural responses only to awaken to the need to rethink and readjust their designs—at very high and painful prices.[3]

Fourth, and recently perhaps most important, senior managers have been consistently exposed to continuous waves of changes and pressures to change their organizations. Not surprisingly, there is a phenomenon of "overkill" and saturation of change programs, of which reengineering is but one, albeit the most influential of the programs. Senior managers, and by diffusion also their middle managers, have gone from one change program to the next, each promising a virtual miracle, and each bringing about changes, many of which were structural.

INADEQUATE SOLUTIONS TO CHANGE PHENOMENA

Sir Winston Churchill was once asked to give his opinion of a most cherished Anglo-American institution: the game of golf. With his usual candor, Sir Winston said that he did not like the game because it was geared toward the frustrating manipulation of a little ball "with implements that were not designed for the task."

Managers today are confronted with successive demands for corporate interventions, in response to changes in their organizations' environment. Yet they respond with inadequate tools and antiquated concepts. In the Churchillian way of thinking, managers are in crisis because their analytical, as well as strategic, tools are inadequate and were not designed for the task of managing in highly turbulent environments. The best executive tools are no more than schemes of classification and categorization. This is because management and organization sciences are relatively new disciplines, and they explore very complex and difficult phenomena. The intricacies of managing a corporation are such that an intervention in one aspect of its operations may precipitate an avalanche of cascading effects, mostly unpredictable and unmanageable.

Add to this the paucity of quantitative measures and techniques that allow managers to obtain a precise view of situations and of their actions and their consequences. Only very recently have management scholars initiated a consistent academic pursuit of mathematical formulations in the organization sciences.[4] Not surprisingly, the areas of concern of the new academic journal on mathematical organization theory are organization design, organizational learning, information technology, and organization evolution and change—all crucial areas for design, redesign, and the understanding of corporate change.[5]

Thus, in this era of almost continuous changes, corporate managers are armed with conceptual, analytical, and synthetical tools that merely provide a broad road map with some general alternatives for action. For instance, Michael Porter's generic strategies and the testing framework for identifying core competencies are two examples of very broad (albeit quite logical) classifications of corporate reality.

The crisis is exacerbated because managers today are faced with much more complex situations in a global and highly dynamic and competitive world than their predecessors or generation of even a decade ago. Yet the tools they command are only somewhat better, in that they explain more of what is happening and they offer additional categorization schema. But they do remain terribly inadequate, thus adding to the frustration of managers and their sense of urgency and crisis.

It is time to stop and rethink the whirlwind of changes, redesigns, and continuous changes that are compounding the crisis in management.

THE CRISIS IS REAL

Why Is It So Difficult To Provide the Tools?

Let's bear in mind that management and organization sciences are relatively new disciplines, still in the stage of classification and the development of crude models that may describe, and to a much lesser degree explain, how the corporate world functions and what managers should do about it. The road from the descriptive to the normative is long and tortuous. Why is it so difficult to create and to develop adequate managerial tools?

One of the reasons is that organizations are by nature complex phenomena which include hundreds of variables, all acting at the same time. The Wharton School at the

University of Pennsylvania, for example, has a computer program which runs hundreds of econometric variables to model some patterns in the economic environment. In modern organizations there are almost as many variables as in a macro system such as a nation's economy. Yet, in part due to disciplinary boundaries and conventions, we treat each category or group of variables separately. In management and organizational research we also assume that we can *isolate* certain variables and focus solely upon them. The most wonderful two words that economists and management/organization scientists use are: *ceteris paribus*—everything else is equal— or, for the sake of our research and our argument, can be ignored and remains essentially unchanged. Human organizations and corporate entities are much more complex and intricate to let us do this with complete impunity. In addition to structural, design, and environmental factors, there are a host of social and psychological variables of the human condition. This is similar to Joshua's call for the sun and the moon to stop in their tracks so he can finish his battle with the Canaanites. In human organizations nature does not freeze, it continues to make matters more complex and complicated.[6]

Management and organization scientists approximate the conditions of reality by employing sophisticated research methods and advanced statistical techniques. In a marvelous book on the intricacies of social and organizational research, Chris Argyris asked a poignant question: "A more profound difficulty is related to the possibility that the conditions that researchers create to generate control are basically no different from the conditions human beings create when they interact with each other or when they create systems to organize human effort to achieve certain goals. But why should this be a difficulty?"[7] Argyris explained that the difficulties and limitations inherent in rigorous research and its applicability to reality of social/organizational conditions are due to the peculiarities of human beings. In particular, he lists the skillful behavior of individuals who respond in a learned mode to given conditions. Such responses may not be replicable in rigorous research. Argyris thus proposes that social scientists should create different models of their social and organizational environments.

However, these inner contradictions are not dependent for their relative solution on a model by which we describe organizations. Argyris advocates new perspectives of, for example, human cognitive processes. If we believe that people in organizations are able to process information and make adequate decisions, we may opt for a less rigid and structural hierarchy, a less, but not totally removed, structural grid. The reason is that regardless of the shift in our perspective on what people in organizations can do, there is still room for a design that respects frailties of human competence, however small they may be.

The issue is focused on the fact that the experience of the last two decades has shown that regardless of new and innovative models, basic limitations persist. E. Geisler and W. Drago, for example, have suggested that as artificiality increases in organizations, so will organizational rationality, leading to more rigid and much less interactive organizations.[8] Thus they claim, in view of the accepted mode of human behavior and regardless of our basic view of organizations, that structural changes will occur. Thus, the models we have generated, such as "garbage can," "resource-based" view of the firm,[9] or "agency theory" perspective,[10] are but variants of some basic principles of the theory of the firm that lead to no more than minor changes in methodology.[11]

In a collection of essays to commemorate the fortieth anniversary of the journal *Administrative Science Quarterly*, Harold Leavitt described "two misguided managerial grails."[12] The first was what he called the myth of the clockwork organization. Managers assume (supported by academic researchers and other consultants) that the firm is an efficient machine whose performance can be improved incessantly if we only discover the exact relations among the parts and the way they work. The second myth was that the manager can make the firm's employees one happy family through a supportive environment.

I agree with Leavitt that these two grails (which are very similar conceptually to the mechanistic-organic continuum) have installed in the minds of managers the belief that the solution is always around the corner, and that there are definitive, perhaps even miraculous, decisions if we only possess the knowledge to declare: "Open Sesame."

A MATTER OF TECHNOLOGY TRANSFER

The difficulty in *creating* adequate tools and usable knowledge for managers to comfortably run their enterprises are compounded by our less-than-successful *transfer* of these technologies to practicing managers.

This is not an issue of the failure of education nor a tale of the inadequacies of training. It is a matter of the process of transfer of management know-how and the results of research effort to practicing managers.

Management know-how (ideas, principles, models, prescriptions, methods, findings, plans for action) is no different than any scientific knowledge or technology. The study of technology transfer has had ups and downs since the end of the Second World War, primarily due to the policies of the federal government and its wish to make federally generated technology more available to private industry. But these efforts were also present within industrial companies and universities. There are three major categories of transfer.

The first is *intra*organizational, where technology (including knowledge and information) is transferred within the firm from one department or unit to another.[13] Many studies were done on the problems that the R&D unit has in transferring its outputs to the new product development unit and to other units in the firm.[14]

The second category is the *inter*organizational, where the transfer occurs between firms. Studies explored the difficulties in forming consortia, coalitions, and other forms of cooperation, even for firms within the same industry where the culture is similar.[15]

Several years ago I was involved in a study funded by the U.S. Air Force (USAF) to ascertain the degree to which major aviation manufacturers who supply the USAF were complying with the congressional mandate for "leader-follower" in technology.[16] This was part of the effort to support small businesses. The concept of leader-follower required the large manufacturers to share some of their skills and technology with small firms they employ as their suppliers. For many reasons, including proprietary rights and unwillingness to spend the time and energy in such transfer, the large companies avoided compliance in some instances by hiring the chief engineer of the small firms—thus eliminating the key person who was able to transfer the knowledge. Other difficulties in the transfer process were also apparent—among them lack of resources, facilities, and sophistication on the part of the small firm to absorb and to utilize the technology, and differences in culture due to size.

The difficulties in transfer within the same industry are magnified when the organizations involved belong to different sectors. This phenomenon is what I have called *intersector* technology transfer.[17] This is the phenomenon that entails the transfer of technology, knowledge, and usable information from one sector of the economy to another. Samples are the transfer between universities and industrial firms, national laboratories and industrial companies, and universities and national laboratories.

In the case of the transfer of technology from universities to industrial companies, recent studies have shown that there are difficulties in establishing a stable and useful transfer process.[18] Differences in culture and internal uniqueness of each sector's way of operating are combined with individual and organizational factors to make transfer a successful and frequent occurrence more of a rarity than commonplace. In addition, knowledge acquisition and adoption is a difficult process that requires commitment in both organizations and the skills, capabilities, and right attitudes to want to engage in such an activity. In my studies of the commercialization of technology from federal laboratories to industrial companies, I consistently advocated the creation of a stimulating and supportive environment in both types of institutions. I have also clearly outlined the crucial role that entrepreneurs play in this process. Without the highly motivated and energetic individuals who are willing to sometimes sacrifice time, position, even careers, not much will happen and technology or knowledge will not be transferred.[19]

Developing adequate and applicable knowledge and tools for managers is therefore a difficult academic endeavor. But compounding the problems of generation are the issues of getting the knowledge to the manager. This is not an issue of more seminars, or additional conferences, or even creation of more "relevant" courses in the business school. This is a much deeper issue of our relative inability to satisfactorily transfer even the knowledge we *do* develop from academia to industry. Technical knowledge is much more amenable to transfer.

Why? Because in both types of institutions the participants in the transaction are scientists who share, to a degree, the culture and terminology of their scientific disciplines. In management we only recently have begun to enjoy a *sui generis* terminology and to engender an academic elite that shares concepts, ideas, and values. But the disciplinary divisions in the business schools still hinder a more comprehensive cohesion of the profession.

In summary, we find it hard to develop and to transfer the tools that managers need to successfully run their organizations. This is a *crisis of knowledge* which is an integral part of the *crisis in management*. The difficulties described above are inherent in the system. We have only recently begun to understand their enormous power as barriers to effective transfer. In the final analysis, managers are left, to a large extent, on their own. They may have a business education and bits and pieces of each disciplinary area (management, marketing, finance, accounting, production, statistics), but they lack the unifying theories and the empirically derived conclusions that are then translated into handbooks and manuals for successful management.

HOW DO MANAGERS MANAGE?

The verb "manage" in this title has two complementary meanings. One is "to manage" as one would run an enterprise, administer an activity or a group of people. The second meaning is the more popular version, in the sense of getting by, making ends meet—in spite of challenges and difficulties.

Today's managers are faced with both meanings of the verb. They must get by and adjust to the difficulties of essentially working in the dark, with few models and tools for the task. How then do managers manage?

Mechanisms for Improvement

There are very few and doubtfully effective mechanisms and channels for executives to update their knowledge and to acquire the tools they need to stay current. There are seminars, continuing education, short courses, and other means to gain formal knowledge. As in the case of technology transfer between universities and industry, there is little "real" transfer. There is a gap between the academic, highly fragmented disciplinary nature of business education, and the empirical/application needs of managers. Ed Schein commented that cultures, primarily occupational cultures in organizations, are a much more important variable than organization scientists had assumed. He also suggested that there are three cultures of management: operators (line managers), engineers (technocrats), and executives (CEOs).[20] Cultural differences among them prevent the smooth occurrence of organizational learning and the adoption of management tools. I agree with Schein, but these internal differences of occupational cultures would be much less of a barrier to learning if we had powerful management tools and the ability to successfully and routinely transfer them.

The gap between academia and managers is generally filled by management consultants. Managers seek help whenever and however they can obtain it. Management consultants interpret the existing knowledge pool and derive workable propositions, ideas, and manuals for action which are supposedly based on the state-of-the-art in management and organization sciences.[21] But they are "hired hands" whose adherence to the practical and workable negates their effectiveness in filling in the gap. Although business schools are constantly modifying their curricula so they will be better tailored to business needs, executives do not embrace such changes with the vigor that allows them to become formal conduits for routine learning and self-improvement. The universities are too academic and fragmented by disciplines, and the consultants are too engrossed in the applicability of their ware—so the gap persists.

Coping with Change

Faced with drastic changes in their environment, managers feel (justifiably so) that they are ill-equipped to deal with them and in a position of utter disadvantage. All they want is tools that would allow them to make sense of these changes, to identify patterns, to discover the logic behind them, and to know how to relatively control their existence within these changes.

A proven method of coping is to develop the company's own way of doing things so that this unique solution would provide them with procedures they trust and understand. Such proprietary solutions end up shaping the culture of the corporation. They are also reinforced overtime by the concept of NIH (not invented here). If a procedure or management technique has not been applied in the company, managers tend to doubt its value and potential contribution.

But the effect on the organization is much more powerful, in that managers tend to commit the two errors of statistics. First, by developing a unique cultural background for dealing with change, they may reject good advice and potentially beneficial techniques and knowledge. The second error may be even costlier, as managers accept and implement doubtful or even harmful ideas, techniques, and programs. This is the case of fads and miracle cures, and perhaps it also applies to Business Process Reengineering.

Another major impact of the organization having to "go it alone" is the reliance on the CEO and his or her way of thinking. When there are few acceptable and satisfactory managerial tools, senior management has to rely not only on intuition and "gut feelings," but also and even more desperately on informal management. The upshot is lessened reliance on systems and routines, and more trust in constantly managing "by exception." Lacking programmed responses to change phenomena is a factor that exacerbates the creation of a culture and a managerial mode of operation patterned after the CEO and senior management's predilections, philosophy, and operational choices.

This phenomenon goes beyond the modeling of the enterprise according to its chief executive. Every corporation charts its way and develops as a response to senior management's leadership and planned design.[22] In other words, the enterprise becomes the reflection of its top management. Yet responses to change phenomena are more than a strategic direction for the corporation. They include "top-to-bottom" as well as "bottom-up" responses of processes and structure. Therefore, when senior managers lack adequate tools to manage change, they delve into their own knowledge, fears, hopes, and capabilities to garner the support of the hierarchy. The resulting culture may be one of "putting out fires," so as to create a constant climate of tension and short-term responses, or one of a more stable work environment. Stability, however, cannot be achieved unless there is routineness and learned responses, and those cannot be fully achieved without adequate managerial tools that can be implemented into the organization's arsenal of routine processes and its structure.

Managers find themselves inadequately armed to deal with changes. When changes do occur, the following effects may simultaneously happen:

- effects on people
- effects on tasks and operations
- effects on competitive position
- effects on market share
- effects on profits
- effects on corporate survival
- effects on the managers themselves

Managers are thus faced with a succession of occurrences that bring about changes in their environment and inside their own organization. They cling to any program or solution that will move them closer to a learned response, and away from the unique "gut" response. They feel the need to routinize and to avoid being caught, over and over, in situations where they must "reinvent the wheel." They are after *patterns, logic, understanding,* and *control.*

So we keep having "fads," straws that are given to managers so they can hold on to them—anything that will make some reason of a bewildered and complex corporate world. Fads keep coming, and like BPR they may be more revolutionary and more earthshaking than before. Fads like BPR are attractive because they do not clash with the on-going culture or with senior management's perspective. There is no need to enmesh them into existing processes. Just let go of the old, welcome the entirely new.

In management, as in medicine, people turn to fads when desperation conquers, and faith in the existing means, techniques, and solutions has all but dissipated. The constant flow of such unscientific and doubtful remedies will probably continue even beyond BPR, thus exacerbating the crisis in management.

PAUCITY OF PARADIGM SHIFTS

Since Thomas Kuhn published his treatise on the way science evolves in 1962 (first edition), the concepts of "paradigm" and "paradigm shift" have assumed an honorable place in the jargon of managers and organization scientists.[23] According to the dictionary, a paradigm is "an outstandingly clear or typical example of archetype."[24] In Kuhnian terms, it is an "accepted model or pattern" (p. 23). Essentially, Kuhn's paradigm is a school of thought which includes the premises, philosophies, methodologies, and the inherent logic for its being.

Transferred to the corporate and organizational worlds, the "paradigm" became a catchall term for a way of thinking. When managers abandon a certain philosophy or belief or method, they are "shifting paradigms."

Allow me to indulge in a play on words. In his response to Karl Marx's historical theology on the historicism of poverty, Sir Karl Popper wrote *The Poverty of Historicism.*[25] Hence the paucity of paradigm shifts.

This term has become so widespread as to describe practically any (however minor) change in mind, attitude, or methodology. There is a popular abuse of the concept to the point of draining most of its original and powerful meaning. Managers do manage and adhere to a set of principles, beliefs, and ways of conducting the affairs of the enterprise—which form a stable configuration. As research into leadership and the matching of leaders to situations has shown, managers/leaders are "set in their ways" and have a difficult time when required to *drastically* change their beliefs and behaviors.[26] The key word is drastically. Minor changes occur constantly and managers, like other people, adjust their thinking and their behavior to the world around them.

But a radical change in thought and action is rare.[27] This is precisely what a shift in paradigm would require: radical departure from existing conventions to a *new* set of beliefs, attitudes, philosophy, and methodology.

Managers do not shift paradigms as often as they change their ties or hire new consultants. Managers usually *adapt* to their environment by continuously implementing minor adjustments to the way they operate. Senior managers build a company, adjust it, and imprint their direction on it over a long period of time. Invariably, it is the organization that is shaped by the CEO, hence it is the organization that has to shift gears.

Moreover, changes in strategic direction or in the approach to the marketplace are hardly shifts in paradigm. Senior executives follow the trends in their industry, or decide to employ a given strategic weapon—as means of maintaining their competitive edge. When the company switches from cost to differentiation strategy, there is no prerequisite for its senior management to switch or shift their way of thinking.[28]

So the crisis in management is compounded by the poor performance of senior managers as *paradigm shifters*. Although the new economy and the business environment of the late 1990s has drastically changed, flexibility in thought and attitudes on the part of senior managers may be a sufficient ingredient for able coping—without the urgent need for shifting paradigms.

G. Hamel and C. K. Prahalad have provided an excellent description of the new conditions that will prevail in the world economies of the third millennium.[29] They join many writers who painstakingly offer a view of the climatic changes the business world has undergone in the past few years, and more to come. The picture they draw is one of shifting and blurring boundaries of authority, control, loyalty, experience, national frontiers, between physical and intellectual and between present and future. Further, they concede that "no one has yet reinvented the practice of management for the information age. There are, as yet, few answers" (p. 237). This, in other words, is the crisis I have been describing: The crisis in management, in knowledge, in tools, in the gap between the changing world of business and what managers can do about it.

THE CRISIS IS REAL

Managers are dealing with a new organizational reality of automation and information technology that is pushing new forms of conducting business and executing processes and operations. Yet the effects of information technology and the business realities of the late 1990s are broader than simple efficiencies of operations and processes, and are creating corporate-wide situations and phenomena that require a comprehensive view of the corporation. Managers in today's corporations are not equipped to be engaged in continuous changes and to conduct changes that redesign the corporation.

The crisis in management is real, and it is reinforced by the whirlwind impacts of Business Process Reengineering. Not only is BPR compelling senior managers to re-create their organization, but to do so with hyperpromises and without the tools needed for a synthetic composition of the corporation.

The time has come to stop and take stock. The crisis in management is not about re-creating business processes and then redesigning and streamlining them with information and computer technologies. This is the stuff that efficiencies are made of. It's neat, it's quick in its results, and it shows improvements in work processes. But it doesn't move the corporation forward; it is not a long-term view of the corporation; and its side effects, when improperly implemented, are enormous.

This book considers the crisis in management and offers a procedure to restore stability and prosperity by cleaning up after reengineering and other changes to impose a systematic, synergetic, and synthetic approach to corporate problems. The focus should be on acutely improving the synthetic skills of senior and middle managers by first achieving a state of balance and by restoring stability and the corporate ability to "come up for air" and regenerate. In essence, the crisis in management will be on its way to a solution by rapidly moving from "reengineering" to "regeneration."

NOTES

1.   Eliezer Geisler, "An Empirical Study of a Proposed System for Monitoring Organizational Change in a Federal R&D Laboratory," unpublished doctoral dissertation, Northwestern University, 1979.

2.   See Bristol Vose *et al.*, "Setting a Course for Radical Change," *Journal of Business Strategy*, 14(6), 1993, pp. 52-57. For an excellent discussion of "analysis versus synthesis," see H. Muller-Merbach, "A System of Systems Approaches," *Interfaces*, 24(4), 1994, pp. 16-25. Professor Muller-Merbach has proposed "Analytic Reduction" versus "Synthetic Integration" bridged by "creative design" confronted by "holistic meditation."

3.   See, for example, Daniel Coleman, "Therapy for Neurotic Organizations," *Across the Board*, 22 (3), 1985, pp. 24-31; also Richard Nolan and David Croson, *Creative Destruction* (Boston: Harvard Business School Press, 1995).

4.   The new journal is *Computational & Mathematical Organization Theory*, 1(1), 1995, published by Kluwer Academic Publishers.

5.   *Ibid.*, pp. 42-51.

6.   See, for example, several discussions of methodological issues in the study and the measurement of management phenomena: E. Geisler, "Measuring the Unquantifiable: Issues in the Use of Indicators in Unstructured Phenomena," *International Journals of Operations and Quantitative Management*, 1(2), 1995, pp. 145-161; also see K. Laverly, "Economic Short Determinism: The Debate, the Unresolved Issues and the Implications for Management Practice and Research," *Academy of Management Review*, 21(3), July 1996, pp. 825-860; and, D. Ketchen and C. Shook, "The Application of Cluster Analysis in Strategic Management Research: An Analysis and Critique," *Strategic Management Journal*, 17(6), June 1996, pp. 441-458.

7.   C. Argyris, *Inner Contradictions of Rigorous Research* (New York: Academic Press, 1980) p. 183.

8. E. Geisler and W. Drago, "Strategic Perspectives of Artificial Management and Organizational Rationality," *The Journal of Information Technology Management*, 6(4), 1995, pp. 45-54.

9. D. Miller and J. Shamise, "The Resource-Based View of the Firm in Two Environments: The Hollywood Film Studies from 1930 to 1965," *The Academy of Management Journal*, 39(3), June 1996, pp. 519-543.

10. K. Roth and S. O'Donnell, "Foreign Subsidiary Compensation Strategy: An Agency Theory Perspective," *The Academy of Management Journal*, 39(3), June 1996, pp. 678-703.

11. See, for example, D. Miller, "Configurations Revisited," *Strategic Management Journal*, 17(7), July 1996, pp. 505-512. He advocated the use of "configuration," defined as common alignments of organizational and strategic elements, guided by a central theme. He also suggested that configuration should be viewed not as an indicator of the type of firm, but as a "quality that varies among organizations" (p. 509), thus providing it with competitive advantage. This is a refined reconstruction of the "organic-mechanistic" continuum and the "cost-differentiation" view of competitive action. It is, however, a good illustration of the dynamics of our conceptual views of the firm, while entailing little methodological change nor a breakthrough in rigorous research and its limitations.

12. H. Leavitt, "The Old Days, Hot Groups, and Managers' Lib," *Administrative Science Quarterly*, 41(2), 1996, pp. 288-300.

13. For example, E. Geisler, "Technology Transfer: Toward Mapping the Field, a Review, and Research Directions," *Journal of Technology Transfer*, 18(3-4), Summer-Fall 1993, pp. 88-93.

14. E. Geisler, "Key Output Indicators in Performance Evaluation of Research and Development Organizations," *Technology Forecasting and Social Change*, 47(1), 1994, pp. 189-204.

15. See, for example, J. Dyer, "Specialized Supplier Networks as a Source of Competitive Advantage: Evidence from the Auto Industry," *Strategic Management Journal*, 17(4), April 1996, pp. 271-292.

16. IASTA Inc., *Source Selection Monitoring and Contractor Past Performance*, Report to the USAF, November 1980.

17. E. Geisler, "Industry-University Technology Cooperation: A Theory of Inter-Organizational Relations," *Technology Analysis & Strategic Management*, 7(2), 1995, pp. 217-230; also see E. Geisler, "Intersector Technology Cooperation: Hard Myths, Soft Facts," *Technovation*, in press.

18. A. Rubenstein, E. Geisler, and A. Cowan, "Patents, Licensing and Cases in the Transfer of Agricultural Technology to Industry," *Proceedings of the Technology Transfer Society International Symposium*, May 1983, pp. 102-111; also see P. Drucker, "Science and Industry: Challenges of Antagonistic Interdependence," *Science* (May 25, 1979), pp. 1110-1116; and E. Geisler and A. Rubenstein, "University-Industry Relations: A Review of Main Issues," in A. Link and G. Tassey (eds.), *Cooperative Research: New Strategies for Competitiveness* (New York: St. Martin's Press, 1989), pp. 43-62.

19. E. Geisler, "Commercializing Technology from Federal Laboratories: A Model and a Study of Mechanisms and Outputs," *Proceedings of the Conference of the Technology Transfer Society*, Huntsville, Alabama, June 1994, pp. 61-68; and E. Geisler, "A Yank into Technology Transfer," *Science & Public Affairs*, The Royal Society, British Association for the Advancement of Science, Spring 1996, pp. 44-45.

20. E. Schein, "Culture: The Missing Concept in Organization Studies," *Administrative Science Quarterly*, 41(2), June 1996, pp. 229-240.

21. Management consultants are also hired for a variety of other reasons. They may serve as "scapegoats" if policies fail or as "objective" observers and analysts. They may also be hired

to defend or support a viewpoint, stand, or perspective of an executive or group of executives, and as a means to justify a certain position or action. Thus, pure transfer of management knowledge is only one of the functions consultants perform in the modern corporation.

22.   The strategic management literature offers an extensive treatment of this issue. See, for example, C. T. West and C. Schwenk, "Top Management Team Strategic Consensus; Demographic Homogeneity and Firm Performance: A Report of Resounding Nonfindings," *Strategic Management Journal*, 17(7), July 1996, pp. 571-576; also see D. Hussey, (ed.), *Rethinking Strategic Management* (New York, J. Wiley, 1995); and D. Hambrick and P. Mason, "Upper Echelons: The Organization as a Reflection of Its Top Managers," *Academy of Management Review*, 9(3), 1984, pp. 193-206.

23.   T. Kuhn, *The Structure of Scientific Revolutions*, 2nd ed. (Chicago: University of Chicago Press, 1970).

24.   *Webster's New Collegiate Dictionary* (Springfield, MA: G&C Merriam Company, 1977).

25.   K. Popper, *The Poverty of Historicism* (London: Routledge and Kegan Paul, 1954).

26.   See, in particular, the work by Fred Fielder and the contingency school. For example; F. Fiedler, M. Chemers, and L. Mahar, *Improving Leadership Effectiveness: The Leader Match Concept* (New York: John Wiley, 1977).

27.   Ironically, Hammer and Champy have, to an extent, placed the blame for the failure of BPR on senior managers' less-than-enthusiastic effort (or even unwillingness) to change their way of thinking. See J. Champy, *Reengineering Management: The Mandate to a New Leadership* (New York: Harper Business, 1995). This is ironic because BPR calls for a revolution in thought and action, yet its creators are surprised when senior executives are not willing or able to change.

28.   See, for example: R. Dooley, D. Fowler, and A. Miller, "The Benefits of Strategic Homogeneity and Strategic Heterogeneity: Theoretical and Empirical Evidence Resolving Past Differences," *Strategic Management Journal*, 17(4), 1996, pp. 293-305.

29.   G. Hamel and C. K. Prahalad, "Competing in the New Economy: Managing Out of Bounds," *Strategic Management Journal*, 17(3), March 1996, pp. 237-242.

4

BUSINESS PROCESS REENGINEERING: WHAT WENT WRONG AND WHY

In their quest for maintaining market competitiveness, companies in almost every industry have resorted to radical change programs. Since 1993, a popular mode of corporate transformation is Business Process Reengineering.[1] In 1994 American businesses spent about $30 billion on reengineering with plans for spending an additional $50 billion by 1996.[2] Over 80% of the Fortune 500 companies have introduced some reengineering activities, with 82% of these companies targeting manufacturing, 61% information systems, and 60% customer service.[3] Senior managers embraced this drastic change program with unusual fervor. Mixed results are nevertheless the norm in evaluating the success of BPR. Some companies have achieved cost savings, have streamlined their processes, and have increased productivity and profits. Many others (perhaps as many as 70%) were not so fortunate. To them, BPR became a source of compounding problems and unfavorable organizational situations ranging from the unsettled to the chaotic.[4]

The aftermath of BPR is a mixed battlefield of some victors and many, perhaps too many, wounded. A classic example is the Mutual Benefit Life Company, which entrusted its reengineering effort to the creator of the concept and the movement, Michael Hammer. The company reengineered its insurance application process, with startling savings and increased efficiency. Yet, soon afterward, Mutual Benefit Life was seized by the State of New Jersey because of insufficient capital, and in effect ceased to exist, although its processes had been streamlined to heightened levels of efficiency.

The aftermath of BPR is a movement in retreat. In the short term there are many companies who exhibit some benefits from streamlined, automated, and redesigned work processes. It is premature, in most cases, to ascertain the effects of such measures and benefits on the company's longer-term survival and success (which were the main reasons for instituting BPR in the first place!). Yet in most companies the aftermath is some improvement in selected processes, compounded by a measure of saturation of the company and its managers.

This chapter challenges the key assumptions that underlie the BPR program of radical change. The chapter combines a review of the relevant literature published on this topic with cases of personal experience of the writer in research and consulting in several companies of various industries. A classification of the reasons for the failure of BPR is then provided, and each reason is thoroughly analyzed.

This chapter also introduces the reader to the basics of the aftermath of BPR. As a major and radical change process, BPR is a bankrupt proposition. At best it has produced some improvements. Yet, as will be discussed later in this book, when we compare these improvements with upheaval and lasting side effects from BPR, the verdict is clear. It is doubtful whether it was worth it.

KEY ASSUMPTIONS

The ardor with which so many companies embraced BPR has given way to frustration and reevaluation. This chapter begins the analysis of the failure of reengineering by challenging the key assumptions underlying BPR. Six such assumptions had been extracted from the vast literature that has emerged following the initial appearance of this radical change program.[5]

Vision Precedes Obliteration

A key assumption of BPR is the existence of a vision by the CEO and senior management, and an agreement with stakeholders as to what the company will be after reengineering. This vision precedes the act of obliteration of the processes and their rebuilding (or reengineering). The vision is conceivably a broad concept that includes the strategic assessment of the value added of processes.[6] In effect, the vision can be viewed as a strategic blueprint on what the company should be *and* how to get there by reinventing critical processes.[7] This means that senior management knows (or should know) before it embarks on the road to reengineering what the improved organization would be when BPR is completed.

Although the vision of the company and where it should be in the future are an integral part of the strategy formulation, senior managers do not link it to work processes at this stage of their thinking. The corollary assumption is that senior management is in possession of adequate and accurate information about crucial work processes. This allows them to set the strategic agenda to a degree that creates a vision of the totally revamped corporation. This assumption is flawed. Such a vision is untenable.

Senior managers are required to have a *complete* vision of the corporation down to its work processes. It is difficult to create in one's mind a picture of what the company should be and where it should go—let alone combine this vision with work processes. In the simplistic view of BPR, reengineering consultants ask managers roughly this question: "If you were to start your company (or unit) over, how would this company (unit) operate: suggest a design of what might have been (or the best of all worlds)." The key to this radical redesign is information (computer) technology.

This is well and good, but it requires a vision of what such a department, unit, or work process would be for, hence how it will operate. In the succession of hierarchical design, work processes start at the top—where the *company* is going and what it is going to do or be in the next *x* number of years. Work processes are not redefined independently. They were created to serve a purpose and to perform a function. Therefore they are tied to the overall concerns and the vision of the corporation. Vision is a prerequisite for reengineering. But vision alone is not enough. There is a need for a "better" vision—that is, a mental picture of the company where the company is more successful, better equipped, and more productive and competitive.

This is essentially what strategic management is supposed to achieve. Its premise is an outlook (or "vision") of where the company would and should be in the time horizon of the planning effort.

Recently there have been arguments for moving beyond strategy to purpose, and in doing so there emerged a more coherent view of the difficulties involved with an all-embracing vision:

The problem is not the CEO but rather the assumption that the CEO *should* be the corporation's chief strategist, assuming full control of setting the company's objectives and determining its priorities. In an environment where the fast-changing knowledge and expertise required to make such decisions are usually found on the front lines, this assumption is untenable. Strategic information cannot be relayed to the top without becoming diluted, distorted, and delayed.[8]

Other criticisms of strategic vision have targeted strategic planning and its fallacies. A particularly relevant fallacy is formalization.

The failure of strategic planning is the failure of systems to do better than, or even nearly as well as, human beings. . . . We think in order to act, to be sure, but we also act in order to think. We try things, and those experiments that work converge gradually into viable patterns that become strategies. This is the very essence of strategy making as a learning process.[9]

A comprehensive vision of the future, much improved organization as conceived by senior management to guide BPR is largely infeasible. Hence this assumption that there is a compelling need for senior managers to start out with a strategic perspective in advance of process obliteration and renewal is patently false.

The fallacy of the assumption is not only due to the difficulties in composing a vision of a better company. It is primarily because even when such a vision does crystallize in the minds of senior managers, there must be a process that will implement or actualize this vision. The strategic management process offers such a stepwise approach, and although it suffers from many shortcomings, it nevertheless has a coherent, logical, and workable procedure. BPR lacks such a procedure. Worse, it calls for *radical* change through obliteration and redesign, so that, by definition, a stepwise procedure is essentially impractical, if not totally infeasible. The fallacy of this assumption thus lies with the essence of the BPR approach itself, in addition to the restricting realities of executive thinking and imagination.

Full Understanding of Work Processes

The successful implementation of BPR relies on the assumption that corporate managers fully understand the work processes that make up the workflow. This is a basic assumption if one is to obliterate, then rebuild, reconstruct, or reengineer these processes so they can be much improved. An illuminating argument may be borrowed from recent criticisms of strategic planning:

Ironically, strategic planning has missed one of [Frederick] Taylor's most important messages: work processes must be fully understood before they can be formally programmed. . . . The problem with hard data that are supposed to inform the senior manager is they can have a decidedly soft underbelly. Such data take time to harden, which often makes them late. . . . Study after study has shown that the most effective managers rely on some of the softest forms of information, including gossip, hearsay, and various other intangible scraps of information.[10]

As in the case of strategy formulation, full understanding of how processes work relies on accurate, timely, and adequate information flowing from the front lines to middle managers and then to senior management. In changing work environments it becomes excruciatingly difficult to clearly dissect and then fully analyze how complex, intricate, and interdependent processes operate—to the extent that we know enough about them to be able (and feel quite comfortable) to reengineer them. Research has clearly shown that we may have in-depth knowledge of certain aspects of work processes, but lack definitive understanding of so many elements of dynamic work processes and the value chain they encompass.

This argument is also very much in force when we consider the contribution of information technologies to the generation and communication of data on corporate processes. As will be later described in Chapter 5 on information technology, too much faith and too much promise have been attached to computer technology. Even when information is relayed in a timely and accurate manner, there is a need to analyze such data and to make decisions based on a thoughtful and considered interpretation. Computer technology is merely a tool that provides better speed, accuracy, ubiquitousness, and volume of data transmitted, received, and stored. But it cannot and has not at this point substituted the executive's abilities to analyze, interpret, and synthesize. It reminds me of the example I use in my classroom to explain the role of information and the differences between data and meaningful information. When a hot air balloonist is forced to land in an open field, he asks a farmer who happens to pass by a simple and straightforward question: "Where am I?" The farmer replies: "You are in a basket attached to a hot-air balloon." The balloonist replies: "This is the most accurate, timely, and most useless piece of information I have ever encountered." In this vein, computer technology can assist in getting the data and even in analyzing it, but it cannot substitute executive talent. In times of rapid change, even the more nimble and qualified executive talent may find it difficult to fully comprehend interdependent work processes.

Unabridged, Unbiased, and Definite Evaluation Criteria

The vagueness of the BPR manifesto gives rise to another false assumption: that managers possess undisputed and definite criteria to evaluate work processes. Many postmanifesto writings have attempted to offer specific action steps and benchmarking techniques.[11] Omitted from these handbook-like publications is a clear description of evaluation criteria. How is a manager to assess the value-worthiness of a work process? How is a manager to evaluate the aspects of a work process that, when reengineered, will surely provide the corporation with some or all of the desired improvements, such as cost cutting, efficiency of operation, and added value to the bottom line? In essence, this is the quest for a principle or principles that would guide the evaluation of the current processes and assess the improvements in processes reengineered.

In his discussion on form and function as analytical components of the new world view, Peter Drucker has commented:

Increasingly, therefore, the question of the right size for a task will become a central one. Is this task best done by a bee, a hummingbird, a mouse, a deer, or an elephant? All of them are needed, but each for a different task and in a different ecology. The right size will increasingly be whatever handles most effectively the information needed for task and function.[12]

A solid principle for change is always welcome, and even one that is fuzzy and broad can be useful in assessing work processes. BPR, however, is a radical redesign for the sake of dramatic improvements. Its purpose is not to simply improve the process but to replace it with a better, newer, and more efficient model, or otherwise simply dismantle it without any replacement. In these cases the criteria for evaluation and decision *must* be much more precise, focused, and well understood. What BPR has given us is a milieu of clichés such as efficiency, improvements, and restructuring. There is a dangerous void where there should be unambiguous criteria for obliteration *and* for restructuring of work processes.

Obsolescence of Current Logic

Any program of radical corporate change brings with it a new perspective of the organization and its future. When the change involves reinventing work processes, it is assumed that the logic which had originally guided their creation has now become obsolete. Logic includes the various criteria that had determined the structure, function, and interaction of the work process with other processes and units. Business processes are the outcome of a painstaking combination of design and experience. They have evolved since their establishment, through adaptation to environmental changes and pressures. To a degree, corporations *routinely* tend to discard or downsize work processes that are blatantly ineffective or superfluous. As in competitive markets, internal work processes are continually subjected to pressures and a dynamic that forces improvements. Under the model of population ecology, many scholars believe that organizations undergo a process of natural selection.[13]

Therefore, as a characteristic of natural selection, work processes are constantly changing to ensure corporate adaptation and sustained survival.

All of these activities are linked by a logic that went into the establishment and the evolution of work processes. How obsolete should this logic become before it is to be totally replaced or discarded? How well is this logic understood by the reengineering change agents? The assumption that the current logic is totally obsolete is therefore false. This presupposes that a team of reengineers can generate a change program that supersedes and is far better than the thinking, logic, experience, and evolutionary power that is embodied in current work processes of a corporation. All this without full understanding of work processes and without unchallengeable criteria for performance, evaluation, and sustained success. It is simply an untenable assumption. My mother always used to say that "a guest for a while, sees for a mile," meaning that a guest for a short while may see defects and problems that are not easily observed nor recognized by the residents of a home or a company. Yet we do not expect the guest to redesign our entire way of living, which we have developed over generations, and which has evolved through success and disasters.

Improvements Are No Longer Enough

There is nothing wrong with improving and even restructuring organizations and their work processes. There is, however, not a shred of evidence that *total* and *radical* redesign—as proposed by the pure form of reengineering—is better than continuous improvements and adaptation to environmental pressures.

For example, Japanese managers have embraced BPR in principle but have failed to implement it in their corporations.[14] Although they are used to continuous improvements in their work processes, they have recently also began to introduce more radical changes. To fully implement BPR like their American colleagues, Japanese managers have to assume that continuous improvements are not enough to assure sustained survival and success. This means that the principle by which the Japanese have operated so successfully for half a century is no longer valid. Continuous improvements, or *kaizen*, is a Japanese concept for gradual and unending improvements. It started as a quality-related procedure to achieve world-class manufacturing and high-quality products. Later on the application extended to everything else in the corporation. The concept presumes that there is always room left to check and to adjust the operation to exceed the previous performance.

Reengineering, on the other hand, calls for reaching much higher performance directly, instantly, and vigorously in order to meet the fast environmental changes. It is much riskier than *kaizen*, and assumes that continuous improvements are not up to the task (see Figure 4.1).

When their system is replaced by BPR, the Japanese are finding that reengineering is an empty shell, without clear content or criteria for action. It's essentially a call to arms, a concept, and a do-it-yourself, ready-to-assemble game without instructions.

Figure 4.1
Comparison Between BPR and Kaizen

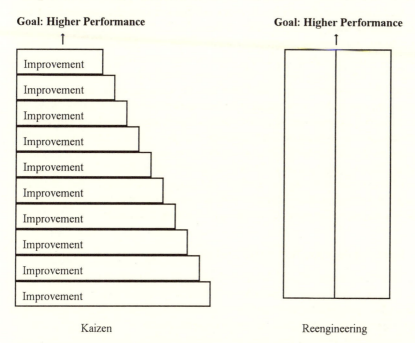

The assumption is that improvements are no longer sufficient because they are merely slight changes in course, and they rely on previous logic and experience. As discussed later in this chapter, many companies, as in Japan, simply introduce improvements to their work processes while inaccurately describing them as reengineering.

TRANSFERABILITY OF CULTURE

Work processes reflect the culture of a unit and the organization. As a web of interrelated transactions, they also determine a given way of doing things and carrying out the work tasks. After a while, a cultural milieu emerges, closely identified with the set of work processes. Even in situations where a new vision is thrust upon the organization, the existing culture remains as an institutionalized frame of mind.[15]

For example, the new democracies in Central and Eastern Europe that emerged from communism to a new vision of a free economy are struggling with the remnants of the existing culture, particularly in the rigidity of work processes. Similarly, the countries in Latin American that reverted from dictatorships to democracy are facing similar problems.

Business Process Reengineering relies on the assumption that the new vision and a redesign of work processes will create a dynamic, renewed, and successful corporation. This disregards the immense power of the existing culture. The entrenched perspective of how work should be done cannot be easily transferrable. The redesigned work processes would entail a different culture, hence the need for a painful transition and a lengthy transformation.[16]

ORIGINS OF REENGINEERING

The concept of reengineering as proposed by Hammer and Champy and applied across corporations in the United States (and now worldwide) is a product of two complementary phenomena: the climate of change as solution, and the failure (or at least inadequacy) of traditional techniques and mechanisms.

Change as Solution

This was described in Chapters 1 and 2, and reinforced in Chapter 3. Business Process Reengineering is a direct product of a continuing stream of programs of change that have been proposed as solutions to the pressing corporate problems of the day. I have previously shown in this book how reengineering has its origins in the pattern of the crisis-solution continuum that includes, among other methods, Total Quality Management and zero-based budgeting.

In order to offer something totally new, reengineering, as a concept, proclaims the inevitability of obliteration and complete redesign. To do so credibly, it proposes to fully utilize the wonders of information technology, which was not entirely available nor as user friendly to previous change programs such as TQM.

I discuss the role of information technology in reengineering in the next chapter. There I clearly show that information technology, as visualized by Hammer and Champy (and all subsequent authors who continued their work), is also anchored in a rationalized process of evolution of corporate and managerial tools and techniques.

Inadequacy of Traditional Techniques

The origins of reengineering are also embedded in the inadequacy, or even failure, of many traditional techniques and mechanisms designed to solve corporate problems and to induce improvements in corporate efficiency and performance.

It is not surprising to see BPR being directed primarily toward improvements in the efficiency of processes. In many instances this is done one process at a time. Rather than becoming the engine for complete overhaul of the corporation, redesign, and "reengineering," BPR is so often seen as merely a tool to downsize and/or redesign some inefficient processes. This blatant misuse of BPR resides, to a large extent, in corporate managers' search for adequate techniques that would allow their processes and their organizations to become more efficient. Overall, as I see it, this use or "misuse" of BPR clearly reflects the paucity of a host of techniques such as operations research (OR), management science (MS), and logistics, and their inability to truly contribute to corporate performance.

Although there is an enormously vast body of literature that has been accumulated since the Second World War on how to optimize, maximize, minimize, satisfy (and a host of other ways and means to improve corporate activities), on the whole the OR, MS, and logistics scholars have embarked on a theoretical pursuit, at the expense of practical solutions. There seems to be an insurmountable gap between the progress achieved by OR/MS scientists and practical problems that are centered around work processes.

For the most part, the development of sophisticated mathematical formulations and the ability to perform high-speed and high-volume calculations with modern computers have been a double-edged sword. These developments have changed the course of research and education in OR, MS, and logistics toward more theoretical problems that now can be easier to tackle and explore by the use of such vastly improved computation devices. Therefore, instead of facilitating the exploration *and solution* of industrial problems, the new devices helped to enlarge the gap between scholars and practitioners. This has also led to a decline in the prestige of OR/MS and similar functions in corporations.

A colleague and I consulted for a major consumer products company headquartered in the Midwest. Our task was focused on assisting the company in the organization of a new unit designed to launch an innovative product. In preparing the various work processes, we inquired as to the assistance from the OR/MS unit at headquarters. The president of the division—who had hired us—sneered:

These operations research people don't understand my business and don't have anything in their bag of tricks that can really help me. The last thing I need is another bunch of formulas. I am building here a new business; I have a winning product; I don't need lofty solutions. I need solutions that work.

This case illustrates a general "malaise" of OR, MS, logistics sciences, and other techniques. The loss of corporate confidence in their ability to solve problems has contributed to the emergence of a vacuum, in which problems were floating and solutions were not forthcoming to solve them. The result was that in the period 1985-1995 many corporations ended up with "defective" work processes because "maintenance" by OR/MS-type functions left much to be desired. Many work processes were inefficient, wasteful, and even unnecessary or duplications of other processes. This was also exacerbated by the flood of corporate changes, mergers, acquisitions, downsizing, and all other dynamics that characterized most companies during this period. OR/MS-type functions didn't keep pace with these transformations and did not or could not offer a definitive solution to recurrent problems by greatly and visibly improving the efficiency of work processes, and thus the performance, profitability, and competitive position of the company.

When BPR appeared on the corporate scene in the early 1990s, the ground was fertile for a totally new and even "shocking" method or concept that promised better work processes and improved performance. Corporate managers could not or would not count on their internal resources, such as OR, MS, and logistics teams. The most advisable way was therefore to look outside and to hire the external gurus of reengineering—to do what many managers wanted their own staff to perform in the first place. It so happened that many managers thus disregarded the "obliterate" dictum of reengineering, preferring to use it as a surrogate for the efficiency experts in their organization—who "let them down."

Have OR/MS and similar traditional techniques really failed? A careful examination of what these traditional techniques have in their arsenal shows that they are well equipped to institute major improvements in work processes and to significantly increase corporate performance. The problem seems to be one of managerial attitudes toward this corporate function, viewed primarily as occasional "firefighters." Although OR/MS teams have performed extremely well in such companies as Federal Express (FedEx), American Airlines, Hewlett-Packard, and United Airlines, the overall perception of OR/MS by corporate management is still that of a superfluous corporate function. If OR/MS Had been called upon to overhaul corporate work processes, they had enough firepower in their arsenal to make the most of these processes and to transform them into efficient conduits of company activities.[17]

There was a lack of internal communication as well as senior management failure to recognize the potential in their in-house capabilities, or even external OR/MS capabilities that could be brought in to help redesign work processes. OR/MS professionals also failed to "sell" themselves to senior management. Finally, the appeal of a totally *new* approach, as reengineering was presented to corporations, outweighed the tired, misunderstood, unappreciated, and perhaps also disinterested OR/MS-type functions.

However, even though BPR ended up replacing a poorly performing corporate function, its failure was also due to several other reasons. BPR was not meant to be a substitute for OR/MS. When it was introduced in the operation, OR, MS, and similar functions rushed to join in the change program and have adjusted their focus to the "new kid on the block." But BPR failed because of reasons that are inherent in the way it was conceived, and in the way it was implemented—as I explain below.

REASONS FOR FAILURE

BPR relies on untenable or even false key assumptions that support the contention of this chapter that reengineering is a far-fetched and unworkable shell of a concept outlining radical corporate change. But BPR is failing because of a combination of several reasons, only one of which is the weakness of the program itself. In addition to the inherent weaknesses, three other main categories of reasons are salient in the literature on postreengineering experiences. All four categories of reasons for failure are summarized in Figure 4.2.

Getting Ready

Preparation for reengineering is usually lackadaisical. There tends to be a buildup of an overly optimistic backdrop to the forthcoming change program. Unrealistic expectations are the norm, with uncritical trust in the wonders of the program and its purported outcomes. More specifically, there is a lack of measurable targeted goals that are widely acceptable and understood throughout the corporation. Instead, the usual situation is one of a top-to-bottom thrust of far-fetched goals and expectations about the speed, scope, outcomes, and benefits from the reengineering exercise.[18] As part of the preparatory scene, there is usually the lack of a coherent package of how senior management envision the resultant corporation.

Many companies dive into this radical change program with high hopes but with little preparation or understanding of what lies ahead.

Implementation

Figure 4.2 shows 11 reasons for failure of BPR under the category of implementation. This cluster has received most of the attention from critics of reengineering. As with any other program of radical change, implementation is difficult and replete with traps that contribute to failure.[19]

Prime candidates for contributors to failure are poor execution of the implementation of reengineering, and the resulting reactions in the corporation. Senior managers seem to shoulder much of the deficiencies in applying the program. They provide lukewarm support and they delegate the task to consultants with little direction. In general, they seem to prefer the easy way.[20] Other misapplications include the selection of a wrong champion, inadequate investments in the program, and focus on cost-cutting rather than the broader and strategic aspects of BPR.[21]

The other side of failure in implementation includes the reaction of employees and middle managers. They show cynicism and resistance to the changes, combined with lack of motivation and involvement. A recurrent theme in criticisms of BPR is the inadequate participation sought of the employees and consequently not given by them. Senior management weaknesses and noncooperation from employees tend to feed on each other and exacerbate the incompetent process of implementation.[22]

As crucial to failure of BPR as it may be, sloppy implementation by itself is not the key to the decline and fall of reengineering. As a rule, organizational change programs are difficult to implement, invariably leading to shortcuts and partial solutions. Yet BPR is a self-contained program, where the change sought is radical, revolutionary, and uniquely comprehensive. Consequently, deviations and inadequate application bring about the collapse of the intended change program.[23] Therefore, the fault lies not in the inevitability of imperfect implementation, but in the rigid attributes of the program of reengineering as an all-or-nothing concept of change. All stages, from the vision of the resulting organization downstream, are interlocked in a seemingly flawless motion of events. The normal flaws of implementation doom the program.

Weaknesses of the Organization

Critics of reengineering have pointed to inherent weaknesses in the organizations as some reasons for failure of BPR. Lack of a coherent strategy, absence of slack resources, and an uncooperative entrenched hierarchy are common in reengineered

Figure 4.2
Categories of Reasons for Failure of BPR

Getting Ready
- Lack of adequate preparation
- Unrealistic expectations
- Lack of measurable targeted goals
- Creation of overly optimistic backdrop
- Lack of a coherent vision

Implementation
- Cynicism and resistance to change on part of employees
- Lukewarm support by senior management
- Delegation of task to consultants without adequate direction
- Lack of employee involvement
- Focus on cost-cutting and narrow technological objectives
- Inadequate investments in cross-functional teams and in information technology
- Choice of wrong champion
- Too little time to implement and evaluate the changes
- Focus on tasks, not processes
- Overhaul of parts, not entire systems
- Generally, taking the easy way

Weaknesses of the Organization
- Lack of coherent organizational strategy
- Absence of slack resources needed for adequate implementation
- Entrenched hierarchy and its rigidity
- Resistance from middle managers who feel threatened

Weaknesses of BPR: Untenable Underlying Assumptions
- Vision precedes obliteration
- Full understanding of work processes
- Unabridged, unbiased and definite evaluation criteria
- Obsolescence of current logic
- Improvements are no longer enough
- Transferability of culture

---

corporations.[24] The issue is not whether an organization is "ready" for reengineering and if it possesses the necessary attributes or strengths to facilitate or even guarantee the success of BPR. If we are to wait for the "right" circumstances in the organization's life, BPR will never be exercised.

Ironically, corporations who are the least able to support the BPR effort are perhaps the most likely to need it (or a similar change program) and maybe benefit from it. Corporations with a coherent strategy, slack resources, and a committed and participative workforce may require some superficial improvements, but hardly a radical transformation. Nevertheless, a weak organization is a detriment to reengineering and tends to contribute to its failure.[25]

Weaknesses of BPR

The six untenable underlying assumptions of BPR were discussed in the beginning of this chapter, and are shown in Figure 4.2.

LINGERING BPR AFTEREFFECTS

Inadequate preparation and weak implementation bring about the decline of BPR as a long-term beneficial radical change program. Several aftereffects have been documented. The combination of massive transformations throughout the corporation and the downsizing and lack of involvement and support from many quarters of the organization creates powerful aftershock and harmful effects. In addition to the untenability of its key assumptions, BPR is also a revolutionary shakeout of the organization.

Although American executives prefer the sudden, frontal attack on the corporate present state (rather than the continuous improvement system of the Japanese *kaizen*), BPR is nevertheless such a radical transformation that it leaves in its wake lingering unhealthy conditions. These conditions are described in more detail throughout the book, in particular in Chapter 6. In this chapter the damage to the corporation from BPR is briefly outlined below.

Low morale, embedded resistance, and deep distrust are some of the more powerful aftereffects. Employees and managers alike are generally unaware of the inherent logic in the BPR exercise, and are also unable to clearly discern, identify, and enjoy the benefits accrued to the corporation from the shakeout they had just experienced. A culture of depressive commitment and wounded loyalties to the corporation is the norm in the post-BPR climate of so many organizations.

Reengineered processes that are supposed to contribute to a leaner and meaner organization may also disrupt the value chain and create disproportionate efficiencies along the chain. The result is usually internal inconsistencies and massive suboptimization. For example, the reengineered delivery and transportation unit of a large service company became much more efficient. Yet the remainder of the company was unable to follow, creating bottlenecks that hindered service to customers, thus negatively impacting performance and profitability.[26]

A third category of such lateral damage is the emerging climate of opposition to any further changes and tinkering with the organization. This leads to difficulties in exercising corrective actions and other less radical changes to navigate the corporation after BPR. There is also a pervasive lack of experienced employees with special skills, who would be the bulwark of any complementary transformation. Because of

BPR and its effects, many such employees are no longer with the organization. Their expertise, vital to any further changes, has been lost. The efficient corporation is also, in many instances, a wounded being, with a much reduced ability to change again, to reenergize, and to revitalize.[27]

In summary, the aftermath of the BPR experience in the average company is a mixed bag of some benefits and much painful and lingering lateral damage. The crisis of management is exacerbated by companies in a state of imbalance and semichaotic disposition of people and units.

In the early days of reengineering, Jill Vitiello had quoted Clelland Johnson, a partner of CSC index (Hammer's former consulting company; he is now president of Hammer and Company) who defined reengineering as "not about slashing headcount, outsourcing activities, revising organization charts." Rather, he said that reengineering is about "developing creative and innovative ways of doing business, managing the organization's human resources through these changes, and implementing the appropriate information technology to support the new environment."[28]

This is a pampered and innocuous definition that in theory is well focused yet totally leaves out the radicalism of the concept. But the reality of reengineering is quite different. Its theory calls for intense redesign which leads to an aftermath of uncertainty, fear, imbalance, and instability—in many instances far outweighing the benefits from BPR.[29]

WHY PROGRAMS FAIL

The failure of BPR is not necessarily an exception to the rule of successful change programs. Quite the contrary, the failure of BPR is but another attempt in the long tradition of corporate-wide programs which overpromised but did not deliver. As shown earlier, BPR's deficiencies were of three main types: conceptual inadequacy, poor implementation, and unfriendly attitudes in the organization. But there is a fourth and perhaps much more powerful reason for the failure of reengineering. This is the main reason why change programs and other such concerted attempts at major improvements are usually doomed to failure.

Simply, these programs do not provide adequate answers to pressing issues and to identifiable problems at all levels of the organization. These programs do not fulfill the *current* or the *planned* needs of corporate management and they are inadequately designed to offer satisfactory solutions to the crisis in management. Hamel and Prahalad have emphasized this apparent gap between what programs we do have and how they can be beneficial to managers by posing poignant questions. They asked: "How would Andy Groves (Intel), Rupert Murdoch (News Corp.), Ed McCracken (Silicon Graphics), or Richard Branson (Virgin) rate our collective contributions? Are they looking to us for answers? Do we even understand their questions?"[30] Moreover, the description of the new competitive economy offered by these authors includes attributes of a changed corporate world that were already present—in full force—in 1993 when BPR appeared on the business scene. Reengineering failed to deal precisely with the problems created by this new world, new economy, and the new way of doing business.

Figure 4.3 provides a graphic presentation of the changes that occurred in our world in the 1990s (and will certainly intensify after the year 2000), versus the methods, programs, and techniques that are currently available in our knowledge arsenal of management and organization sciences. The figure is a bird's eye view of some advances in our knowledge about management and organization, as they are roughly compared with the new world managers face today and will increasingly face in the near future. There are no direct matches in the figure because the methods and programs are spread across the vast tapestry of what we know about how corporations behave, why they succeed or fail, and most important, what can be done to master their destiny.

YET TO COME

In addition to an overall graphic display, a crucial facet of Figure 4.3 is the methods and programs yet to come (YTC1 ... YTCn). As our methods and our pool of knowledge grow and evolve, new and as yet unknown methods, techniques, and programs shall emerge. This pattern is similar to the Periodic Table of Elements in which as yet undiscovered elements of matter can be identified and positioned in the overall table. Some of these unknown methods and programs may be but variants of those currently in existence, but others will be radically different in concept and in projected impacts.

Why? Because the accumulation of attributes of the totally new world of business and global economy produces a host of new questions and a host of hitherto unknown situations for which we lack the experience or the tools with which to offer adequate solutions.

The perpendicular axis in Figure 4.3 was left without an insert that explains its meaning. This was done with a reason: I don't know which factor is the criterion for the evolutionary flow of management methods and programs. There are several possiilities. *Complexity* is a plausible explanation. As the situations created by the new business world become more complex, there is a need for more creative and revolutionary solutions. Another possibility is the degree of *urgency* of the new business environment so that its effect on management is such that their anxiety and frustration raise the level of urgency in procuring new methods and solutions. Negative experiences with existing programs may also lead to pressures on the creative elements in business and in academia to engender innovative solutions. Perhaps it is a combination of these and other factors.[31]

CONTRIBUTIONS TO KNOWLEDGE

In the evolutionary view of the development of management tools and management knowledge, change programs may be assessed by the degree to which they contribute to the epistemological growth—that is, to the accumulated pool of

Figure 4.3
An Evolutionary View of the New Business World and Key Management/ Organization Methods/programs

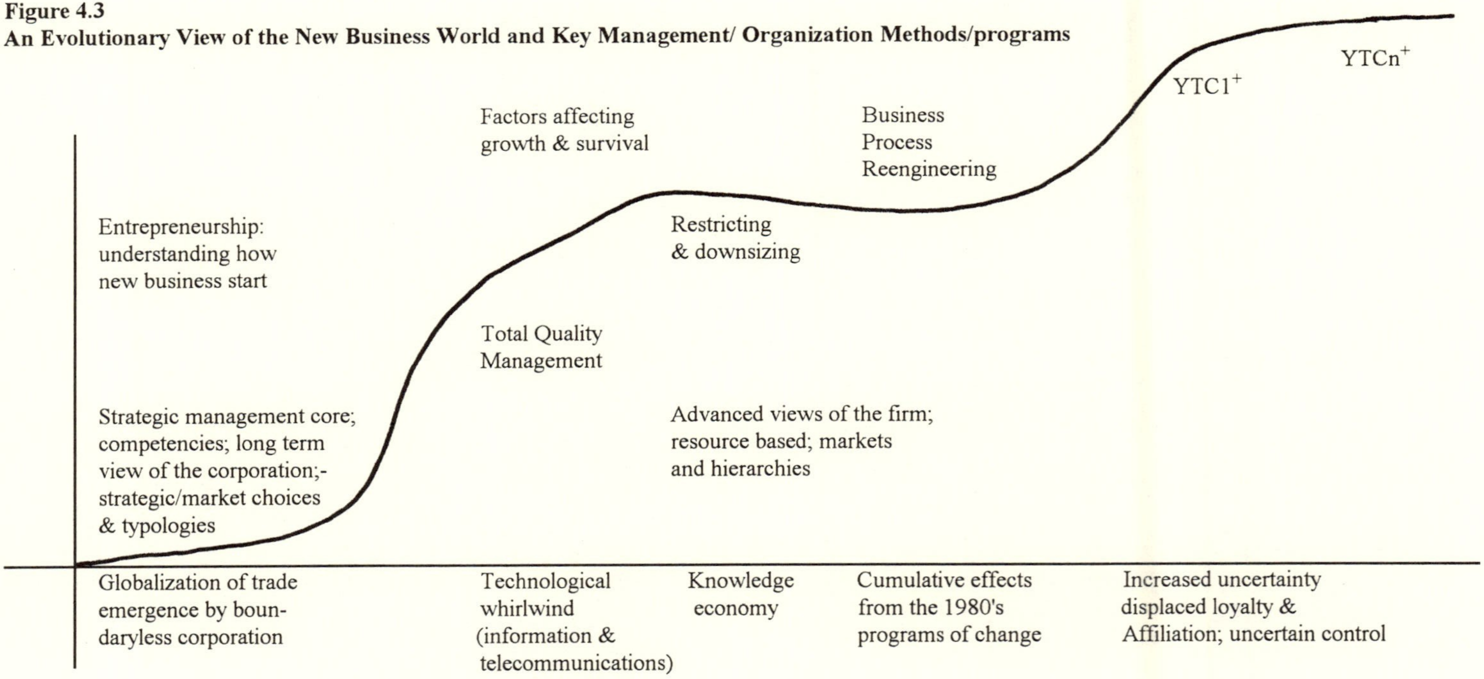

YTCn$^+$

YTC1$^+$

Factors affecting growth & survival

Entrepreneurship: understanding how new business start

Strategic management core; competencies; long term view of the corporation;- strategic/market choices & typologies

Total Quality Management

Restricting & downsizing

Business Process Reengineering

Advanced views of the firm; resource based; markets and hierarchies

Globalization of trade emergence by boun- daryless corporation

Technological whirlwind (information & telecommunications)

Knowledge economy

Cumulative effects from the 1980's programs of change

Increased uncertainty displaced loyalty & Affiliation; uncertain control

*YTC: Yet to come: Methods and programs yet to be created.

knowledge. This phenomenon, which some authors have named "evolutionary epistemology," is roughly shown in Figure 4.3.[32]

Normally, the ascension along the curve is incremental, with each additional technique, program, or piece of knowledge adding to the growing pool. The evolutionary component is reflected in the learning that occurs with each addition to the knowledge pool. In this manner, managers learn from their experiences as do scholars and consultants. Some scholars refer to this by the overall term: "organizational learning."[33]

Yet learning and evolution of the knowledge pool occur when there are successes as well as failures. To paraphrase a popular phrase: when I make a mistake once, I can blame many factors other than myself; when I make the same mistake the second time, shame on me. Thus, management programs or interventions are useful if they contribute to the organization's learning and to evolutionary growth of its knowledge. This is valid for successes as well as for failures.

In a study conducted several years ago, my colleagues and I surveyed about 50 R&D departments in major corporations. The purpose of the study was to identify factors that impinge upon the R&D unit's successful mission as producers of new products. Our methodology called for dyads of projects, one successful, the other a failure. We found ourselves hard pressed to have the companies clearly identify projects that "failed." Finally, we substituted the term "failed" with "less than successful." This euphemism suddenly helped to uncover dozens of such projects. Nevertheless, most R&D managers we interviewed conceded that they had *learned* a lot more from the projects that were "less than successful" than from those that succeeded.

Business process reengineering, on the whole, failed because it did not contribute to the evolutionary growth of the knowledge pool. By obliterating the existing conditions in favor of some obscure ideal organization, BPR was neither success nor failure, from which management could learn and add to their improved view of the world.[34]

In this, BPR lacked what the military jargon calls *debriefing*, and what organization scientists in general call learning. In both cases the idea is that each detail of the results of an intervention may be of little significance by itself, but when added to a tapestry of facts it provides the element for a cumulative value of the effort. Thus information becomes knowledge, which allows the drawing of conclusions as well as the identification of patterns and logic in the seemingly dispersed elements. BPR did not provide (at least at this stage) for the conditions, tools, or information that allow managers to effectively learn and add to their knowledge pool.[35]

In this broader picture, BPR is but one of many programs designed to offer solutions, but to a situation quite different from the emerging world of the late 1990s and early 2000s. As Figure 4.4 shows, the cumulative effects of the knowledge gathered in the existing pool lead to a better understanding of the gap between what we know and what we need—but not necessarily to answer the emerging questions.[36]

ARE ALL PROGRAMS DOOMED TO FAIL?

BPR joins a host of other respectable change programs that could not match available tools to the needs of management and their problems. Examples include restructuring programs and those which emphasized group work and other motivational techniques. Some benefits were always derived from all these programs. Total Quality Management and Group Think produced improvements in productivity and redesign of work processes. These and other techniques may offer some solutions to situations arising from the new world of business. But they are far from solutions that comfortably match current and future needs. Moreover, the cumulative impacts of the development of management tools lead to applications, but not to radical thinking or a shift in paradigm.

All such programs generally fail because they offer present solutions to future problems. In order to succeed, these programs must have a "real" shift in paradigm, not simply a call to obliterate what exists for a foggy idea of what is new. BPR in particular failed because it was out of tune with the new world of business and the new world economy. Not only was BPR not the solution, but in 1993 BPR *was already obsolete.*[37]

The evolutionary development of management knowledge (as shown in Figure 4.3) is not only incremental but also progresses in saturation stages. As in the evolution of science, the contributions by the existing pool of knowledge—the state-of-the-art—tend to reach a degree of saturation, after which only radical movement can elevate it to a higher plain.[38] This is very similar to the concept of the scientific paradigm discussed above. In the next section I will utilize the notion of paradigmatic "leaps" to illustrate the changes in corporate and managerial knowledge and the failure of BPR to partake in this process.

REAL SHIFTS IN PARADIGM

"Real" shifts in the paradigm of management thought and knowledge are rare occurrences. New thinking emerges only as a leap in the evolutionary scale. In Figure 4.3 these leaps are shown for the cumulative effect of several programs, and for each of the yet-to-come knowledge pool.

Shifts are rare because of two main reasons. First, managers are entrenched in their thinking and in the picture they have of their world. They, their consultants, and even most scholars have much intellectual capital invested in this approach or paradigm. So real change is hampered by strong interests in favor of the status quo.

Second, training and education are based on current thinking. The educational system (and management education is hardly an exception) emphasizes stability over revolution and conformity over leapfrogging. In addition, the training itself is conducted with present tools and knowledge that are obsolete at the moment of transfer to the next generation.

So, how does new thinking emerge and how is a paradigm replaced? When a paradigm does shift, it is in a way of looking at the world and in the way of understand-

Figure 4.4
Current Knowledge and Future Solutions

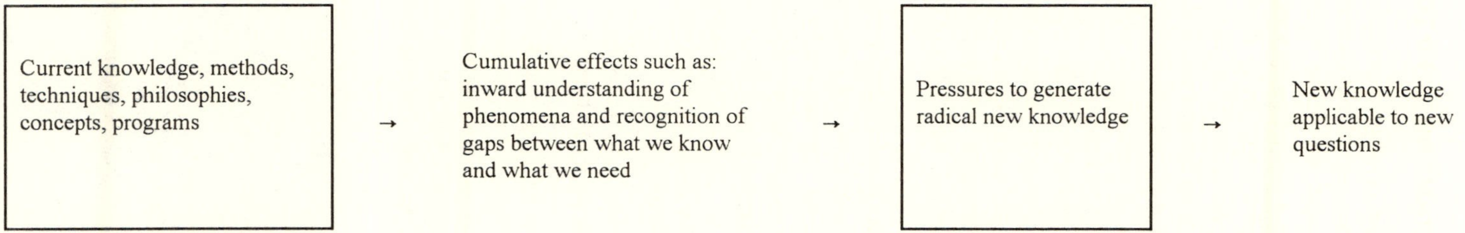

Current knowledge, methods, techniques, philosophies, concepts, programs

↑

Cumulative effects such as: inward understanding of phenomena and recognition of gaps between what we know and what we need

↑

Pressures to generate radical new knowledge

↑

New knowledge applicable to new questions

ing it, so that patterns and logic are totally new and the existing pattern and logic are no longer valid.

A friend of my family in the 1950s owned and operated several plants in Europe. The company manufactured and sold vacuum tubes, cathode-ray tubes, and diodes, all for the television and radio sets of that era. His company had contracts with major manufacturers in Europe, such as Blaupunkt and Grundig. In an attempt to improve the plants' productivity, he sought the advice of management consultants who recommended overhauling the line and the introduction of variants of his products. In an attempt to improve the plants' productivity, he invested heavily in the redesign of the production line and ancillary functions. The first of these new plants was inaugurated several months before the appearance of solid state technology, which made his entire operation totally obsolete—overnight.

A shift in the paradigm is not only due to the advent of a new technology. It is the appearance and then dominance of new questions. Instead of asking: what type of factory should I build? one asks: should I be in this business at all? Instead of asking: how can I lower my cost of making VCRs? one asks: what lies beyond VCRs? It is a new perspective, with totally new views of what the world is like and of how and why things appear and work the way they do.

Kenneth Clark gave an excellent illustration of this point in his treatise on the development of Western civilization.[39] Through descriptions of the evolution of the visual arts and architecture, Clark focused on the year 1100 when radical changes occurred in European culture, in architecture, in sculpting, and in the manner in which people perceived their environment, themselves, their religion, and their place in the constellation of events. Suddenly, Clark noted, within one lifetime, such change occurred. This change was not due to some technological breakthrough—just a fortuitous release of energy and a leap to a higher plane.

Real shifts in scientific paradigms appear as a whirlwind activity of a great scientist who redesigns the world in his or her head. Isaac Newton and Albert Einstein are such revolutionaries who led us to a totally new direction. Is this feasible in management?

PARADIGM SHIFTS IN MANAGEMENT

Radical change in management occurs as a happenstance combination of a leap in technology *and* a shift in management philosophy, outlook, and perspective. When the two merge in a fortunate manner, we then have radical change. Some scholars believe that such changes are due to environmental turbulence, in a manner similar to the great discontinuities in biological evolution that may be attributed to major changes in the earth's environment (end of the ice-age or the attack of meteorites).

The emergence of schools of thought in management which I discuss elsewhere in this book may serve as an illustration to such radical changes in management. The merging of technology leap and management philosophy changes does not generally occur simultaneously. There is usually a gap in time between the occurrence of these two dimensions of the radical shift in management paradigm.

For example, Douglas McGregor established the idea of "Theory Y" as opposed to "Theory X." His description of "Theory Y" proposed a new perspective of how managers view their employees. It was a totally different view of what motivates people at work and how to manage them.[40] But the effects of the shift to a more human-relations view of corporate workers did not fully crystallize until adequate breakthroughs in technology in the 1960s and 1970s allowed companies to make radical changes in the way they operate, produce, *and* treat their employees.

Shifts in management paradigm are a very lengthy and complex process, seldom attributable to one innovator or even to a single decade in time. They are evolutionary, not revolutionary. They are incremental, not sudden. They happen through methodical improvements, by trial and error. The triggering dimensions of technology and change in management philosophy come from *outside* the corporation and its executive pool. Management scientists and consultants digest such potential changes into a long-term indoctrination effort which results in shifts in paradigm.

Although there are "gurus" in management, there are no Newtons or Einsteins, or Johannes Keplers, or Benoit Mandelbrots.[41] Knowledge in management and organizations is still a fragile assortment of methodologies and findings from various disciplines. The integrative framework is yet in its infancy to allow for the emergence of a revolutionary scholar with the ability to radically change the field. Add to this the complex array of questions in the disciplines and the inherent inability of the field of management and organization at present to formulate simplistic yet encompassing models of how corporations operate.[42]

What complicates matters is that, at any given time, there are not one but several paradigms present in management and organization scholarship. Some of these are convergent, others conflicting. Thus a radical shift is unlikely when there are diverse intellectual forces pulling in different, even paradoxical, directions.[43]

BPR WAS NOT A PARADIGM SHIFT

Proponents of Business Process Reengineering believe that their program of change has ingrained in it a propitious encounter of leaps in both technology and management thinking. They believe that such a conjuring of events has occurred in the early 1990s, and that BPR *is* the propellant to a shift in paradigm.

Absence of Intellectual Alternative

BPR is *not* a paradigm shift because of at least two central reasons that emerge from the discussion above. The first reason is the paucity of knowledge in the arsenal of management and organization scientists. When BPR obliterated the existing processes and their connecting structure, and when it called for a new culture to emerge, it lacked the supporting knowledge base that would allow its implementers to build the new organization. Proponents of BPR have also suggested that senior managers lack the "vision" to create the redesigned corporation. But what senior managers lacked were the intellectual tools for the job.

At the time BPR appeared on the corporate scene there were no leaps in management thought, and BPR did not provide any such contribution of intellectual transformation. Unlike other (political/economic) manifestos, BPR failed to offer an alternative intellectual framework.[44]

As I previously argued, paradigm shifts in management are very rare and incremental. BPR started out with this disadvantage, with the cards stacked against it. But the lack of adequate knowledge and tools would have hindered BPR's attempt to transformation even if there was a combination of events in the early 1990s that would qualify for the preconditions of leaps in technology and transformation in management thought.[45]

Level of Entry

A second reason is the level at which BPR entered the organization. In theory, BPR is the responsibility of senior management who undertake the redesign and restructuring of the corporation. But, as I discuss throughout this book, the implementation of BPR (as any change program) is carried out at all levels of the organization. In particular this is crucial at the level of middle management. Therefore when a radical change program like BPR is introduced, its effects transcend the narrow confines of senior executives, reverberating down the organization at all levels of management.

In the context of the concept of multiple paradigms in management and organization theory, one can extend this to the hierarchy of the corporation. Middle managers generally have different perspectives than senior managers on what the organization is, does, or should be doing. Middle managers thus have a management paradigm of their own, which may or may not coincide or match that of their superiors.

In a ten-year study which started with my doctoral research, I discovered that senior managers' perceptions, views, or representatives of corporate phenomena differ from those of middle managers. This finding held even when age, tenure in the organization, gender, and other personal characteristics were considered. I have also found that there were similarities between the perceptions of senior managers and those of nonsupervisory employees. This leaves middle managers as a unique group of corporate members who have a very specialized view of their organization—divergent from and even conflicting with their superiors.[46]

Therefore, when BPR was introduced at the senior management level, in addition to problems with diffusion and implementation, the middle managers were confronted with a threat to their own paradigmatic representation of the organization. Unless BPR was able to address this phenomenon, there was hardly a paradigm shift in middle managers.

SUMMARY

Business Process Reengineering was doomed to failure when it was introduced in the early 1990s. Its basic premises were unattainable. Its implementation collapsed from the weight of poor guidance.

But above all BPR was an obsolete solution to a set of questions, perhaps way ahead of this program on the evolutionary scale of management knowledge. BPR had little, if any, knowledge tools to tackle these problems. It lacked an intellectual alternative to the structures it demolished. It was sold to managers as a shift in paradigm or even as a manifesto for change. *It was neither.*

Like any other revolutionary program for change, BPR lacked from its inception, and by design, the ability to bring about a shift in paradigm. As I argued in this chapter, BPR was an impossibility from the very start. Paradigm shifts in management are rare, but they do happen—incrementally and over time. BPR was certainly not one of them.

NOTES

1.   M. Hammer and J. Champy, *Re-engineering the Corporation: A Manifesto for Business Revolution* (New York: Harper Business, 1993).

2.   R. Mathews, "Does Reengineering Really Work?" *Progressive Grocer*, February 1995, pp. 32-38.

3.   B. Smith, "Process Reengineering: The Toughest Challenge," *HR Focus*, February 1995, pp. 24-25.

4.   C. Clemons, "Using Scenario Analysis to Manage the Strategic Roles of Reengineering," *Sloan Management Review*, Summer 1995, pp. 61-72; and A. Vogl, "Reengineering: Light that Failed?" *Across the Board*, March 1995, pp. 27-31.

5.   See, for example, A. Du Bain, *Reengineering Survival Guide* (Cincinnati: Thompson Executive Press, 1996); also M. Hammer and S. Stanton, *The Reengineering Revolution: A Handbook* (New York: Harper Business, 1995); and J. Champy, *Reengineering Management: The Mandate to a New Leadership* (New York: Harper Business, 1995).

6.   M. Klein, "10 Principles of Reengineering," *Executive Excellence*, February 1995, p. 20; and J. Gilmore, "How to Make Reengineering Truly Effective," *Planning Review*, May-June 1995, pp. 39-40. Also see G. Hall, J. Rosenthal and J. Wade, "How to Make Reengineering Really Work," *Harvard Business Review*, November-December 1993, pp. 119-131.

7.   This is the key theme in the writings of Hammer and Champy. The stages or principles of BPR reflect both a strategic perspective of the organization after its reconstruction, and a generalized road map to put there.

8.   C. A. Bartlett and S. Ghoshal, "Changing the Role of Top Management Beyond Strategy to Purpose," *Harvard Business Review*, November-December 1994, p. 8.

9.   H. Mintzberg, "The Fall and Rise of Strategic Planning," *Harvard Business Review*, January-February 1994, p. 111.

10.   *Ibid.*; pp. 110-111.

11.   Reengineering advice and handbook-like publications cut across industries. For example, see J. Uzzi, "Reengineering Doesn't Have to be a Dirty Word," *National Underwriter*, April 17, 1995, pp. 49-51; B. Gale, "Quality Profiling: The First Step in Reengineering and Benchmarking," *Planning Review*, May-June 1995, pp. 37-38; and, A. Thayer, "Industry Group Weighs Reengineering Value," *Chemical and Engineering News*, May 15, 1995, pp. 15-18; also see R. Westcutt, "Whole System Architecture-Beyond Rengineering: A Guidebook for Designing Work Processes and Human Systems for High Performance Capabilities," *Quality Progress*, April 1995, pp. 125-127.

12.   P. Drucker, *The New Realities* (New York: Harper & Row, 1989), p. 261.

13. G. Carroll and M. Hannan, *Organizations in Industry* (New York: Oxford University Press, 1995).

14. J. Boyd, "Reengineering: Japanese Style," *Information Week*, December 5, 1994, pp. 39-46.

15. J. Martin, *Cultures in Organizations: Three Perspectives* (New York: Oxford University Press, 1992).

16. Illustrative publications on managing change are: P. Nutt, *Managing Planned Change* (New York: Macmillan, 1992); K. Lewin, "Group Decisions and Social Change," in J. Maccoby, T. Newcomb, and E. Hartley (eds.), *Readings in Social Psychology* (New York: Holt, Reinhart and Winston, 1958); and G. Lippitt, P. Langseth, and J. Mossop, *Implementing Organizational Change* (San Francisco: Jossey-Bass, 1985). Also see C. Argyris, *Overcoming Organizational Defenses* (Needham, MA: Allyn and Bacon, 1990).

17. I had previously written about this phenomenon. See Eliezer Geisler, "Measuring the Unquantifiable: Issues in the Use of Indicators in Unstructured Phenomena," *International Journal of Operations and Quantitative Management*, Vol. 1, No. 2, 1995, pp. 145-161. Other writers have also discussed the issue of gap between theory and practice. See, for example, A. Blumstein, "The Current Missionary Role of OR/MS," *Operations Research*, Vol. 35, No. 3, 1987, pp. 926-929. Professor Muller-Merbach from Kaiserslautern University in Germany has pointed out to me that there have been many valuable contributions of OR to BPR. Among the salient examples: network analysis, simulation, stochastic processes, queuing theory, and principles of systems approach. He contends that these are blatantly overlooked in today's BPR scene.

18. A. Ascari, M. Rock, and S. Dutta, "Reengineering and Organizational Change: Lessons from a Comparative Analysis of Company Experiences," *European Management Journal*, March 1995, pp. 1-30.

19. L. Barton, *Crisis in Organization: Managing and Communicating in the heat of Chaos* (Cincinnati: South Western Publishing Company, 1993).

20. J. Kiely, "Managing Change: Why Reengineering Projects Fail," *Harvard Business Review*, March-April 1995, p. 15; also see J. Rosengard, "The Missing Link Is Reengineering," *Financial Executive*, March-April, 1995, pp. 15-20.

21. K. Peterson, "Reengineering: The Razor Edge," *Executive Excellence*, February 1995, pp. 12-13.

22. S. Longo, "After Reengineering—Dejobbing?" *CPA Journal*, March 1995, p. 69; also see J. Champy, "Reengineering Management: The Mandate for New Leadership," *Industry Week*, February 20, 1995, pp. 32-42; and B. Stuck, "Collaboration: Working Together Apart," *Business Communications Review*, February 1995, pp. 9-12.

23. M. Moravec, "From Reengineering to Revitalization," *Executive Excellence*, February 1995, pp. 18-19.

24. S. Barr, "Grinding It Out: Why Reengineering Takes So Long," *CFO*, January 1995, pp. 26-31; also see B. Ettore, "Reengineering Tales from the Front," *Management Review*, January 1995, pp. 13-18; J. Hendry, "Process Reengineering and the Dynamic Balance of the Organization," *European Management Journal*, March 1995, pp. 52-57; and J. Kotter, "Leading Change: Why Transformation Efforts Fail," *Harvard Business Review*, March-April 1995, pp. 59-67.

25. J. Hyatt, "Real World Reengineering," *Inc.*, April 1995, pp. 40-53; also see G. Scott, "Downsizing, Business Process Reengineering, and Quality Improvement Plans: How Are They Related?" *Information Strategy*, Spring 1995, pp. 18-34; and J. King, "Reengineering Focus Slips," *ComputerWorld*, March 13, 1995, p. 6. Experiences of companies who have undergone BPR are told in J. McHale, "Straight Talking about the Reengineering Revolution," *People*

Management, April 6, 1995, p. 52; and B. Spiker and F. Lesser, "We Have Met the Enemy . . .", *Journal of Business Strategy,* March-April 1995, pp. 17-21.

26. E. Naumann, *Creating Customer Value* (Cincinnati: Thompson Executive Press, 1995). Much of the damage caused by inconsistencies and suboptimization is usually attributed to poor application of logistics and poor implementation of reengineering programs. However, massive change programs, such as BPR, are inherently unable to avoid differences in efficiencies and inconsistencies, and other results of the different reactions of units and people to corporate radical changes. See, for example, H. Mintzberg, *Structure in Five: Designing Effective Organizations* (Englewood Cliffs, NJ: Prentice-Hall, 1993).

27. P. Frost, V. Mitchell, and W. Nord, *Managerial Reality* (New York: HarperCollins, 1995).

28. Jill Vitiello, "Reengineering: It's Totally Radical," *Journal of Business Strategy,* 14(6), 1993, pp. 44-47.

29. R. L. Manganelli and S. P. Raspa, "Why Reengineering Has Failed," *Management Review,* July 1995, pp. 39-43.

30. G. Hamel and C. K. Prahalad, "Competing in the New Economy: Managing Out of Bounds," *Strategic Management Journal,* 17(3), March '1996, p. 242.

31. See, for example, the Price Waterhouse Change Integration Team, *The Paradox Principles: How High Performance Companies Manage Chaos, Complexity, and Contradiction to Achieve Superior Results* (Chicago: Richard D. Irwin, 1996). This book was written by a group of consultants, thus benefitting from their experiences and episodes in their practice. Although they concentrate on discussing issues of information technology, the book nonetheless provides some integration of the factors listed here, such as complexity and urgency. See, for example, J. Osterlund, *Competence Management by Infomatics Systems in R&D Work* (Stockholm: Royal Institute of Technology, 1994).

32. In particular, the pioneering work of Donald Campbell. See for example, D. T. Campbell, "How Individual and Face-to-Face Group Selection Undermine Firm Selection in Organizational Evolution," in J. Baum and J. Singh (eds.), *Evolutionary Dynamics of Organizations* (New York: Oxford University Press, 1994) pp. 23-38.

33. See, for example, A. Miner and S. Mezias, "Ugly Duckling No More: Pasts and Futures of Organizational Learning Research," *Organization Science,* 7(1), 1996, pp. 88-99; also see C. Nass, "Knowledge or Skills: Which Do Administrators Learn From Experience?" *Organization Science,* 5(1), 1994, pp. 38-50; and C. Argyris and D. Schon, *Organizational Learning* (Reading, MA: Addison Wesley, 1978).

34. For example, L. Yelle, "The Learning Curve: Historical Review and Comprehensive Survey," *Decision Sciences,* 10(3), 1979, pp. 302-328; also see A. Van de Ven and D. Polley, "Learning While Innovating," *Organization Science,* 3(2), 1992, pp. 92-116.

35. See K. Sissell, "Reexamining Reengineering: Down to Microsurgery," *Chemical Week,* 158(22), 5 June 1996, pp. 29-33; and A. Blackburn, "BPR—New Wine which Missed the Bottle," *Management Services,* 40(5), May 1996, pp. 18-21.

36. See D. Tobin, *Transformational Learning: Renewing Your Company Through Knowledge and Skills* (New York: John Wiley, 1996).

37. For example, "Reengineering Use Starts to Decline," *Chemical Marketing Reporter,* 249(3), June 3, 1996, p. 5. This article reports a survey by Bain & Co.

38. See, for example, a recent article that summarizes some relevant aspects of this issue: J. B. Quinn, P. Anderson, and S. Finkelstein, "Leveraging Intellect," *The Academy of Management Executives,* 10(3), November 1996, pp. 7-27. The authors have concluded that "while managing professional intellect is clearly the key to value creation and profitability for

most companies, few have arrived at systematic structures for developing, focusing, leveraging, and measuring their intellectual capabilities" (p. 25).

39. K. Clark, *Civilization: A Personal View* (New York: Harper & Row, 1969).

40. D. McGregor, *The Human Side of Enterprise*, New York, McGraw Hill, 1960.

41. A key developer of chaos theory and fractal geometry. See B. Mandelbrot, *The Fractal Geometry of Nature* (New York: Freeman, 1977).

42. There is, of course, a heated discussion in the management literature on where the field is and where it is going. For example. M. Hitt, "Comment: Academic Research in Management/Organizations: Is It Dead or Alive?", *Journal of Management Inquiry*, 4(1), 1995, pp. 52-56.; also see A. Westerholz, "Paradoxical Thinking and Change in the Frames of Reference," *Organization Studies*, 14(1), 1993, pp. 37-58; and M. Zald, "Organization Studies as a Scientific and Humanistic Enterprise: Toward a Reconceptualization of the Foundations of the Field," *Organization Science*, 4(3), 1993, pp. 513-528. For a different criticism, see R. Aldag and S. Fuller, "Holding a Mirror to Management Research: On Creativity, Elitism, and the Defense of Dogmatism," *Journal of Management Inquiry*, 4(4), December 1995, pp. 341-344. Aldag and Fuller have valiantly indicated the problems in the field by sharing the blame. They say: "Hitt (1995) concludes that relevant valuable research is being conducted by management scholars, but that channels for dissemination of that research are not well developed. Such a perspective is comforting because it largely externalizes our apparent impotence. However, we do not feel the fault is in the stars . . . we feel we should reach not for a telescope but for a mirror" (pp. 343-344). In this connection also see J. Pfeffer, "Barriers to the Advance of Organizational Science: Paradigm Development as a Dependent Variable," *Academy of Management Reviews*, 18(3), 1993, pp. 599-620. A counterview is given in A. Canella and R. Paetzold, "Pfeffer's Barriers to the Advance of Organizational Science: A Rejoinder," *Academy of Management Review*, 19(4), 1994, pp. 337-341.

43. R. Quinn and K. Cameron (eds.), *Paradox and Transformation: Toward a Theory of Change in Organization and Management* (Cambridge, MA: Ballinger, 1988).

44. I am referring here specifically to the work by Karl Marx from whom the term "manifesto" may have been borrowed by Hammer and Champy in their original book. See K. Marx and F. Engels, *The Communist Manifesto* (Moscow: Progress Publishers, 1971). The original manifesto published in 1848 offered a new economic and political philosophy that would replace the existing system. Although this new system ultimately failed, it was nevertheless—at the time—a seemingly viable alternative.

45. See, for example, T. Galpin, *The Human Side of Change* (San Francisco: Jossey-Bass, 1996).

46. The results from this series of studies are being computed and will soon be published. See related research in I. Palmer, and R. Dunford, "Conflicting Uses of Metaphors: Reconceptualizing Their Use in the Field of Organizational Change," *Academy of Management Review*, 21(3), 1996, pp. 691-717; also see R. Daft, and K. Weick, "Toward a Model of Organizations as Interpretation Systems," *Academy of Management Review*, 9(2), 1984, pp. 284-295.

5

INFORMATION TECHNOLOGY: RATIONALIZING THE IMPERATIVES

THE "RITCHIE INCIDENT"

In the annals of military history there is an incident that occurred in the Second World War in which a battle was lost. The incident hinged upon information, its distribution, interpretation, and value.

Anthony Cave Brown, in his marvelous account of the clandestine war of deception conducted by the Allies against Germany, described the effect of Ultra: the British cryptographic agency that cracked Hitler's ciphers and was thus able to read most communications to and from the German military.[1] On the eve of the battle of Alam Halfa, in the North African Desert, the British 8th Army was commanded by General Sir Neil Ritchie. He was facing Field Marshal Erwin Rommel, the "Desert Fox." In late May 1942, Ritchie received substantial information from his superior, General Auchinlec, based on the deciphered communications provided by Ultra. For security reasons, Ritchie, a field commander, didn't know of Ultra's existence. Ultra was able to decode Rommel's battle plan, which was duly relayed to Ritchie. Not knowing the source of the information—although he now possessed all necessary information for a great victory and the avoidance of Rommel's trap—Ritchie decided to ignore the data on Rommel's intentions.

On June 13, 1942, Ritchie committed his army to battle and fell into the trap. He lost 300 tanks, his army retreated toward Egypt, and the British Army endured a defeat that triggered swift changes in command throughout the Middle East and Africa.

How would a military commander, in possession of what we might call "complete information" on his opponent's plans, nevertheless act in a manner that defies common logic, ending up in defeat and humiliation?

This incident clearly shows the following truisms. First, that the possession of information doesn't guarantee that it will have value in promoting sound decision making. Second, that information is only as valuable as its acceptance, interpretation, and utilization by decision makers. This truism is in addition to issues of risk-taking propensity and the biases involved with the framing of problems and the nature of the problems themselves.

The "Ritchie incident" is a case that shows the need for a revision of the traditional theory of information processing. This theory explores the transfer and communication of information, focusing on such attributes as message clarity, encoding, decoding, modes of transmission, and the like.[2] The "Ritchie incident" adds a new dimension: the value of information as a component in critical decision making.

INFORMATION TECHNOLOGY AND REENGINEERING

Business Process Reengineering, as devised by Hammer and Champy, heralded information technology (IT) as the *enabling mechanism* that allows corporations to reinvent themselves. Since the original creators of the reengineering movement have provided only a cursory description of how information technology will serve as the engine for their proposed change program, there emerged recently a wave of studies and writings on what is being called "second generation reengineering,"[3] and a host of approaches in which various tools are used to implement BPR.

Information technology is the enabling technology, at the core of what reengineering promises to achieve. The redesign of the work process, the elimination of processes with little or no value-added, and the overall redesign of the organization that follows—all depend on the existence and support provided by ubiquitous information technology.

The fallacy of this contention is composed of two major dimensions that help to explain the inherent failure of BPR as a comprehensive cure for corporate problems: (1) the "Ritchie incident" phenomenon, and (2) the pattern of evolution of information technology in the organization.

The "Ritchie Incident" Phenomenon

General Ritchie had acted like any senior manager who is confronted with a crisis. He assembled all information available to him; weighed the value of each piece of data; assessed the validity, reliability, and trustworthiness of each; weighed the risks involved—and made a decision. In the case of the Ultra information, he had all the information he needed for a successful campaign. There were no problems in the clarity, understanding, transmission, or interpretation of the information received. The data were clear, relevant, understandable, received, decoded, and complete.

The equivalent in the corporate environment is information about work processes, jobs, organization units, and strategic options. Reengineering supporters claim that the fact that there is new, available, adequate, and sophisticated technology to generate, transfer, store, and retrieve information finally allows corporations to exercise BPR, and to extract its promised advantages. As the "Ritchie incident" phenomenon shows, this is hardly the case. Information technology is only the technology that carries information faster, better, more of it, clearer, and that allows for more sophisticated manipulations. But reengineering is an exercise in crisis management. Hammer and Champy indeed had emphasized the crisis mode in which reengineering is implemented. It is a battle that looms ahead in the war of global competitiveness. IT, in general, is an enabling technology, but it's not a substitute for managerial decision making.

Hammer and Champy, and other writers on the topic of reengineering, have indeed recently turned their attention to the role that executive reasoning and decision making plays in the successful application of reengineering. They have recognized the need for executive involvement in the reengineering program. Thus there is an emerging recognition of the fact that the mere introduction and proliferation of IT in the company is not enough of an engine to promote reengineering nor to assure its success.

In other words, a manager may be in possession of all the information he needs about an inefficient work process, yet decide against any interventions. This decision may be, and probably is, highly biased by the executive's assessment of the information, the role that the process plays in the overall strategy of the company, and other such factors (see Figure 5.1).

In fact, IT may have a much stronger effect in changing the way business is conducted and organizations behave than its effect as a dynamic force in reengineering. This means that if Hammer and Champy regard IT as a very powerful force that *already* exists in organizations, and their BPR scheme is designed to take advantage of this powerful technology ("ride the wave"), they may be correct. But correct insofar as to join all other executives and scholars who for the past 20 years have struggled with the role that IT plays and should play in the business enterprise.

What Hammer and Champy contend, however, is that IT enables information to become ubiquitous, allows generalists to make expert decisions, and allows for speedy and more detailed operations. All fine and good, but, I repeat, not enough to become the essential component of reengineering.

Figure 5.1
Why Information Technology Cannot Compensate for Inherent Flaws in Reengineering

---

The "Ritchie Incident" Phenomenon

- Even the best, complete, timely, correct, and clear information is not enough to fuel reengineering.
- If reengineering is already flawed, as a concept and major change program, information technology and the ubiquity of information will not overcome these flaws.

Evolution of it in Corporations

- IT initially introduced for "back-room" cost-cutting efficiency purposes.
- IT gradually evolved in corporations.
- From "back-room" to front-end and strategic user for overall corporate performance, corporations advanced on the learning curve.
- Take away the radical advantage of IT, and reengineering is stripped of its engine.

Why? Because if the other dimensions of a reengineering program are flawed (as I advocated in the previous chapter), then IT is not capable of salvaging the change program just because it allows information to become ubiquitous, speedily transmittable, and so on. If reengineering, as a concept, is feasible and produces great results with minimal side effects, IT may serve as a technology that facilitates the execution. But if reengineering is *already* a proposition flawed internally, then, as in the case of General Ritchie, even the "best" information given to you in a complete and timely fashion, cannot save the day.

Evolution of IT in the Corporation

QVC is an on-line shopping network with sales in 1995 of $2 billion and a worldwide search organization that purchases goods everywhere in the world. QVC is a business shaped by information technology and the innovations and spread of telecommunications and computers. The next logical step for QVC is the Internet. QVC cannot operate without information and telecommunication technology. (I prefer this term because it encompasses the essential component of telecommunications. The acronym ITT is more descriptive than IT, although in this book I use both.) QVC relies not only on the existing ITT, but also on the emerging technical developments, techniques, hardware, and new capabilities in equipment and in software.

As a member of a very large group of businesses that emerged from the ITT revolution and depend on its continuing growth, QVC is a type of company that redesigns and regenerates itself as ITT changes. The regeneration is driven by the technological imperative (as organization scientists like to call the technology dimension in organizations). Companies like QVC have no choice but to transform themselves as the ITT changes, and to the tune of such changes.

However, most other companies are not as dependent on ITT. To them, ITT is a technological trend that has provided solutions to automation/computerization of activities in the corporation. Beyond automation, ITT allowed the enterprise to rationalize work, streamline operations, and open opportunities for activities and processes to benefit from ITT's capabilities of logic, speed, ubiquity, and increased reach.

When one reads the manifesto that Hammer and Champy have proposed to reengineer the corporation, it seems that information technology is suddenly discovered and that its potent capabilities can *now* be mastered by the reengineering team of experts.

The realities are that ITT arrived in corporate America (and throughout the world) very gradually.[4] ITT was initially introduced in corporations as a tactical tool to rationalize and to automate the "back-room" operations of accounting and payroll. Only in the period 1985-1995 did ITT expand its functions to support front-end operations, and to begin its support of strategic actions (see Figure 5.2).

Figure 5.2
Evolution of Information and Telecomunication Technology in Corporations

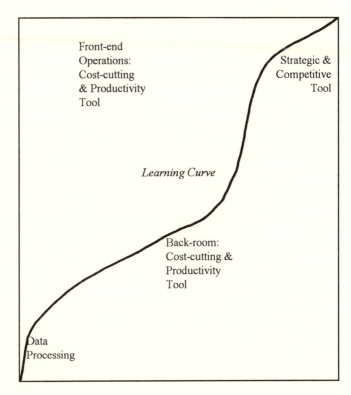

Front-end
Operations:
Cost-cutting
& Productivity
Tool

Strategic &
Competitive
Tool

Levels of
Sophistication
and User-
Friendliness

Learning Curve

Back-room:
Cost-cutting &
Productivity
Tool

Data
Processing

Time →

Information Technology: Cost-Cutting and Productivity Tool

ITT is, and has been for almost a decade, a corporate reality. Companies have accumulated knowledge and experience on how to utilize ITT in various capacities and for various functions. Not only was there a learning curve, as shown in Figure 5.2, but the evolution of ITT was incremental and cumulative. Data processing and back-room improvements are still practiced, but companies have mastered the intricacies of these functions as they move along the sophistication curve toward using ITT as a strategic tool.[5]

In many ways, therefore, ITT is used in reengineering in a "one-step-forward-two-steps-backward" approach. Although Hammer and Champy intended for ITT to assist reengineering and to facilitate it along the entire spectrum of its capabilities (including as a strategic weapon), the results had generally been disappointing. As corporations learned to utilize ITT to improve the efficiency of their operations, they tended to put ITT to this use when implementing reengineering. Moreover, as reengineering had been largely implemented piecemeal, the main emphasis in each work process was cost-cutting and productivity enhancement. Tools are used where they are needed and where they produce the best results. ITT is no exception, and corporations preferred to use it in the manner in which they had been accustomed and in which they had progressed along the learning curve. Hence also the striking results in some cases where reengineered corporations posted notable improvements in productivity and had substantially cut costs.[6]

RATIONALIZING THE TECHNOLOGY IMPERATIVE

In this chapter I have advanced the argument that ITT cannot be claimed by reengineering proponents as the key mechanism that enables it to successfully achieve its promised benefits. ITT is a set of enabling technologies that was gradually introduced into corporations at a tremendous cost in learning and adaptation. Reengineering proponents seem to suggest that they have "discovered" ITT and its wonderful (perhaps uncharted) capacity to promote the proposed radical change, and to finally bring about "new rules" of a brave new world.

These new rules had been unfolding and slowly evolving in corporate life for more than a decade. Thus, proponents of reengineering are discovering an existing reality and simply co-opting it to their scheme of radical change.

In another angle, Hammer and Champy have suggested that reengineering is proposed as a new model that rejects the traditional industrial paradigm. This, they propose, can be achieved by harnessing the potential in information technology.

Yet the new paradigm of industrial organizations is also an already established view, at least in the minds and writings of organizational scholars. Peter Drucker introduced such ideas in 1988,[7] and a host of other scholars have since discussed the nature of the new organizational format. They include the virtual organization, and the move toward the knowledge-based structuring of work.[8]

If reengineering indeed rejects the traditional industrial organization and makes use of ITT to reinvent the corporation according to a new format and a new model, then it must start out with such a model in mind, before radical change is imposed. This is not what happened.

Information technology has been utilized in reengineering in precisely the same mode as in the early days of its introduction into corporate life. ITT was again primarily used to increase efficiency and to cut costs. There has been no significant radicalization of a new model of the corporation. An excellent example is Ford Motor Company, which in April 1996 reengineered its information systems operation by introducing a client-server software from an external vendor to replace its in-house systems for its core functions (e.g., manufacturing).[9] The move to packaged software was made to cut costs and increase the level of flexibility of its systems, in a rapid environment. Another goal of the move was to cut the "time-to-market" of a new car from 37 months to no more than 24 months.

Although in the auto industry cost cutting and reduced time-to-market will ultimately have profound strategic effects, the reengineering effort of this case was not geared toward a new model of work organization. Clearly, some effects of a change to packaged and perhaps more friendly ITT will occur. People in the corporation will acquire additional skills, improve their reach, and even change their behavior to some extent.[10]

In addition to increased efficiency and cost cutting, ITT also generates a rationalization of work processes and the work environment in general. The characteristics of ITT, such as speed, accuracy, computing capacity, ease of use, and ubiquity, combine to produce capabilities for both people and units within the corporation to introduce rationality into current processes. It now becomes easier and more attractive to view work in rational terms, to reduce the effect of subjective reasoning, and to enhance logic as a guiding mechanism for the design or redesign of work flows.[11]

In a classical sense, rationality is the questioning in a skeptical mode why a certain process exists and how it accomplishes it objectives. In an operational sense, rationalization calls for finding a better way to do it.[12]

Rationality, ITT, and Behavior

What ITT accomplished in the corporation is a blend of effects that seem to overlap. Professor Drago and I have recently proposed a model of the way ITT influences behavior.[13] We suggested that ITT increases rationality, thereby acting as a *modus operandi*, influencing individual and group behavior, and fostering routineness of operations. Managers become more interactive, yet are also more likely to rely on "canned" or packaged solutions, which are considered more rational and efficient. The trend is toward standardization, routineness, and rationality.[14]

Therefore, these effects of ITT do not create a novel corporate format. They do influence behavior and open up opportunities and new ways of accomplishing given corporate tasks. The impacts of ITT have also evolved to the point where they facilitate strategy decisions. ITT is thus an enabling technology, but not a substitute for careful and considered managerial actions. ITT is a limited tool, whose influence on the organization has been gradual and therefore temperate.

Moreover, as I have already mentioned, ITT had created enough changes and discontinuities in the organization as to cause uneasiness and uncertainty, compounded by the effects of executive change programs. Streamlining, routineness, and rationality are powerful change phenomena in themselves. They have modified behavior and have made some skills obsolete, while elevating many other, new skills to the vanguard of corporate desirability. This was the situation that the reengineering movement encountered upon arrival in the corporation of the early 1990s.

The Technology Imperative

ITT is a technological imperative in the corporation. Its absorption by the reengineering movement as the enabler of the radical transformation programs simply added an extra component of rationality to reengineering. Put somewhat differently, the reliance of BPR on ITT as its engine of transformation, provides it with a dimension of rationality. Without ITT, reengineering becomes the proverbial king in his new clothes. What ITT gives the reengineering effort is a mantle of rationalization of the technology imperative. When devoid of ITT, reengineering is merely a call to arms, directed at a nonexistent army, without weapons or a battle plan. Reengineering is a "manifesto" to redesign and reinvent work processes, which relies on ITT to provide the necessary tools, or conduits, for the proposed dramatic change programs.

Yet, as I advocated here, ITT has not lived up to the high expectations bestowed upon it. Once ITT is removed from the arsenal of that which makes reengineering really work, it remains the domain of the reengineering analysts who are now encumbered with the task of reinventing the corporation. The main task is now mainly dealt with on a subjective basis, whereas it should be rationalized and deterministic.

The Japanese Example

In 1995, Peter Cooper and Lynne Markus described the case of a CEO of a Japanese soy sauce manufacturing company, Higashimaru Shoyu, who reengineered his company through the help of his workers rather than reengineering consultants.[15] In this case the authors have stated that "increasingly, it is becoming clear that the engine of reengineering is not reengineering analysts, but managers and the people who do the work."[16] In the case of Higashimaru Shoyu, the authors have described five techniques used by the CEO of the company to implement radical change: (1) group leader meetings, (2) price control system, (3) tornado program (allowing group leaders to review their performance), (4) draft system (increasing level of self-worth of participants), and (5) cutting-in-half game (promoting creative thinking on part of the participants). This Japanese example shows the unrelenting need in American corporations for examples of successful reengineering, even though it's a Japanese company with its similar culture and idiosyncratic mode of management.

In another description of the Japanese experience with reengineering, John Boyd in *Information Week*[17] has suggested that one of the reasons for the failure of BPR to take hold in Japanese companies is their reluctance to implement IT. Boyd believes that this is due, in part, to the Japanese language, which is less direct and more complex than Western languages. In addition, Japanese managers maintain much more frequent personal contacts than their counterparts in the United States and Europe.

In essence, I believe that Japanese companies have rejected BPR "American style" because they applied redesign and reconfiguration of their business processes in their own way. Boyd cites the examples of Fujitsu in electronics and Kao in cosmetics as companies that implemented redesign, by whatever means that worked.

Similarly, if we accept the premise that the Japanese aversion to ITT, particularly e-mail and voice mail, is a key reason for not implementing BPR in the American format, then this reinforces my contention in this chapter. I have reiterated that without ITT as its driving engine, BPR is reduced to just another plan for improved efficiency to be carried out by trained consultants with fuzzy road maps and a lot of subjective assessments of organizational reality. The Japanese experience clearly supports my contention. Companies such as Fujitsu and Toyota avoid layoffs, utilize internal teams to create change, and have "reengineered" themselves with minimal use of ITT.

I cannot but overemphasize the immense role that the reengineering concept attaches to ITT, and, conversely, the totally different realities of ITT in the corporate work environment. It should be clarified that, in my view, reengineering in American companies, as a rule, didn't generally have such a high rate of failure because BPR analysts had not fully employed the power of ITT. The more prosaic picture is that there are no miracles built into ITT, and most of its impacts and benefits had *already been absorbed* by companies and managers during the long period of incremental usage and diffusion of these technologies.[18] Reengineering did move to the front burner the notion of rationalization: the steel-cold analysis of tasks, means, ends, and their justification. This notion has great appeal to executives who yearn for quantitative, sensible, and rational descriptions and explanations of corporate phenomena.

THE SEARCH FOR QUANTITIES

Another aspect of the rationalization of work processes is the constant search by managers of quantitative descriptions of corporate situations, problems, and phenomena. The search leads to the overwhelming preference by managers of *ratios, indexes*, and other quantitative descriptions.[19]

This is very understandable, since managers who daily confront a turbulent environment desire a rational and, if possible, numerical representation of the world around them. If it's quantitative, so the belief goes, it can be measured, comparisons can be made, and it inspires a higher degree of confidence.

The implementation of reengineering as a radical program of change brings about the necessity to generate measures, preferably quantitative. Thus, any improvement in the performance on efficiency of a unit or work process needs to be determined and measured. Ratios have long been the hallmark of productivity measurement. In addition, measuring progress, performance, and efficiency is carried out against preestablished standards and *benchmarks*.[20]

All of these benchmarks and ratios are doubly important for reengineering as well as any change program. They allow the corporation and the reengineering analysts to establish two main descriptions: (1) what's wrong with work process and unit performance, and by how much; and (2) how reengineering has improved this situation, and by how much.

However, managers should be aware of the fact that the use of such ratios as measures of performance may lead to unexpected and unwelcome consequences, which are not tied to a specific index or ratio. Rather, the discussion here focuses on the inherent problems which may arise when indexes and ratios of any kind are used *to evaluate* the performance and efficiency of any corporate unit or function or used to assess the contributions of reengineering. There are six main problems that may arise in the use of ratios and indexes in the capacity of evaluation tools, which are summarized in Figure 5.3.

Figure 5.3
Problems Inherent in the Use of Ratios and Indexes as Measures of Evaluation

---

- Once established, measures become "sacrosanct"

- "Contamination" phenomenon leads to behavior that is geared toward satisfying the measure rather than improving the activity being measured

- Biases are commonly due to the choice of measures

- Leading to wrong solutions

- Total picture of the activity or organization is blurred, while "local solutions" take precedence, leading to suboptimization

- Raiffa's error of the third kind

"Sacrosanct" Measures

When ratios and indexes are made into measures of evaluation, there is a tendency to think of them as "givens," and to relate every other measurement to these basic quantities. This problem is exacerbated when these measures are declared benchmarks. Against the benchmarks everything is compared. In the process, managers tend to forget how the benchmarks had been established, and refer to them as "God's eternal truth." Another difficulty arises when benchmarks are external to the corporation. This is particularly the case with industry benchmarks used as a point of departure or as a measure of performance to which we should aspire.

For example, in a consulting project for a Fortune 300 company, we discovered that the industry benchmark for "time to market" of new products was 28 months. Senior management insisted that any change in the R&D, as well as engineering, platforms must abide by this standard. As consultants, our task involved the redesign and improvement of the R&D and engineering functions. This was before reengineering had entered the corporate scene. When taking into account the overall strategy of the company, which emphasized quality as a differentiating characteristic of its product, and the constraints of its European customers, we concluded that quality is the most important guideline in our redesign program. We also discovered that when we take into account available resources and a reconfigured and downsized platform, we can do perhaps 30 or 32 months in "time to market."

Management rejected the redesign plan and insisted on 28 months *or less*. It was futile to compare the benefits that would accrue in launching a new product two months later—yet of high quality and almost zero defects—to the premature launch. The benchmark was a "holy figure," around which everything else had to conform.[21]

"Contamination" Phenomenon

A much-studied phenomenon of ratios and other quantitative measures used in evaluation is the "contamination" of these measures. Briefly described, people tend to behave in a way that is geared toward satisfying the evaluation measure, rather than to improving the activity being measured.[22] This is particularly true when these measures are used to assess human performance, which in turn translates into monetary and promotion rewards.

In one mid-size company headquarters in California, senior management had instituted a performance evaluation system whose cornerstone was the teamwork activities of the company's middle managers. The standard measure was set at 20% of activities, so that a middle manager cooperates with his or her peers. The objective of this personnel policy was to encourage interunit cooperation. The results were quite unexpected. Middle managers tried to outperform each other by spending more than half their time in all forms of "cooperative work," such as endless meetings, needless joint projects, and "social events" that counted toward teamwork credits.

Contamination can also occur in other activities of the corporation, not necessarily involving personnel actions. For example, a large metropolitan hospital, for whose director I recently consulted, was operating under the ratio of patients admitted per patients discharged as a measure of effectiveness of care. The closer the ratio to 1:00, the more effective the hospital. So, in order to improve the ratio, the hospital could manipulate the nominator (admissions) and/or the denominator (discharges). The first consisted of turning away terminally ill patients who might affect the ratio if they die during their hospital stay. The latter consisted of discharging patients who are beyond help, so as to avoid their death within the confines of the hospital. In both examples, there is behavior modification (personal as well as corporate) to accommodate the measure of evaluation. As seen, ratios are more maneuverable since they allow manipulation of two components—nominator and denominator.

Creating Bias

Measures are selected through a combination of rational processes, politics, and a large dose of compromise. Ratios and indexes are quantitative measures of relatively complex phenomena and their use creates a biased outlook.

A colleague recently consulted for a midsize manufacturer of auto parts. In agreement with the union, the shipping department was evaluated according to a ratio of crates arriving, per crates shipped, per hour. Although this measure at first sounds rational, my colleague discovered that a relatively slow process could release a crate within 20 minutes. Since the standard in the company was two crates per hour, much could be done to improve the flow. The measure did not reflect what the shipping process was designed to do.

Leading to Wrong Solutions

Quantitative measures that are used as absolute measures of a process or unit may also lead to wrong solutions. As in the case of the shipping department, measures may not represent the true problem in the unit.

For example, in the case of a pharmaceutical company with which I am familiar, the corporate R&D department was subjected to performance ratios such as: number of patents produced per scientist and engineer; and number of publications per scientist and engineer. The focus in these measures was the prestige of the scientific group. Yet the main problem of the company at the time was a lack of new products in the innovation pipeline. There was *only one* such new product with some potential of being approved by the U.S. Food and Drug Administration. A decision process regarding the R&D activity should have looked at its contribution to new product development rather than scientific prowess.

In another example, the marketing department of a large travel agency used the ratio of executives above a certain rank, company income, and nationwide branches as a composite index of a company's economic viability and its potential for travel. The marketing plan therefore targeted those companies with a high index. The plan was less than successful because, as it was later discovered, the planning solution totally disregarded the companies' policies on travel. Over half of the companies targeted had recently issued strict curbs on executive travel! As later reemphasized, when such measures are a stand-alone quantity that influences decision making and policy, severe problems may occur.

Total Picture Blurred

Suboptimization is likely to occur when quantitative measures are solely used for evaluation purposes and when they focus on local solutions.

A large manufacturer of electronic components for complex optical devices such as lasers for military use was concerned with the efficiency of its inventory management system. The company was caught in the euphoria of just in time (JIT), and the marvel of savings that would accrue to its inventory. Clearly, the mathematics were undeniable—the company could save 25-30% of its inventory costs. The company thus used inventory loadings benchmarks to create a sophisticated JIT system. While this was unraveling, the company also installed a rigid Total Quality Management program. It was quickly discovered that the added efficiency of the inventory function had been harmful to the supply of quality parts, primarily because the vendors were chosen by their ability to provide parts in a speedy manner, rather than highest quality possible. Speed versus quality, local success versus overall corporate threat.

Raiffa's Error of the Third Kind

The sixth problem is Raiffa's error of the third kind.[23] Instead of the wrong solution to a problem, executives provide reasonable solutions to the wrong problem.

For example, a candy manufacturer had been observing a decline in the sale of certain types of candy in all areas of its market. Senior management thus interpreted these measures as a decline phase in the life cycle of the product and hastened to introduce a new product to take its place. Sales of the new products were disappointing and no change downward was observed in the original product. The problem happened to be that the marketing manager was assigning the original product (which he assumed had a good reputation since it had been in the market for many years) to new and inexperienced sales representatives. The causal link between the phenomenon of reduced sales and life cycle of the product was in error, leading to a reasonable solution to the wrong problem.

QUANTITATIVE MEASURES AND REENGINEERING

How does all this relate to reengineering? Ratios, indexes, and other quantitative measures are essential to the measurement and assessment of corporate phenomena. In the previous section I outlined the peril of using them as assessment tools.

Information technology seems to offer the ability to reduce some of the problems associated with the usage of quantitative measures because they allow for better measurement and manipulation of these measures. Yet its qualities and attributes notwithstanding, ITT cannot overcome the problems inherent in the use of such quantitative measures.

The relation to reengineering is straightforward. According to Hammer and Champy, reengineering is starting with a clean slate. So, in theory at least, existing measures of inefficiency, benchmarks, and such are disregarded and *new* measures shall be formed. However, in order to analyze the benefits accrued to the unit and the corporation from reengineering, there is a strong comparison with the past performance and past practices. Improvements are shown in percentages and other figures. How, then, can we protect against the six problems discussed above and summarized in Figure 5.3? At the completion of reengineering, how can we be sure that contamination, biases, wrong solutions, and suboptimization have not occurred?

We cannot, and they do occur, very frequently. Moreover, considering that BPR promises so much and therefore is in need of a "success accounting," there are tremendous pressures to show such improvements by the utilization of quantitative measures as much as possible in a strong evaluation mode.

Hence, the use of quantitative ratios, indexes, and other quantitative measures is emphasized and greatly increased where the benefits from reengineering are to be calculated. ITT is recruited to enhance the use of such measures, but all of this cannot reduce the impacts of the lateral damage and the side effects that are generated by reengineering.

INFORMATION TECHNOLOGY AND THE PARADIGM SHIFT

Franz Kafka wrote a classic book about the adventures of a Mr. Joseph K. Here's a passage:

Their remoteness kept the officials from being in touch with the populace, for the average case they were excellently equipped, such a case proceeded almost mechanically and only needed a push now and then; yet confronted with quite simple cases, or particularly difficult cases, they were often utterly at a loss, they did not have any right understanding of human relations, since they were confined day and night to the workings of their judicial system, whereas in such cases a knowledge of human nature itself was indispensable.[24]

Information technology specialists in the corporation (IS and MIS [information systems and management information systems] units and professionals) are to some extent self-contained in a cultural and organizational isolation. Information technology is not conducive to a paradigm shift because it is not a tool in the arsenal of managers that would push for or even enable them to shift to a new paradigm. Contrary to the claim made by Hammer and Champy, I argue that IT has not yet reached the point of being the tool that brings about a paradigm shift. My argument is based on three key reasons: cultural gap, imperative rationalization, and evolutionary weaknesses.

Cultural Gap

The first key reason for IT's failure to generate or even support a shift in management paradigmatic thinking is the gap in the cultures between the IS/MIS function and the senior management of the corporation.[25]

IT does have many effects on the culture of the organization and on the way work is performed, analyzed, and evaluated. But these effects are concentrated at the level of the work flow. They tend to seem so powerful at times that many observers of these corporations believe that these effects mark some more powerful impacts on the strategic direction of the corporation and on senior management's paradigmatic thinking. This is not the case. As my own studies and many others have shown, the gap in culture between the IT function in the firm (represented by the IS or MIS function) and senior management's philosophy and perspective are still very much in existence and almost impossible to bridge.[26]

The influence of IT on how work is performed is manifested in changes in priorities, time frame, and productivity measures. There is also the emergence of a certain "climate" in the organization that is typical of an IT-intensive workplace. However, the cultural gap between the professional function such as IS and senior management persists despite the changes that occur throughout the working organization.[27]

This cultural gap arises from deep differences between the way the chief executive officer and other senior managers perceive IS/IT in the organizational context, versus how IS/IT managers perceive it.[28] In a mode similar to what we have observed in the case of R&D, senior managers perceive IS to be a *support* function, of essentially secondary value to the strategic priority of the firm. This perception is translated roughly into: "It's good to have" and "We must have it, but it's a pain and a drain on our resources."

On the other side of the house, the IS professionals and managers view their function as absolutely essential to the performance, success, vitality, and survival of the firm. Moreover, as their R&D colleagues before them, they are often amazed at the fact that their views are not totally shared by senior management.[29]

Senior managers do not completely understand how the R&D and the IS functions operate in their organizations. Attempts by consultants and organizational members to "force" senior managers to pay more attention to IS/IT usually fail. Spending more time with the IS/IT people will not make a substantial dent in senior managers' inherent inability to sufficiently grasp what IS/IT is all about—beside, of course, their view that it is a support function designed to maintain and improve efficiency of operations.

I recently completed a comprehensive study of the strategic implications of information technology.[30] The study explored over 100 service companies in four sectors: banking, investments, insurance, and transportation. The main purpose of the study was to measure and understand the antecedents of the gap between the strategic impact of IT on the corporation. Instead of using the usual methodology in which managers are questioned on their "strategic" use or perception of IT, this study concentrated on the criteria actually used by the sample company to evaluate their information technology.

The findings clearly showed that, by and large, service companies evaluate their IT as contributors to efficiency, cost savings, cost cutting, and productivity. Little attention is given to IT as a major force in shaping the strategic survival and performance of the company in a volatile and competitive business environment.

Another explanation may be that senior managers and IT managers have different paradigms of what their function does to contribute to corporate success. In any event, there is a pervasive and inherent difference between IS and senior managers in the way they perceive the corporate or business value of IT.[31] Integration of IT with business strategies is close to impossible, no matter how hard one tries.

Therefore, because of this gap IT cannot influence the change in senior management's paradigm. IT cannot even influence the *strategic* management of the firm—let alone affect the way senior managers think.

Imperative Rationalization

This is a fancy name for the simple fact that IT in the corporation usually becomes an end in itself, not the means for something else. As is the case with R&D, IT becomes to its professionals and managers the end or purpose of what the corporation is and should be.[32] The link between IT and corporate goals and objectives is somehow lost.

There is an interesting paradox that can be observed in this regard. As information technology has advanced in the past decade, to a point where it is more complex, ubiquitous, and sophisticated than ever before, its professionals and managers were more inclined to isolate themselves and to withdraw to a position of "magnificent insularity." Their main concern has become the continuing improvement of their discipline and their methods.[33] The complexity of information systems and technology coupled with the rapid expansion of its usages and the waves of innovations in products and systems have created a highly dedicated caste of IS/IT professionals. They are specialized in the profession, yet lack the time, energy, or skills needed to maintain some concern with the business strategies of the corporation. Hence, as IT budgets continued to grow and justification is restricted to what IT does best—namely improved efficiency and cost savings—IT professionals and managers have not felt the pressure to link their activities and their outcomes to corporate overall objectives. IS/IT is rationalized as a necessary function which has the seemingly unlimited ability to improve efficiency and productivity, and to benefit the organization also by cutting costs.

Owing to this phenomenon, IT cannot act as a mechanism in shifting the paradigm of senior management. IT is barely managed by its own professionals and managers who are busy making sure that they are in control of recent developments to avoid obsolescence, and that they at least contribute to improvements in efficiency of operations.

Evolutionary Weaknesses

The third key reason for the failure of IT to provide a substantial contribution to the shift in senior management's paradigm is the current stage in IT's evolution.

IT is essentially a set of tools in the process of evolution. It has not yet achieved a stage of development that would allow its professionals and managers to venture beyond their limited confines, to influence others. IT is still in the early stage of its evolution, preoccupied with itself, constantly changing, and in need of focus.[34]

The recent academic literature on management information systems and management of information technology clearly indicates that scholars in this field view their discipline in a state of flux. The rapid changes in technology, coupled with a spiraling number and types of organizational applications, point to a state of immaturity of the discipline.

Although it is true that IT had multiplied in the past decade and even in the early 1990s, there has been a real revolutionary growth in its applications in the business world. Yet we ought not confuse such unbridled growth with the maturity of IT to affect a change in management thought—as essentially claimed by the proposers of reengineering.

My recent visit to a high-tech company in the electronics and telecommunications industry will illustrate my argument. While discussing with a team of very competent and successful programmers and systems analysts the state of their products, I mentioned the advantages of voice-generated commands. I said:

At present we have a menu that is very restrictive. In order to perform simple work and processing tasks, I have to make somewhere between 8 and 10 selections from a menu, always starting from scratch. Imagine if I were in a restaurant and the server would keep asking basic questions such as: what kind of meal would you like? each time the server returns to our table. In my interaction with the computer it should be enough to say: "type a letter." What if the secretary would answer: In what language? Are you sure you want to fax it? and so on.

The systems analysts were amazed that the concept of a menu would be challenged. They were so set in their ways that their entire effort was directed toward improving menus, rather than questioning the concept and moving on to a higher order of integration. Hence, if IT professionals are so hard pressed to shift their paradigm, how can one expect their ware to generate a shift in senior management's paradigm?

WHY IT CANNOT BE A CATALYST FOR BPR

Information technology cannot and did not act as a catalyst for BPR, as advocated by proponents of this change program. Information technology is still in a developmental stage, lacks operational maturity, and suffers from a debilitating gap in culture between senior management and its functional and organizational position in the corporation.[35]

In order to facilitate the application of reengineering (or any other radical corporate restructuring), IT must fulfill at least the following three criteria: (1) *acceptability* by all levels of management based on adequate understanding of what IT is and what it can do, (2) *availability of* an arsenal of *tools* which are easily implementable, and (3) *generation of outcomes* which create an environment in which IT is responsible for more than just ubiquitousness of information or efficiency of operations, but also contributes to strategic and conceptual redesign and restructuring of processes, units, and activities. Figure 5.4 summarizes these criteria.

Acceptability by Management

Figures 5.1 and 5.4 show this criterion to be a major hurdle in making IT an effective catalyst for a radical change program such as BPR. Even when the information is usable, and in addition to the phenomenon of the "Ritchie incident," IT has failed to gain ample acceptance at all levels of the corporation. As I have discussed earlier in this chapter, cultural gaps have precluded senior management (and even some middle managers) from gaining an understanding of what IT is and what it can do for the corporation. IT is viewed merely as a technical support function, whose job is to routinize processes, make them more efficient, and by doing so contribute to the bottom line by cutting costs and adding savings.

This lack of acceptance by management hardly qualifies IT to become the engine that drives a radical restructuring such as BPR. At best IT may help to improve the efficiency of some processes and some selected operations. But IT cannot and has not become the engine that drives a major restructuring of the organization.

Figure 5.4
Why IT Cannot Be a Catalyst for Business Process Reengineering

---

Criteria Not Met by IT in Today's Corporations

Acceptability by All Levels of Management

- Understanding what IT is and what it can do
- Understanding the link of IT to business needs
- Integration of IT into corporate strategies

Availability of Arsenal of Implementable Tools

- Having tools that are easily implementable
- Having tools that allow managers to make decisions in a confident and comfortable manner
- Having tools that are acceptable and usable

Generation of Outcomes Beyond Efficiency

- Outcomes that create an environment in which IT contributes to strategy at the senior levels of the corporation
- Outcomes that contribute significantly to conceptual redesign of processes, units, activities
- Outcomes such as reliable models of executive actions; routinization of most activities to free managers at middle and senior level to engage in strategic management—thus creating a climate of management beyond mere efficiency matters.

Availability of Tools

Again, I mention the act that IT has failed to provide the corporation with an arsenal of tools, systems, and techniques which are easily implementable and which allow for nonroutine decisions.

The stage in the evolution of IT, discussed earlier in the chapter, is still below marketing, so that the tools IT has to offer are not yet sophisticated enough for the task of major restructuring. In the area of expert systems for managers, it has become a common practice to shy away from the development of comprehensive systems with generic applications—and to concentrate on specific, task-oriented expert systems.[36]

On this evolutionary scale we are still far from the development of usable intelligent systems which would support radical restructuring. Ubiquitousness, speed, and other such attributes are not enough to foster and to provide the vitality needed by managers in their effort to restructure the corporation. As IT is now, it is not a sufficient arsenal of tools for either a revamping of the organization, nor for the less lofty task of taking over a substantial number of routine decisions.

Generation of Outcomes Beyond Efficiency

The third criterion not met by IT in today's corporation is the need for outcomes that create a climate of management beyond mere efficiency. To reiterate the previous criterion of availability of tools, IT at present has not generated outcomes which move the corporation beyond simple improvements in productivity and efficiency.

Specifically, there are two outcomes: (1) Reliable models of executive actions showing what executives do and how to apply models in situations that are routine as well as nonroutine. By outcomes I mean the resultant climate that emerges when information becomes ubiquitous, when it becomes possible to manage information with increased speed, accuracy, and volume. These attributes bring about a much improved environment where information is much more, and better managed. But they do not produce outcomes such as expert models of managerial actions. (2) Routinization—concomitantly, these attributes do not generate and have not produced the substantial routinization of managerial activities so that managers can devote their efforts to strategic thinking. Nor do managers have the adequate IT tools to engage in such strategic endeavors—*which are essential for a radical restructuring of the corporation.*

In summary, IT has not been a catalyst for BPR, as advocated by Hammer and Champy. This is not to say that IT has failed as a dramatic change force in the corporation. Quite the contrary, IT has brought about many changes in culture and in the way work is performed. But all this was not enough to become a driving force and an enabling technology for radical redesign of the organization.[37]

When added to the inherent flaws in BPR, the failure of IT to be the mechanism that makes reengineering a vibrant possibility becomes a crucial reason why BPR has failed. IT cannot "carry" reengineering. IT cannot and has not saved the day. IT is pervasive in the contemporary organization and its effects and impacts are still unfolding. But, as of now, IT is not what makes reengineering feasible nor the character in a children's book that "saved Christmas."

NOTES

1. Anthony Cave Brown, *Bodyguard of Lies* (New York: Bantam Books,1975).

2. There is a vast literature on communications and information processing. See, for example, P. L. Tom, *Managing Information as a Corporate Resource* (Glenview, IL: Scott, Foresman, 1987); F. Jabin, L. L. Putnam, K. Roberts, and L. Porter (eds.), *Handbook of Organizational Communication* (Newbury Park, CA: Sage Publications, 1987); and F. Luthans and J. Larsen, "How Managers Really Communicate," *Human Relations*, February 1986, pp. 167-168.

3. See, for example, S. Park and R. Bhaskar, "Reengineering Through Information Engineering: Experience from a Division of Narcotics Enforcement Case," *Journal of Information Technology Management*, 5(7), 1994, pp. 1-10; and H. Cypress, "Reengineering," *OR/MS Today*, February 1994, pp. 18-25.

4. See, for example, E. Geisler (ed.), *Strategic Management of Information and Telecommunication Technology*, Special publication of the *International Journal of Technology Management*, 1992.

5. There is an extensive body of publications on this topic. See, as an illustration, W. R. Synnott, *The Information Weapon* (New York: John Wiley, 1987). Five years before the appearance of BPR, William Synnott, a former chief informations officer at the Bank of Boston, described the transformation of ITT from a primarily cost-cutting tool to a competitive weapon that can be used to advance the company's strategic goals.

6. Thomas Davenport, *Process Innovation: Reengineering Work Through Information Technology* (Cambridge, MA: Harvard Business School Press, 1993).

7. Peter Drucker, "The Coming of the New Organization," *Harvard Business Review*, January-February 1988, pp. 45-53.

8. See, for example, N. Venkataraman, "IT-Induced Business Reconfiguration," in M. Scott-Morton (ed.), *The Corporation of the 1990s* (New York: Oxford University Press, 1991).

9. See Doug Bartholomew, "Ford Retools," *Information Week*, April 1, 1996, pp 14-16.

10. Bill Gates, chairman of Microsoft, expressed this view in an article in the *Chicago Tribune*, March 31, 1996. He contended that the technology embedded in personal computers provides a range of possibilities to users that vastly improves their environment.

11. E. Geisler and W. Drago, "Strategic Perspectives of Artificial Management and Organizational Rationality," *Journal of Information Technology Management,* 7(4), 1996.

12. Of the vast literature on this and related topics, see for example, Robert E. Quinn, *Beyond Rational Management* (San Francisco, CA: Jossey-Bass, 1988); and J. Elster, *Ulysses and the Sirens: Studies in Rationality and Irrationality* (Cambridge University Press, 1979).

13. Geisler and Drago, *op. cit.*

14. See the example of Ford Motor Co., in which packaged systems had replaced tailored, organization-specific yet more expensive software. Also, note the case of *groupware*, which allows for ample interactions via ITT without personal/physical contact. See, for example, Stephanie Stahe and John Swenson, "Groupware Grows Up," *Information Week*, March 9, 1996, pp. 14-15. They contend that the multiple platforms available to users improve the quality and comprehensiveness of usage.

15. Robin Cooper and M. Lynn Markers, "Human Reengineering," *Sloan Management Review*, Summer 1995, pp. 39-50.

16. *Ibid.*, p. 39.

17. See, for example, John Boyd, "Reengineering: Japanese Style," *Information Week*, December 5, 1994, pp. 39-46.

18. There is an excellent illustrative account of the diffusion of "intranets" in corporations, where they are turned into a useful managerial tool: Amy Cortese, "Here Comes the Intranet," *Business Week*, February 26, 1996, pp. 76-84. Cortese describes the experiences of Eli Lilly, where 3,000 desktops in over 20 countries were transformed into an internal network, and a similar program at Visa International.

19. I recently described the issues involved with measuring quantifiable phenomena in E. Geisler, "Measuring the Unquantifiable: Issues in the Use of Indicators in Unstructured Phenomena," *International Journal of Operations and Quantitative Management*, 1(2), 1995, pp. 145-161.

20. There is a vast literature on this and related topics. A marvelous book edited by my colleague, Dr. Tom Kiresuk, and his coauthors discusses the intricate issues of measurement and scaling in evaluation: T. Kiresuk, A. Smith, and J. Cardillo (eds.), *Goal Attainment Scaling: Applications, Theory and Measurement* (Hillsdale, NJ: Lawrence Erlbaum Associates, 1994).

21. Much as been written about these measures when they become the driving force of any change activity. For example, see C. Strauss and C. Cordero, "The Difficulties of Quantifying Quality," *Business and Health*, 10(12), 1992, pp. 30-36.

22. See, for example, T. Cook and D. Campbell, *Quasiexperimentation: Design and Analysis Issues for Field Settings* (Chicago, IL: Rand McNally, 1979).

23. H. Raiffa, *Decision Analysis* (Reading, MA: Addison-Wesley, 1970).

24. F. Kafka, *The Trial* (New York: Alfred A. Knopf, 1964 [originally published in 1937]), pp. 148-149.

25. There is a growing literature on the relation between information systems and the senior executives of the company, particularly in terms of the link between IS and strategic management. See, for example, R. Boar, *The Art of Strategic Planning for Information Technology* (New York: John Wiley, 1993); and A. Hax and N. Majluf, *The Strategy Concept and Process: A Pragmatic Approach*, 2nd ed. (Upper Saddle River, NJ: Prentice-Hall, 1996), in particular Chapter 20, pp. 360-375. Also see M. Cherbrough and D. Teece, "When is Virtual Virtuous? Organizing for Innovation," *Harvard Business Review*, 74(1), January-February 1996, pp. 65-74.

26. See, for example, E. Geisler, "The U.S. Information Superhighway: An Industry Analysis," *Journal of Information Technology Management*, 6(2), 1995, pp. 1-9; and E. Geisler, "How Strategic Is Your Information Technology?" *Industrial Management*, 36(1), 1994, pp. 31-33; also see A. Barua, C. Kriebel, and T. Mukhopadhyay, "Information Technologies and Business Values: An Analytic and Empirical Investigation," *Information Systems Research*, 6(1), 1995, pp. 3-23.

27. See a summary of the academic distinctions between the concepts of "climate" and "culture" in D. Denison, "What Is the Difference Between Organizational Culture and Organizational Climate? A Native's Point of View on a Decade of Paradigm Wars," *Academy of Management Review*, 21(3), 1996, pp. 619-654.

28. Information systems (IS) and information technology (IT) are used here interchangeably. I am aware of the differences between the two concepts and functional presence in the firm, but have opted to list them in this way in order to facilitate the discussion on their relation to strategic thinking.

29. In the area of the R&D-corporate cultural gaps, see, for example, S. Bergen and C. McLaughlin, "The R&D/Production Interface: A Four Country Comparison," *International Journal of Operations and Production Management*, 3(1), 1992, pp. 5-13; also see R. Burton and B. Obel, *Strategic Organizational Diagnosis and Design: Developing Theory for Application* (Norwell, MA: Kluwer Academic Publishers, 1995).

30. E. Geisler, "Strategic Management of Information Technology in Service Companies: An Empirical Reexamination of the Issues," Working Paper, 1996.

31. Some writers have further attempted to better explain this link between IT and corporate performance or the lack of it. See a more recent book by Gerald Hoffman, *The Technology Payoff* (Burr Ridge, IL: Irwin, 1994). Hoffman calls for integration of IT strategy with business strategy. Yet he recognized that "unfortunately, this seldom happens. Many senior executives simply do not see the potential of information technology to influence business strategy. . . . The only IT strategy they are interested in is one designed to cut costs" (p. 53).

32. See, for example, W. Souder and J. D. Sherman (eds.), *Managing New Technology Development* (New York: McGraw Hill, 1994).

33. An illustration of this overwhelming concern is D. Ballou and H. Pazer, "Designing Information Systems to Optimize the Accuracy-Timeliness Tradeoff," *Information Systems Research*, 6(1), 1995, pp. 51-72.

34. See, for example, D. Cray and G. Haines, "The Relationship Between Environmental Complexity and Information Processing Structure and Its Effect on Performance: The Case of Canadian Pension Fund Managers," *The Journal of Information Technology Management*, 6(4), 1995, pp. 1-12.

35. E. Turban, E. McLean, and J. Wetherbe, *Information Technology for Management: Improving Quality and Productivity* (New York: John Wiley, 1996).

36. See, for example, J. Felli, L. Brennan, G. Hoffman, and A. Rubenstein, "An Architecture for the Functional Design of Intelligent Machines," *The Journal of Information Technology Management*, 6(4), 1995, pp. 55-66; also see E. Geisler and A. Rubenstein, "Barriers to the Adoption of Intelligent Support Systems by US Lawyers," *International Journal of Computer Applications in Technology*, 6(1), 1993, pp. 45-49; and A. Rubenstein and E. Geisler, "Users' Needs for Intelligent Systems (UNIS): A Study of Potential Adoption by Professionals," in A. Rubenstein and H. Suhwaertzel (eds.), *Intelligent Workstations for Professionals* (Berlin: Springer-Verlag, 1993), pp. 6-25.

37. S. Molloy and C. Schwenk, "The Effects of Information Technology on Strategic Decision Making," *Journal of Management Studies*, 32(3), 1995, pp. 283-312. These writers explored the effects of IT on major strategic decision stages such as identification, development, and selection. They concluded, however, that "for decision makers to use information technology effectively, they should have experience with the specific information technology in question" (p. 302). They also restricted their study to problem decisions and crisis decisions. Finally, the authors agreed that impact on decisions that involve major organizational phenomena (restructuring or retrenchment) need further study. Also see D. Knights and G. Morgan, "Strategy Under the Microscope: Strategic Management and IT in Financial Services," *Journal of Management Studies*, 32(2), 1995, pp. 192-214. The authors studied U.K. companies and concluded that "commitments to IT strategy were readily abandoned when market changes were interpreted largely through the corporate strategy as a whole as urgently demanding immediate and IT-intensive product developments. Regardless of the importance of the IT strategy to the corporation, it had to be abandoned in order to meet other strategic goals" (p. 211). This conclusion supports my argument about the gap between IT and senior management, hence the weakness of IT regarding its ability to serve on the engine for BPR.

6

THE AFTERMATH OF REENGINEERING

DOUBTFUL ACHIEVEMENTS

As stated in the previous chapters, the aftermath of Business Process Reengineering is a mixture of some achievements and many, perhaps too many, side effects. In this chapter I will outline these side effects and the "lateral damage" they have caused in so many companies.

Every change program and every intervention in the organization is bound to create ripple effects and some lateral damage. The magic formula for intervention to be considered a relative success is:

> **PROJECTED ACHIEVEMENTS − LATERAL DAMAGE =**
> **ACCEPTED OUTCOMES**

This formula has a built-in element of risk and a large dose of intuitive decision making, coupled with a high degree of certainty that we know how to compute all these components of the formula. The question that comes to mind is: can we quantify these elements in the formula to an extent that will allow reasonable conclusions?

As seen in Chapter 5, solely using quantitative measures may not be the best solution. Targeted achievements and lateral damage should be considered complex phenomena that ought to be assessed by a mix of quantitative *and* qualitative measures, objective *and* subjective criteria. This is why such declarations of accomplishments as x% improvement in a work process are essentially meaningless to the corporation, except for the process itself.

Put differently, consider a company that has achieved a 20% improvement in a work process. Even if this improvement directly contributes to the bottom line of the corporation, it is still of little value unless it is closely tied with what the corporation is, what it does, and what its business is all about.

There is a long-standing story of a miser who goes to the telegraph office to send a telegram. In discussions with the clerk the miser continually omits words as he tries to save money. Why should I say who is sending the telegram? I know who is sending it. Why waste words on the address? Everybody knows my cousin in that town. At the end of the story the telegram is a bare-boned, unintelligible, useless collection of disparate words.

If projected or actual achievements have not been in line with the company's overall strategy, they are even more undesirable when substantial lateral damage is present. Since reengineering has been hailed as a provider of drastic improvements, its achievements thus far have been bound by the limitations of efficiency gains in selected work flows. Shrinkage, downsizing, and leanness that followed or accompanied reengineering may have provided the companies with some competitive advantages, but at what cost? In many instances the situation resembles the "miser's telegram"; in other cases there is much lateral damage.

LATERAL DAMAGE

A senior manager in a Fortune 500 company with whom I recently consulted has succinctly expressed his company's situation:

We had downsized three years ago. This year we went through reengineering. It began when our CEO decided that it's time to do it. We've heard about it but we didn't really know what in the world the whole thing entailed. I keep up with what's happening, but I didn't know the details. The consultants seemed very professional, so we trusted them. Our industry is doing well. Everywhere you look sales are good and we are gaining market share. But here, everything is in a mess. Reengineering left us, and I mean managers *and* employees, in a state of chaos. We don't know what we accomplished with reengineering. To me it looked like a bad case of downsizing.

Popular opinion and the popular press are mostly focused on the human aspect of reengineering and on the effects of downsizing. Stories appear in *Business Week, The Wall Street Journal,* and a variety of other publications in which people who have been "downsized" are interviewed. In a story about economic anxiety, *Business Week* quotes an unemployed chemist: "All the economic indicators are up . . . except mine."[1] The anxiety that has engulfed the American workforce, hence its reflection in the press and even in the political arena, is very understandable. Consider that since 1980, about one in five workers in the largest companies was let go because of some form of restructuring, and three of every four such employees were white-collar. Was this the culmination of Peter Drucker's prophecy of a very flat business organization?[2] Hardly, since to a large extent restructuring did eliminate some layers of hierarchical position, but at the same time it transferred most of these positions to different forms of interactive managerial spots.

The arguments that I bring in this book to describe the scenario of the failure of reengineering are focused on the *internal* corporate difficulties in the aftermath of reengineering. This is not meant to discount the tremendous side effects that resulted from laying off nearly 4 million workers since 1980 by the group of Fortune 500 companies. There is a heavy *social* cost to such layoffs.[3]

But the failure of reengineering is particularly manifested in the internal corporate difficulties and dislocations, as they are caused by BPR's side effects.

There are five phenomena of lateral damage that directly result from reengineering: (1) low morale, (2) declining unit performance, (3) discrepancy in performance, (4) increased overall cost of human resources, and (5) threats to overall core competencies and competitiveness (see Figure 6.1).

Low Morale

The first side effect to appear in most companies that have undergone reengineering is low morale, which is generally apparent by an increase in the number and intensity of complaints from employees and middle managers. These complaints are sometimes also accompanied by a growing and pervasive lack of trust in the company and its leaders. Other indicators of low morale are the growing unwillingness to work longer hours, an increase in the rate of absenteeism, and an overall feeling of sluggishness.

Although morale is a difficult concept to measure, the acceptable indicators are very potent and lend themselves to precise measurement and reasoned interpretation. Thus, an indicator such as rate of absenteeism and decline in loyalty to the corporation can be safely interpreted as indications of decline in morale.

Figure 6.1
Phenomena of Lateral Damage Resulting from Reengineering

- **Low Morale**
  - Sense of loss and alienation
  - Sense of debilitating uncertainty

- **Declining Unit Performance**
  - Downsizing liaison functions
  - Misuse of the concept of core competence

- **Discrepancy in Performance**
  - The Hawthorne effect
  - Informal communications

- **Increased Cost of Human Resources**
  - Redesign and managerial behavior
  - Redesign, orchestra, and behavior

- **Threats to Core Competencies and Competitiveness**

Some of these effects of lower morale may be attributable to the downsizing effects of restructuring in general (and reengineering in particular), and to the uncertainty that accompanies such change programs. Reengineering, however, is a much more powerful program than mere restructuring because it is usually heralded in the corporation as a major change effort, received with heightened anticipation, and is said to be applied *throughout* the organization. This means that employees expect a radical change effort that will essentially affect *everybody*, regardless of their unit or position in the hierarchy. Thus, when the downsizing hammer falls, the effects are more powerful in the perception of the workforce and reverberate with greater intensity throughout the corporation.

Low morale also tends to spill over to other areas and activities in the corporation. Motivation in general is affected.[4] Productivity tends to suffer and an overall climate of discontent takes over in the corporation. In some instances the phenomenon starts in the unit which had first or mostly been reengineered.

In a Fortune 300 company in the paper and pulp industry, the acquisitions and supply decision at the central office was reengineered. Downsizing of about 20% of human resources was instituted. Work processes were streamlined so that efficiency improved. The cost of this function to the company dropped by 15% in eight months. The savings from the BPR program became the talk of the company and a shining example of successful reengineering. Then problems started. The remaining workforce had to work harder, longer hours, always fearing the next phase of reengineering and its potential effects on their jobs. The division was processing more requests per day, at a lower cost per request. But workers in other divisions noticed an isolation and alienation effect of the acquisition personnel. They complained of worsening working conditions, increased fatigue, and stress. In a short time this division became an example of "what we may be next" to other divisions. Morale fell throughout the corporation as a result of the reengineered division.

Other side effects seem to accompany the decline in morale. They include a sense of loss and alienation, a sense of chaos, and a strong sense of debilitating uncertainty.

These are particularly unwelcome when they are found in middle managers, since they tend to serve as examples to their subordinates and to transfer their feelings to the rank and file.[5] These side effects also tend to disrupt the entrepreneurial spirit of many middle managers. With a pronounced sense of loss and a decrease in loyalty, these middle managers reduce their level of enthusiasm and the innovativeness with which they conduct their activities and with which they move and shake the company's business.[6] Such effects contribute to a decline in performance.

Declining Unit Performance

Kim Cameron has proposed a typology of downsizing strategies composed of three types: (1) workforce reduction, (2) work redesign, and (3) systemic.[7] In essence, reengineering combines all three types of downsizing—at least as it is practiced by most companies. The first type is a short-term approach that includes layoffs, early retirements and buy-out packages. In the second type the company attempts to reduce its employee workforce by combining functions, merging units, redesigning positions, and by eliminating layers of supervisory personnel. Cameron argued that the third kind is a longer term restructuring effort that includes a bottom-up change and involves the entire organization.

However, he reports that in half the companies he studied, productivity and overall performance have dropped, and that morale, trust, *and* productivity have declined in no less than three-fourths of the downsized companies.

As I argue in this book, reengineering was utilized by many companies as an umbrella framework for change, in which the main component was a reduction in the number of employees and their managers. Regardless of the term used to describe such a move— "downsizing," "rightsizing," or even "dumbsizing"— the results were almost always a reduction in force and the process to make the organization lean. Unit performance usually suffered because of the following actions embedded in the reengineering program: (1) different emphases in changing different units, (2) deep changes in individual units, and (3) systemic failures.

The first action involved different degrees of emphasis in the changes imposed on different units. This tended to cause a breakdown in the relationship between units, in the form of either links in a chain or cooperating departments. In the case of the chain, when one unit underwent deep changes in the form of cuts in personnel, changes in its work processes and even its purpose and mission, the units linked to it in the chain were impacted. The performance of all tended to suffer.

For example, my students analyzed the case of a state-owned electric utility which had undergone some form of reengineering. The human resources department was chosen to bear the brunt of the change program. Its restructuring through deep reductions in force and radical changes in procedures and work flows affected other departments linked to it through the value chain and the logistic flow of the company. Morale and performance declined throughout the company.

The second action concerns deep changes in individual units that lead to a drop in the unit's performance. Many managers and scholars have suggested that a drop in performance is a by-product of reengineering and is to be expected (at least in the short term). Therefore it is considered a "normal" occurrence. But when such decline persists and is seen to be extreme in selected units, there is an urgent need to explore the reasons for such a drop. This lateral damage from reengineering is supposed to be manipulated by the theoretical focus of BPR. Namely, when the *entire* organization or even operation is restructured from the new starting point, such dislocations in change emphasis should not occur (by definition). Yet they *do* occur and they create dangerous declines in performance.

The third action is a systemic failure. This is an extension of the first action described above. Performance of a unit sharply declines because of what I call *systemic breakdown*. Broadly defined it is inherent in the inability of reengineering to carry out its promises, thus creating a cascading effect in which unit performance declines throughout the corporation. When a selected unit is reengineered, other units tend to undergo changes that are usually unplanned, in order to cope with the reengineered unit. The reengineering effort thus reverberates throughout the organization.

In 1993, G. Hall, J. Rosenthal, and J. Wade cited the examples of Banca di America e di Italia (BAI), AT&T, and Siemens Nixdorf to propose five keys to successful reengineering.[8] The authors are consultants with McKinsey & Company in New York. Their keys to success are (1) aggressive targets, (2) commitment of 20-50% of the CEO's time to the reengineering efforts, (3) review of customer needs and market trends, (4) senior executive in charge of implementation, and (5) conduct a pilot of the new design. These suggestions are essentially the basic guidelines for *any* comprehensive change program. In my view, as clearly expressed in this book, these suggestions would not salvage the lateral effects of reengineering, nor would they prevent systemic breakdown.

Why? Because although there is support from top management and there are other recommended foundations for successful implementation, it is utterly impossible to implement BPR in the *entire* organization with one redesign effort, as outlined in the original concept of reengineering. A compromise is normally the outcome, which means that BPR is applied unit-by-unit, serially, and in stages. Therefore, regardless of how implementation is successfully carried out, there will be differences and gaps between the unit being reengineered and other units in the network of interdependency that characterizes the modern corporation. Systemic breakdown is thus *inevitable*.

Downsizing Liaison Functions

Moreover, systemic breakdown also occurs because reengineering usually conceives and promotes downsizing, in which the first victims are liaison functions. These are linkages between units that are sharply curtailed in the first cut of resources and positions intended to cut costs and improve efficiency. Such functions are generally not recognized as an integral part of a work process, and they tend to easily escape scrutiny in the redesign of the workflow, being considered nonessential activities.

A marvelous example of this phenomenon of restructuring is an episode in the television comedy *The John Larroquete Show*. The key protagonist is John Hemingway, the manager of the bus station in St. Louis, Missouri. He is confronted with the retirement of an old-time employee, whose function in the organization seems to be unknown to all other employees. John Hemingway goes through the exiting employee's box of belongings, in an effort to discover what his job was. He finds some articles, including some traffic signs. On the night following the employee's departure, a bus veers off and crashes into the station's restaurant. The bus driver staggers out of his cabin, asking: "Where is that little man with the stop sign?"

Sometimes liaison functions are called "boundary-spanning roles" by organization scientists. They allow units to communicate across hierarchical constraints, and to maintain the vitality of value chains. They allow for R&D units to relate to marketing and product development functions, for marketing and manufacturing to communicate, and they facilitate the flow of information up and down the hierarchy of the formal structure and among work teams in the informal structure.

These functions are similar to those of umpires in baseball games and referees in basketball games. Clearly, the game can be played without them, just as work processes can be carried out without liaison and other nonessential functions that are not *directly* involved with getting the work done, but they are essential for the entire picture to emerge, in which there is linkage and closure with other units and functions—for a total systems performance.

Many organizations find that reengineering has led to the elimination of these functions, whereas in the longer run (sometimes in quite a short term) there is breakdown in the system, as would be bound to happen in a game without a referee.

In their criticism of reengineering, M. G. Benuvides and P. Rossler have stated that "there are no limits to being lean,"[9] and "secondly, the realization that all systems require a bit of fat to function naturally is often overlooked."[10] The necessity for some "fat" is generally discussed in the management literature in terms of "slack resources." These are essential for flexibility and skills of adaptation of the corporation to changes in its competitive environment. The problem encountered in the aftermath of reengineering and downsizing is that such liaison and supportive functions are not included in the logical redesign and the strict analysis of work processes, all aimed at eliminating duplication, waste, and inefficiencies. By definition, in order to function properly, systems (such as value chains) require some support functions that may fall into the broad definition of slack resources because they indirectly contribute to the welfare of the system.

Misuse of the Concept of Core Competence

In a seminal article in 1990, C. K. Prahalad and G. Hamel proposed the concept of core competence of the corporation.[11] They defined the concept as the roots of competitiveness, and recommended redeployment to exploit these competencies. They concluded:

Once top management (with the help of divisional and SBU [strategic business unit] managers) has identified overarching competencies, it must ask businesses to identify the projects and people closely connected with them. Corporate officers should direct an audit of the location, number and quality of people who embody competence. This sends an important signal to middle managers: core competencies are *corporate* resources and may be reallocated by corporate management.[12]

This message and the concept of focus on core competencies and reallocating or eliminating other resources, thus considered marginal, had been misused in the rush to reengineer and to downsize. The concept of core competencies becomes a powerful tool that *justifies* deep cuts in resources, therefore contributing to systemic failure. Although the concept of core competencies, as clearly defined by Prahalad and Hamel, is a corporate strategic concept that leads to corporate actions (reallocations and restructuring) aimed at the overall competitiveness of the firm, the actual use of the concept in many instances is localized in selected units. The analysis of resources that ensues generally eliminates many functions not deemed in the "core" of the unit or the process. Furthermore, the distance between the operational units and corporate strategic conceptions tends to act as a gap between *intentions* and *actual activities* that follow the analysis of core competencies. Much is lost in the translation between strategic corporate planning and the needs and activities of the operational units.[13]

Finally, the concept of core competencies relies on measurements of the payoff from unit resources and actions triggered by such calculations. In most cases the contributions of resources (human and other) are a complex web of clearly identifiable *and* more obscure, less measurable payoffs on their investment. Inability to arrive at a sound methodology to compute such quantities is one of the reasons the concept of core competencies is misused—with devastating consequences.

Some authors have attempted to deal with the decline in unit performance because of reengineering by focusing on group dynamics, individual motivation, and empowerment of employees who participate in change programs.[14] These are actions with some degree of effectiveness, but they cannot and do not counteract the decline in performance that accompanies reengineering. They are a good antidote for the wrong problem.

Discrepancy in Performance

A different set of lateral damage phenomena is the discrepancy in performance, which may also be defined as intensive suboptimization.

The Hawthorne Effect

In many corporations that have undergone BPR programs, there appeared dramatic disparity in the performance of key units, as well as along critical value chains. This phenomenon is similar to the "Hawthorne effect" discovered by organizational scientists over half a century ago.[15] This effect was observed in the Western Electric Hawthorne plant outside Chicago, Illinois. In the early 1930s a team of social scientists from Harvard University, led by Eldon Mayo, conducted some experiments at the plant, with the objective of increasing productivity. Following Taylor's *scientific management* approach they manipulated physical working conditions for some production units of the plant while keeping other units unchanged to serve as control units in their experiment. Over many months of such planned interventions, Mayo and his colleagues discovered that productivity levels wildly oscillated in both the experimental and the control units, primarily because there was open communication between the two categories of units, leading to a convergence of expectations. The units throughout the plant were unaware of the objectives of the experiments.[16]

Mayo also discovered that informed leaders and their work groups had a very strong influence on setting productivity levels. Later his work contributed to the rise of the *human relations* school of management.

The reason I have dusted off a 50-year-old finding is that Mayo's intervention at Hawthorne was almost identical to present-day reengineering programs. The objective was then, as now, redesign of work to improve productivity, cut costs, and enhance overall performance. Implementation was also similar, as selected units underwent the planned intervention whereas other units remained unchanged. Finally, lack of adequate information across units led, in both cases, to the emergence of an informal network of information sharing as to the purpose of the intervention and its potential consequence. Downsizing and loss of jobs was ominous at Hawthorne, because the experiments were conducted during the depression years.

As in the Hawthorne experiments, units that have not been reengineered seek to match those that have, leading to a vast array of changes in behavior of both people and organizations. Problems arise in communication and coordination. The results are confusion, mistrust, uncertainty, and an overall sense of puzzlement: why is all this happening?

In addition, when compensation and other benefits are linked to performance and are given to those units that were reengineered, this leads to increased distrust, dissatisfaction, and conflict. Overall, the outcome is discrepancy in performance and interunit breakdown of critical flows, communication, and coordination.

Informal Communications

The discrepancy in performance is not caused only by defective implementation. Much of its occurrence is due to the inherent inability of BPR to exercise its redesign intervention throughout all the organization, and with perfect and complete information provided to *all* the participants. It is an utterly impossible task. Even if such a task is attempted, there will always be interunit differences, and there will always be some effects from the workings of the informal structure that inhabits any organizational framework. Information flows in the form of innuendo, whispers, interpretation of the official line, and the formal corporate explanation and description of what is about to happen—all of these freely flow inside and between units.

Moreover, the more the sensitivity about changes, and the more organizational members are nervous about corporate intentions, the more such informal communications will proliferate, distort official stories, and generate discrepancies in performance through defensive behavior on the part of people and units.

How much damage do such effects cause? The inability of reengineering to prevent an informal "takeover" of corporate communications is a very powerful occurrence. The effects of such distortions in communications are usually strong enough to enhance discrepant performance levels, and to promote confusion and mistrust. They also lead to mistrust in change processes in general, which makes any additional implementation of reengineering in *new* units much more difficult, with added discrepancies in performance.

Increased Cost of Human Resources

Another lateral damage incurred in the application of reengineering is the increased cost of human resources. This sounds counterintuitive, since a primary result of BPR is usually downsizing, leading to a smaller workforce.

The phenomenon I describe here is hardly new. In the past few years surveys of companies that have downsized have shown many who have rehired employees. Some surveys show up to 40% of companies questioned have rehired many of their downsized employees and managers. Perhaps some of these rehires are in different positions and do conform to the restructured and perhaps "revitalized" organization.[17] In four companies out of six with whom I have consulted in recent years, all of whom have undergone BPR programs, there had been a continuing trend to increase the workforce after the initial drastic cuts.

However, the phenomenon that I describe here is not merely the rehiring of employees and middle managers—as if to overturn or reverse the sought-after benefits of reengineering: the lean organization. Rather, I describe here a rampant, albeit still poorly documented, practice by managers throughout the reengineered corporations.

In essence, middle managers, and even some senior executives with overall corporate authority, restore some or much of the resources downsized during reengineering. They usually do so by replacing formerly full-time employees with part-time employees and consultants. Since reengineering depletes their unit or function of some critical skills that were embedded in many positions and employees that were let go, managers counteract by exercising *creative hiring*.

As I discovered in a large company, a manufacturer of home appliances, the overall head count was lower than that before reengineering, but the overall cost of human resources had sharply increased. The employees who had survived the reengineering program were overworked, risk averse, and looking for ways to decrease their constraining lack of resources and skills.

Overworked and confused employees make more mistakes, and when fewer controls are effectively in place there is consequently an overall increase in costs. The benefits from the downsizing and restructuring brought about by reengineering, primarily in terms of higher efficiency of operations, may be overshadowed by increased costs of resources.[18] This is an example of defensive behavior by managers up and down the hierarchy and throughout the corporation.

Redesign and Managerial Behavior

Middle managers in particular tend to pad their units with slack resources, especially slack or redundant positions. They do so in order to protect their power base and to forestall cuts in their budgets, as well as to insure the performance of their unit in adverse times and uncertain conditions. They tend to build a web of activities, so that even when some restructuring occurs, there are other positions that take the place of those that were eliminated.

The metastructure becomes the norm that guides the behavior of managers and units in such a way as to occupy managerial talent in finding creative means for defensive maneuvers. This behavior is exacerbated when change programs are either planned or actually exercised in the corporation.

An illustration from the experience of a manufacturer of home appliances exemplifies this behavior and its consequences. Reengineering had improved the efficiency of the shipping department by increasing the speed with which the finished goods were shipped to warehouses. It was found, after a while, that the cost of the supporting units had increased, because the managers of these units overreacted to changes in speed and costs of the shipments by creating protective mechanisms of control through massive acquisitions of information technology (equipment and software) and by hiring specialists—all in order to protect themselves and to adjust to the redesigned department in their value chain.

Although redesign of work processes through the reengineering program is supposed to account for such behavior and to create a structure that defuses or at the least allows for such behavior to be incorporated into it—there are limits to the redesign of organizations. This is also true with the application of information and telecommunication technology as tools that offer managers an advantage of high-tech communications, thus (presumably) diminishing or even eliminating the need for defensive behavior.

The reality is much more prosaic and counterproductive. In times of a radical change program in the corporation, managers find themselves in an environment of increased uncertainties, thus they reenergize their defensive behavior. Moreover, since the framework they build, with slack resources and a defensive perimeter of functions and activities, is disrupted by the restructuring effort, their levels of personal uncertainty and confusion sharply increase. This is because the reengineered structure does not offer an *alternative* or a substitute for such a framework. Managers therefore feel wounded, incapacitated, and vulnerable. The ultimate outcome is a higher cost of running a reduced workforce.

Redesign, Orchestra, and Behavior

In his seminal article in 1988, Peter Drucker compared the new organization to an orchestra.[19] With the high level of professionalism pervading every aspect of the modern corporation, each employee is a consummate professional, and the CEO, like the musical conductor, directs the overall effort of all players toward the desired wholesomeness of the strategic purpose of the orchestra (corporation).

In this era of BPR, the reengineering effort is aimed at redesigning the corporation, so that professionals are thus able to perform as best as they can, with the help of information technology. Work processes thus become highly efficient, making wholesome music like a well-rehearsed orchestra.

However, corporate realities and the failure of BPR combine to create a totally different picture. First, in recent years there has been a growing consensus among organization scientists that no design of the corporation is totally adequate for all conditions and circumstances. There are limits to how the structure of the organization can be of use when environmental conditions are changing. Hence the periodic need for changes and redesign programs. The reengineering concept, however, contends that a "better" structure can be achieved by starting over. This is an illusion. BPR does not start over. It utilizes the same core of people and other resources, and it works with the same environment and constraints that confronted the previous structure.[20]

Therefore, redesigning the work process itself, without *total* revamping of everything else in the corporation, is an exercise in futility—if we take BPR at its word. All we are able to accomplish in BPR is a measure of improvement (if at all), since organizational redesign is inherently limited in what it can do and how much it can solve the organization's problems.

Second, organizations are not orchestras (at least not yet)! Although professionalism in corporations has dramatically increased in recent years, and information technology enables professionals to better perform their tasks, the overall acuity of a corporation is far from that of a musical orchestra. In the case of an orchestra, each and every musician has an extremely well-defined part, thus working in an absolute division of labor. Thereare no overlaps, and by definition the "score" is totally known to all. In other words, there is complete information, *fully* disseminated to *all* the members of the orchestra. Control is totally concentrated with the conductor, although the parts for each player are preestablished.

In the corporation, however, parts are not as well defined, nor are they as strictly preestablished. Intrapreneurship and personal leeway are encouraged. Overlaps are common, and interpersonal as well as interunit cooperation are not dictated from above in the way it is done by the conductor of the orchestra. Uncertainty, different interpretations of the direction, and mode of operation of the organization are common.

In my view, organizations more likely resemble a flock of birds in flight; they are moving in one direction, yet each flies with some leeway of movement, while changing directions in a sequence of small adjustment within the overall direction.

The redesign of work processes does not preempt the defensive behavior of managers and consequently also cannot reverse the rise in the costs of human resources.

Threats to Core Competencies and Competitiveness

A pharmaceutical company with whom I consulted had undergone a comprehensive reengineering program. A past reengineering review had shown that most of the lateral damage described above was indeed present in this corporation. Morale was low, employees became irritable and self-absorbed, whereas the number and severity of on-the-job accidents increased, as did the rate of absenteeism. The product development unit was the first to be reengineered, followed by the marketing unit, followed by the research unit.[21]

The reengineering effort had produced a dangerous situation by creating a side effect that proved a threat to the company. Specifically, the restructuring of the corporation had almost destroyed the linkages between research and new product development (NPD), and between NPD and marketing. The aim of the restructuring effort was to improve the work processes to cut costs and eliminate waste and duplication. A 28% reduction in force was accomplished in several months across the three units. The threat of downsizing was omnipresent in the company.[22]

As a result, the following happened. First, employees and managers became withdrawn and retreated into their unit's boundaries. They created a protective wall around their unit, in what organization scholars refer to as "local-patriotism." They placed emphasis on their own unit and intense interunit competition became commonplace. Second, as the executive in charge of research explained, the unit was criticized for too lengthy tests and retests of compounds, above what would be required by the Food and Drug Administration (FDA):

The upshot was that we felt we have no choice. We abandoned those compounds where we thought that we would invest too much, and we concentrated on those two or three compounds that showed promise. What's more, we nearly severed all relations with NPD. Their new director is a product of the reengineering exercise. She has no appreciation for what we do here. She is a bean-counter. We couldn't work together, so I tried to have something quickly and throw the compound to her and let her deal with it. Needless to say, the compound was not ready for her people to play with, so we gave her another. That's all we had. The pipeline was dry

This pharmaceutical company reengineered itself by placing the focus on new product development and research functions as the place where radical improvements were needed. Consequently, a massive reorganization of these units occurred. The units were redesigned with the aim of cutting the time-to-market and of making their activities more cost-efficient.

However, the core competence of this company was, and is, its innovativeness. Its success and competitive position in the marketplace depend upon new and revolutionary products. Inefficiencies and suboptimization were not the issues for this company's success. Here, Prahalad and Hamel are correct, in that by identifying, recognizing, and emphasizing its core competence, a company reinforces its competitive stance. This pharmaceutical company was highly innovative. Its work processes had, over the years, somewhat deteriorated into some inefficiencies, overlaps, and "fat."

But the company had cohesion along the idea-to-market continuum: its critical and basic value chain. It benefitted from direct lines of communication between research and NPD, and between NPD and marketing. These, and the quality of its innovation process, were the core competencies of the company. Reengineering ended up destroying these competencies in a methodical way. People in the company had reacted the way one would expect them to react: by protecting themselves and their turf, and their units. The result was almost disastrous, as the core competencies of the corporation were slowly eroded and nearly destroyed.[23]

LONG-TERM EFFECTS

Lateral damage due to reengineering is perhaps only the "tip of the iceberg." Much more pervasive and permanent are the long-term effects. The aftermath of BPR in the longer term harbors four main categories of negative effects: the human factor; retrenchment into a climate of efficiency perspective; industry distortions; and technology caging.

The Human Factor

Earlier in this chapter I listed in Figure 6.1 and in the related text some of the people effects in the aftermath of BPR. Low morale, uncertainty, alienation, and discrepancy in performance are what may be called "immediate" or proximal effects. They occur shortly after the implementation of BPR, sometimes within months of its application in the corporation.

However, long-term effects which involve the human factor are far-reaching in their impacts on people and organizations.[24] In this category there are three main groups of negative effects.

The first is the creation of a *climate of fear*. This goes way beyond low morale and alienation. It is a persistent climate in the organization that involves deep psychological damage to the members at almost all levels. It is silent, slowly involving the people and their perspective of the corporation and of work in general.

How are people affected? There is first of all an ingrained feeling of suffering and disbelief that this is occurring. It may be comparable to the pain involved with the loss of a dear relative or friend. Disbelief, denial, anger, and a sense that one is powerless and even useless seem to proliferate. Longer term impacts are the development of feelings of fear and mistrust. Organizational members develop an adversarial relationship with their workplace—typical behavior as a consequence of a climate of fear.[25]

Second, such a climate generates a *loss of confidence* in any program or intervention, even those that are targeted toward specific and well-defined improvements in processes or activities. Such interventions may be very beneficial, yet scorned by employees and opposed in many innovative ways.

The loss of confidence and the psychological effects in the longer term are not just the province of a few disgruntled or malcontent workers. Unfortunately, these are the attributes of a climate that is embracing the entire organization, the full effects of which are yet to be felt. The damages are cumulative and are yet to appear in a destructive eruption or, more probably, in waves of disruptions in performance and stability of the corporation over time.

Third, the effects on people create a *climate that is difficult to reverse*. A senior manager in a large company in the commodities industry has suggested to me that "everything can be reversed and every wound can be healed." True, time and appropriate interventions ultimately will reverse even the longer term damage. However, when a climate of fear, uncertainty, and loss of confidence in the future persists over time, it becomes ingrained in what scholars call the "organizational memory." This climate is then transferred to the next generation of employees as a "tradition," through regular socialization and indoctrination procedures and rituals. When this climate is pervasive throughout the organization, socialization occurs at the levels of middle management and first-line supervisors—with detrimental consequences of the perpetuation of uncertainty and fear.

The psychological effects are caused not only through the direct effects of downsizing, restructuring, and the broken promises of reengineering. There is a more complex process by which these planned changes trigger a host of organic changes in a cascading effect.[26] These organic changes include a variety of structural and process changes to accommodate the new climate of fear in the corporation.

For example, lingering uncertainty over a long period of time leads employees and their managers to create processes and mechanisms (formal and informal) that facilitate internal communication. These mechanisms tend to siphon resources from formalized and routine channels, causing delays in the information flow of the firm and even distortions—both planned and unscheduled. The longer this situation persists, the more it is likely that the "clandestine" processes will take over and become the routine avenues for information exchange.

In one firm I visited following BPR, the first-line supervisors now customarily approved changes in logistics by signing the same request five times. Interviews revealed that they were terrified of making mistakes. Control became an obsession. Information was routinely withheld and often "sweetened" for transmittal to middle management. "If this company is going to the dogs, it won't be because of me," said one first-line supervisor. Two years after BPR, the scars were visible, but the damage was deeply ingrained. It manifested itself in what became (and was acknowledged by the workers) "strange behavior." As a management consultant, I was intrigued by the complexity of the control and communication mechanisms and double, nay, triple and quadruple safety valves along the way. As I concluded in my preliminary report: "This was one scared bunch of people."

Retrenchment into Efficiency Trap

A second group of negative effects that are manifested in the longer term is the eventual retrenchment of the organization into a mode of favoring efficiency and productivity improvements over all other possible avenues of action. Over time there develops a lack of understanding and lack of support for the broader issues and situations that a firm faces in the rapidly changing world marketplace. In what Hammer and Champy described as lack of executive vision, senior managers retreat into the new comfortable and results-oriented restructuring and reengineering of selected processes. Savings and improved efficiency become the guiding light.

As an illustration, my students and I conducted a literature search of the business and engineering computerized databases. In 1995 we found 962 papers in scientific and professional publications on how to better reengineer your work processes, with better software and other tools for increased efficiency. Cases of 12% in a given process, for example, are touted as the long success story. Everybody is impressed, and the cases keep coming and we continue to report them and to wonder at their contribution to the bottom line. Managers at all levels were also impressed. They feel that this is a winner, this is the way to go, so they want more of the same.

Over time the savings are less and less dramatic, until they are not more than a trickle. But the *frame of mind* is still there: efficiency is the key to success (personal as well as that of the firm). This frame of mind creates a climate of retrenchment, as managers distance themselves from risky undertakings, and from a more strategic view of their activities and their corporation.

A good example is the recently heralded balanced scoreboard.[27] R. Kaplan and D. Norton had proposed this method in 1992.[28] In essence, the scoreboard is a multi-perspective approach to corporate performance, by which four basic perspectives of the firm are explored: financial, customer relations, internal business, and innovation and learning. These are criteria for success that have been chosen opportunistically by Kaplan and Norton to allow some measures of cross-links among different, sometimes competitive, goals and directions the company follows. These perspectives or criteria include the latent fads of the early 1990s such as customer satisfaction, time to market, and financial capabilities.

Although Kaplan was coauthor of an important book in 1987 on the obsolescence of management accounting, and his coauthorship of the 1996 paper linking the balanced scoreboard to strategic thinking, there is still much in the scoreboard that exemplifies management's retrenchment into efficiency type reasoning.[29] In their book T. Johnson and R. Kaplan have argued that contemporary cost accounting systems are not providing adequate nor accurate information about the internal operations of large companies, thus leaving them exposed to fierce and successful competition from smaller and more aggressive companies who enjoy a more focused information and accounting system. In the 1987 book the authors proposed a scheme for performance measures, in particular focusing on nonfinancial indicators. This was the beginning of their thinking about the scoreboard and the multiperspective approach.

Yet, although Kaplan and Norton have stressed the strategic implications of their scoreboard, their main argument is that the scoreboard supersedes and is more strategically performing than management's reliance on financial measures alone. This may be a step above financial ratios but a closer look at the measures included in the scoreboard reveals a preponderance of efficiency measures (e.g., time to development cycle time, unit cost, engineering efficiency, actual schedule versus plan).

These are examples of the internal business processes that were the target of BPR. Kaplan and Norton claim that these measures "move companies forward" (p. 79) and that they put strategy rather than control as their focus. But measures of internal processes and segmentary performance outcomes tend to support, and thus perpetuate, the nonstrategic view of what makes the company succeed. BPR has acted on some of these measures by increasing their efficiency and performance. Processes that decrease the time to market, cycle time, and that reduce unit cost and engineering efficiency are the main targets of BPR, as well as the showcase for its dubious and short-term successes.

How do we tie the measures (and information thus provided) used in the scoreboard for management to think beyond productivity and efficiency improvements? In fact, a summary view of what the scoreboard has contributed shows that the questions asked are still in the realm of "how better to do what we are doing?" than "why are we doing this and is their another way to compete?" When senior managers are consistently fed a diet of methods, approaches, and performance measures that emphasize how better to do what they are doing, they continue to suffer the effects of BPR and to retreat into an insular view of their firm.

Industry Distortions

A third category of persistent long-term harmful effects of reengineering is the possible development of distortions in the industry's base of companies that have undergone BPR. The phenomenon is largely magnified as a result of the trend of mergers and solidification in many of the leading American industries. Figure 6.2 shows the ten biggest mergers since 1984.

When some companies undergo reengineering and others in the same industry refrain from radical restructuring, there is a strong possibility that structural distortion may appear in the industry makeup. In particular it appears that when companies on different sides of the reengineering continuum (one that reengineered and the other did not) enter into a merger, the result is an imbalance that tends to accentuate the negative impacts of reengineering.[30]

Figure 6.2
Ten Biggest Mergers in the United States

Companies Merging	Date	Value[1]
1. RJR Nabisco with Kolberg Kravis Roberts & Co.	1989[2]	$25 billion
2. Bell Atlantic and Nynex	1996[3]	$22.7 billion
3. Walt Disney and Capital Cities/ABC	1996[2]	$19 billion
4. SBC Communications and Pacific Telesis Group	1996[3]	$16.7 billion
5. World Coin Inc. and MFS Communications Co.	1996[3]	$14.4 billion
6. Wells Fargo and First Interstate Bank	1996[2]	$14.2 billion
7. Warner Communications and Time Inc.	1990[2]	$14.11 billion
8. Kraft Inc. and Philip Morris	1988[2]	$13.44 billion
9. Gulf Oil and Standard Oil	1984[2]	$13.4 billion
10. Chase Manhattan and Chemical Bank	1996[2]	$13 billion

1. In US Dollars, unadjusted for inflation. Values are those registered at the time of the merger.
2. Completed.
3. Announced.

For example, a recently merged company in the financial services, BigBank (not its real name) had undergone extensive reengineering of its processes, while its partners to the merger remained unrestructured. BigBank had several processes reorganized to an extent that they looked less like a financial company's processes and more like a highly automated manufacturing plant. When the merger took place, the merging partner adapted itself to BigBank, with the resulting disaster in which a pocket of unserviceable and isolated processes emerged. This has neutralized any benefit from the merger, leading to massive cuts in personnel, and a perilous desertion by some of the bank's preferred customers.

In addition to effects on mergers, the industry distortions also appear when a group of companies (where BPR had been intensely applied) becomes highly efficient in certain aspects of its operations, versus the remainder of the industry. This creates a situation whereby industry standards are changed—without basis in ultimate success experience. Such distortion provokes other companies into action to match these new standards, although they are not prepared nor structured for such changes. One such phenomenon is the change in the production to market cycle. In some industries companies have reduced the time it takes a new or improved product to arrive on the shelves. The advantages of "first moves," as I describe elsewhere in this book, are vastly overshadowed by longer term effects on the company's innovative capability and on the industry's ability to introduce innovations that would satisfy the marketplace.[31]

The imbalance caused by the implementation of BPR in only a part of the industry may also generate a long-term distortion in the evolution of the industry. Organization scientists who espouse the perspective of the population-ecology of organizations will recognize the dangers inherent in unintended modifications of only selected parts of the population. The evolution of the industry may become subjected to the fleeting short-term improvements in the efficiency of some companies at the expense of long-term growth and real advances in the marketplace. Mergers, acquisitions, and strategic alliances are then based on uninformed, even misleading, criteria of success and long-term survival.[32]

Technology Caging

The fourth category of long-term effects is the "caging" of technology. I have used this term to describe a situation in which the technological base of the corporation is encaged in an organizational space which confines it to lack of growth and expansion.[33] This leads to deterioration, anemic development, and persistent obsolescence.

To use a model of human physiological processes, BPR is supposedly acting as a lypolitic (fat burning) agent, whereas in reality over time it consumes the critical muscles, making them weak and arresting their development. Technology is such a muscle. The effects of BPR on technology caging act in the following modes.

First, there is the factor of *outsourcing* which I have discussed elsewhere in the book. When efficiency is the reigning criterion for transforming the organization, technological outsourcing becomes a key ingredient in this program. Outsourcing is usually more economical and also allows for drastic reductions in the number of technical and administrative employees from the functions and units that are outsourced. In the longer term the capabilities of the company in the technical area that was outsourced drastically diminish, because there is no longer a core of specialists who can successfully apply a learning process to the technology.[34]

Second, technology becomes encaged when the functions and processes that normally provide it with support are gradually transformed to the point of shrinkage or selective abandonment. By reengineering key work processes in the corporation, managers presumably cut the "fat" and those activities and subprocesses that are unnecessary or superfluous. Many of the processes thus labeled are those which directly or indirectly support technological activities. Support comes in many ways, some in the form of channels through which the technological content for new products and processes usually flows. By reengineering these supporting functions and processes, the corporation in effect drills holes in its network of channels, creating massive leaks that hemorrhage the new product development system.[35]

Essentially, the long-term impacts on the technology base are such that it "freezes" in some sort of a "time capsule." The technology base continues to function, but it cannot reach beyond the confines of its cage. Innovation and new product development become nominal functions, with little or no impact on the competitive stance of the firm. However, since the skeleton of technical competencies remains and continues to function, it becomes very difficult to detect such a pattern of decline, at least in the short run. In the longer term the effects of this deterioration are felt in the business performance of the company, as they start to be reflected in a collapsed technology-marketing interface, decreased market share, and sagging profitability.[36]

AFTERMATH DAMAGE AND CORPORATE PERFORMANCE

Up to now I have focused on the short-term and the long-term negative effects of Business Process Reengineering. In this section I extend the discussion to the link between the persistent and longer term damage from BPR and the performance of the corporation. Clearly, the damage caused in the aftermath of BPR is most important insofar as it impacts the long-term performance of the corporation. As already mentioned, this type of damage may be the more difficult to detect and to repair.

The management literature has devoted a great deal of effort to the variables that contribute to performance. Yet, when we speak of the performance of the corporation, it's as if we are all in agreement on what constitutes performance. Perhaps in the short run there are financial indicators such as earnings, value of the stock, and return on stockholder investment that constitute performance when they are joined by marketing and strategic variables (e.g., market share).[37] Thus, performance of the corporation has generally been equated with profitability, survival, market share, and overall success in gaining in the competitive global economy.

However, in addition to measurable and quantifiable indicators of performance, such as those listed above, the long-term survival and ability to compete need to be measured by indexes that are less manageable and easily attainable.

What Is Long-Term Performance?

Long-term survival and extended ability to compete are indicators of performance that materialize *after* the time period in question has passed. It is difficult to assess the probable occurrence of these indicators several years in advance. This is particularly true when a major change program is implemented in the corporation. Senior management is concerned with the longer term effects. Thus, short-term profitability, increased productivity, and a larger market share do not necessarily indicate a bright longer term future, survival, and downstream competitive abilities.[38]

So long-term performance is primarily survival *and* having the ability to compete. Survival itself is not a good predicator unless it denotes successful survival. If we decide that a long-term time horizon is over one year, the issue becomes less acute. This is a result of the definition of the relevant time horizon as a function of the dynamics of the corporation's external environment, characteristics of the industry, and the degree to which it implements aggressive change programs. In highly innovative industries one year is a very long time frame indeed (e.g., computers and consumer electronics). Many companies, however, relate their time horizon to their budget cycles. Anything under that is short-term, over is long term. There have been numerous criticisms of American executives who exercise purely a short-term view of their business to satisfy Wall Street and their stockholders eager for immediate gratification.[39]

Yet the preference of executives for short-term appraisal not withstanding, there is a long-term performance which should be defined and perhaps evaluated before its effects gradually or suddenly appear, to the surprise and even detriment of management and the corporation.

A good illustration is the assessment of the long-term impact of the R&D function on the company. Traditionally, R&D had been evaluated by its immediate outcomes, which were equivalent to the short-term indicators of performance. These included scientific outputs such as publications, reports, and patents.[40] However, the corporation demanded a better way of assessing the longer term impacts of R&D. In other contexts, such as those of public research organizations, the pressure was also on the generation of methods and indicators which would provide assessment of long-term performance.[41]

Currently the most promising methods are those that employ multiple indicators over several stages of the organization's outcomes. These stages may extend over a long period of time, and they measure progress as outcomes from such stages are generated. In addition, the multiple indicators may be combined into indexes for macroindicators, which are then compared against benchmarks or standards for performance.[42]

In the public sector these benchmarks are determined by the organization as well as by how the political/administrative system establishes its needs and priorities. But in the private sector, corporations determine benchmarks through a complex process of what might be considered "the invisible hand" of the market. Thus the questions: how much performance is considered minimal and how much is good or excellent? are essentially answered by the marketplace, through a process of trial and error. Those companies whose performance levels fall below the industry minimum may be eliminated by adverse competitive forces.

Long-term corporate performance is then the ability to sustain a competitive position in the marketplace by accomplishing outcomes that are above market benchmarks needed for survival. If fallen below such benchmarks, the corporation will be rejected by investors, customers, and suppliers, as well as pursued by regulators.

In summary, although difficult to preassess and to predict, long-term performance is key to corporate sustained presence in the market as a viable competitor. As such, therefore, any factor that contributes to this capability or poses a threat to it must be vigorously understood and managed.[43]

How BPR Impacts Long Term Performance

The four categories of impacts described in the previous sections were human effects, efficiency, dislocations, and technology caging. When these combine, they form a powerful influence which translates into long-term and lingering impacts on the following factors:

- Lowering the arsenal of skills and capabilities of a less motivated workforce, so that the decline in both categories and level of sophistication of skills is cumulative.

- Weakening of the network of channels of communication and information flow, and deterioration of the quality of information that flows through them.

- Deterioration of the technology base, leading to a less innovative company.

- Weakening of whatever links existed between units and factors to a coherent corporate strategy.

- Decline in main indicators of financial and market performance, cumulative over time.

What BPR seems to cause is the weakening or even elimination of the lay factors that influence longer term outcomes, hence sustained performance. So the main concern corporations face in this aspect of BPR's damage is how to assess and to identify the long-term impacts.

Issue of Imputation

As a program of change with substantial impacts, BPR has not been in existence long enough to produce hard-core cases of long-term detrimental effects on corporate performance. In the three years in which BPR has been widely applied, there have emerged many cases that allow for a learned analysis of what the effects will be.

However, there is an issue of *imputation*, which is the linking of two distinct, seemingly unrelated events into what we declare to be a cause and effect phenomenon. How do we know that BPR was responsible for the poor performance down the line, two or three years after its implementation in the corporation? Issues of imputation are pervasive in the social sciences, particularly when we study two events separated in time.[44] In the case of BPR, the intensity of the program and its invasiveness throughout the organization were so powerful as to allow for a causal link to be established.

Early-Warning Indicators

Even in the case of BPR, where causality is relatively easier to determine, there is a need for a system of early warning signals to alert the corporation that long-term and cumulative effects are brewing and will eventually result in powerful and devastating damage. Such a set of indicators is designed to go beyond the evaluation after the fact, as now practiced by corporations through a variety of "audits" and similar assessment frameworks.

How do we build a system of early-warning indicators? As indicated above and in various attempts in the literature, the indicators are designed into stages in the progression of the organization. In the case of R&D, early-warning indicators of outcomes are shown in Figure 6.3. The output indicators in the figure are only measures of the results from the R&D activity. They, and any indicators of outcome or performance, become early-warning indicators if they abide by the following criteria:

- *Availability*: Data for these indicators are available in organizational archives or can be obtained from members. They also must be available over time, so that lagged measurement can be accomplished.

- *Measurability*: Another criterion is whether these indicators can be measured. This does not imply a scientific approach—rather, these indicators lend themselves to any form of measurement with the tools we currently have for this task of measurement.

- *Benchmarks*: Existence of some acceptable form of benchmarks or standards against which the indicators will be compared.

- *Interpretation*: Existence of a system of values and criteria to be used in interpreting the trends of the indicators, thus providing meaning to the raw measures.

Figure 6.3
Illustrative Early Warning Indicators for Research and Development Outputs

---

Immediate Outputs

1. Number of publications in refereed journals
2. Number of patents
3. Number of citations in refereed journals
4. Number of new products conceived
5. Number of key improvements suggested
6. Number of new and improved test methods, models, and standards
7. Number of problems solved
8. Number of complaints by clients/users

Intermediate Outputs

1. Number of improved/new products produced by the company as a result of R&D's outcomes
2. Number of improved/new test methods
3. Actual cost reduction/savings in products and processes
4. Actual improvements in productivity of materials/equipment/techniques or people in the company
5. Judgments by other organizations

Source : E. Geisler, "An Integrated Cost-Performance Model of Research and Development Evaluation," *Omega*, 23(3), 1995, p. 285.

Many of the indicators in a system such as the "balanced scoreboard" may be used as early-warning indicators. The key factor for the set to be effective is the joint or cumulative effects of a *group* of indicators moving in a similar direction, hence representing a clear phenomenon. For example, if there is a marked decline in such components of the balanced scoreboard as: (1) percent of sales from new products, (2) percent of products that equal 80% sales, (3) quarterly sales growth, and (4) engineering efficiency (I selected one from each of the four perspectives), then the joint decline of the set over a given time period signals clear danger to the company. The persistent trend—over, say, two budget cycles—may be interpreted as unusual and as early warning.

Moreover, early warning may be interpreted when a set of indicators shows a common pattern in only *one* time period. This is the power of the set for it presumably represents a broad spectrum of the company's activities and categories of outcomes. Hence the need to employ multiple indicators from multiple perspectives. The more that indicators show a perilous trend, the more dangerous the situation.

A Proposed Early-Warning System

I have argued earlier in this chapter that the balanced scorecard fails to capture all the potential damages from BPR. Limited to financial and marketing indicators, the scorecard leaves out a host of organizational and managerial factors.

In order to predict the longer term damage from BPR, the company would need a system of early-warning indicators that is capable of alerting it to potential harm, long before such danger materializes.

The illustrative indicators proposed below are partly borrowed from my doctoral dissertation and from a ten-year study I have conducted on the monitoring of organizational phenomena.[45] Figure 6.4 shows the proposed indicators, *in addition* to the set of financial and marketing indicators already in use. Thus, the proposed system will encompass both the set proposed in Figure 6.4 and financial marketing.

The indicators in Figure 6.4 are not exhaustive and reflect only key outcomes and developments in the corporation. The emphasis is on structural indicators which tend to change over a longer period of time, with dramatic effects on corporate survival and competitiveness once these indicators occur.

Clearly the interpretation of what these indicators mean to corporate health and success rests on comparison with a given preestablished set of benchmarks or standards. For example, indicators of morale in Figure 6.4 may differ by industry and type of firm. However, a sharp change in the number and trend of an indicator does raise a red flag and should be analyzed within the larger picture of what happens to the other indicators.

A case in point is Dinner Delight (not the real name), a major manufacturer of food products. In 1994 the company initiated a major restructuring effort by a team of BPR enthusiasts, with the active support of the CEO and senior management. In mid-1996 the company agreed to collect some data on selected indicators and to regard them as early-warning signals.

Although productivity in some manufacturing processes has improved, and the financial indicators for 1995 and early 1996 were optimistic, the CEO was concerned. "It's my gut feeling that we are doing something wrong." Profits had improved in the 1994-1995 biennial and the company's stock was strong in the bull market.

The analysis of the data collected at Dinner Delight has produced the following results:

- Due to severe cuts in internal investments, training intensity and vertical mobility have sharply declined.

- The average age of the workforce has increased by about 25% (employees were retained by seniority and Last In First Out criteria).

- Control and formalization have sharply increased.

- The customer base was shrinking as many of the firm's customers maintained personal relations with downsized employees.

Figure 6.4
Illustrative Indicators of Corporate Performance as Early-Warning for Long-Term Effects

Structure

1. Degree of vertical integration
2. Degree of horizontal differentiation
3. Number of hierarchical levels

Formalization

1. Number of corporate forms
2. Number of different organizational units

Control

1. Ratio supervisors/employees
2. Ratio middle managers/employees

Human Resources

1. Training intensity (manhours/years)
2. Vertical mobility (no. of promotions/employees)
3. Age composition (average age)
4. Gender composition (ratio per employees)
5. Ethnic composition (ratio per employees)
6. Professional competencies (no. of professionals/ employees)
7. Professional updating (no. professionals hired in past 2 years)

Morale

1. Rate of absenteeism
2. No. of accidents/employees
3. Rate of resignations (per employee)
4. Rate of personnel actions for tardiness and other/ employees
5. Rate of intra-company transfer requests/ employees
6. Rate of formal complaints by employees/per employees

Reputation/customer Relations

1. Number of complaints by customers
2. Number of products/outputs returned/total shipments
3. Number of clients/customers who terminated relations/ total number of customers

These and other indicators, when woven into a larger picture of a threatening trend, have convinced the CEO that his feelings were correct. Although the financial performance was sound, the structural and human indicators pointed to a dangerous future. The company was changing into a sharply controlled, uninnovative, and ossified organization. Something has to be done now, before these indicators turn into a watershed that would probably lead to disastrous paralysis. As I wrote this chapter, the company was considering its options for a long-term effort to correct the situation. In essence, any system of early warning is acceptable as long as the indicators fulfill the four criteria listed above (in the "Early-Warning Indicators" section) and are representatives of a wide variety of corporate activities and perspectives.

Avoiding the Trap of Benchmarks

As a key criterion for making sense out of the change indicators, benchmarks are a highly beneficial means to assess the severity and intensity of trends. However, benchmarks may also become a trap, leading the analyst to wrong conclusions.

Benchmarks or standards may be derived from several sources: industry practices, corporate experience, external demands, and special configuration.[46]

Industry practices are commonly applied as benchmarks. Examples are production yields, sales quotas, and financial indicators such as debt ratio. These benchmarks offer a sense of safety insofar as they denote the company's position in a competitive mode. "If the industry's practice is such and we are at or above it, we *must* be doing well."

A trap may develop when industry practices are skewed due to a decline in the entire industry or a decline phase in the life cycle of the industry or many of its companies. This happens to new, entrepreneurial firms in a mature industry, whose performance may transcend existing benchmarks. Indeed, these firms represent the portion of the industry which is in revival. Such companies must apply different standards to their performance and avoid those of older firms.[47]

Corporate experience is also a commonly used approach for determining and establishing benchmarks. This criterion relies on "past performance" of the company, and on what becomes the culture or the "way we do it in this company" aphorism. Such experience is fine and good when there is an uninterrupted history of performance whose indicators may be easily plotted as a time-series graph.

However, it is abundantly clear that following a major restructuring event, such as BPR, there are radical discontinuities in such historical data.[48] A possible trap is to rely on "antebellum" benchmarks used before the change. Such action disregards the new realities of the company. Similarly, in cases of mergers and acquisitions, the acquired company may be forced to adopt standards used by the other firm. Such standards of performance may be inadequate for its beneficial use.

A problem that emerges in the case of major discontinuities is how to compare the performance following the change. If historical corporate benchmarks are no longer adequate, the forthcoming performance should be compared against which corporate experience? Also, how should a vibrant new company just acquired by a larger competitor compare its performance with lower standards of the acquiring corporation? Generally, senior managers should consider these issues on a case-by-case method, and by putting additional weight on the other sources (industry, external demands, and in particular: special configuration).

External demands are a strong source for establishing benchmarks for corporate performance. These demands or pressures may come from regulators, suppliers, customers, and, increasingly today, from partners in strategic alliances who are from different segments or even industries.[49] Similarly, such demands also exist internally in a company that is vertically integrated.

External demands may create a trap for the company when the benchmarks thus enforced are over- or underestimations of the degree of performance they require or represent. For example, a midsize manufacturing company, maker of electrical parts, has adopted some performance standards of its European customers, as part of its effort to obtain certification through the ISO-9000 process. In addition to the establishment of a rigorous quality control system, the company had also introduced benchmarks for manufacturing, packaging, and even employee compensation—all borrowed from its customers. This company overestimated the power of these benchmarks and their applicability to the American scene and its specific corporate environment. The result was a mismatch between productivity and compensation, leading to conflicts and to an ultimate decline in overall performance.

Special configuration is a less popular source for the establishment of benchmarks. The criterion in this source is the combination of circumstances in an organization or a unit which requires special benchmarks. Professional and high technology units present their special configurations as a case for different standards. Research functions usually request different rules, criteria, and standards for the performance of their units and their professional staffs (less control, relaxed atmosphere, and special performance measures due to the uncertainty and long time horizon embedded in their activity).

A possible trap in this type of benchmark is the widespread application of these standards beyond the confines of the specialized unit. The usual erroneous argument is: "if it works in A it should work in B." The company may avoid this trap by keeping a strict limitation on different benchmarks, and by making certain that they apply to specialized functions or activities—after intense scrutiny.

The aftermath damage from BPR inflicts long-term and measurable negative consequences on corporate performance. There is an urgent need to assess such consequences and to prepare a program that would deal with them and attempt to correct them—*before* they become the devastating storm that cripples the corporation. This is what the remainder of this book intends to do.

SUMMARY

Reengineering brings about several side effects that create lateral damage in the corporation. Some of these side effects are embedded in the behavior of the individual, while other effects are manifested in the organization.

The individual effects include devastating psychological impacts on the workforce. Low morale, increased uncertainty, absenteeism, sense of loss and chaos, and the will to retreat into oneself are but some of these effects. There is a decline in risk taking, in intrapreneurship, and in communicating across unit lines.

The organizational effects include decline in unit performance, discrepancies in unit performance, increased costs, and threats to core competencies.

As I have reiterated in the chapters five and six, these side effects are not caused only by poor implementation of reengineering. Although Hammer and Champy, in their more recent publications, have suggested ways to improve implementation (thus, in their view, eliminating or at least attenuating these side effects), the main damage is caused by the reengineering program per se. The damage is inherent in what BPR does to the organization, *however effective or efficient is its implementation.* Corporate redesign is inherently a bearer of shock and chaos; lateral damage is inevitable, yet *not* irreversible.

Finally, I must reemphasize that I am not against restructuring or redesign of the corporation. Like birds in flight, organizations must perform periodic course adjustments, some major, some minor. They must: (1) maintain the integrity of the flock, (2) keep to the overall direction, and (3) adapt their flight to changing conditions. This means that change is integral to the normal operations of an organization—if it wishes to succeed and to survive.

What I do oppose is a change program that is inherently faulty and which brings about short- and long-term side effects that far outweigh the overpromised benefits from the program.

In the chapters ahead I outline a program for *cleanup after reengineering*, and I propose the way to restore stability and to repair the damage inflicted upon the corporation.

NOTES

1. *Business Week*, March 11, 1996, p. 50.
2. See Peter Drucker, "The Coming of the New Organization," *Harvard Business Review*, January-February 1988, pp. 45-53.
3. See *Business Week, op cit.*, pp. 50-56.
4. There is a very large literature on employee and managerial motivation. For example, see D. Kolb, I. Rubin, and J. McIntyre, *Organizational Psychology*, 2nd ed. (Englewood Cliffs, NJ: Prentice Hall, 1974) and C. C. Pinder, *Work Motivation: Theory, Issues, and Applications* (Glenview, IL: Scott Foresman, 1984).
5. An excellent book on middle managers is F. J. Aguilar, *General Managers in Action*, 2nd ed. (New York: Oxford University, 1992).
6. I wrote an article on the entrepreneurial activities of middle managers: E. Geisler, "Middle Managers as Internal Corporate Entrepreneurs: An Unfolding Agenda," *Interfaces*, 23(6), 1993, pp. 52-63.
7. K. Cameron, "Strategies for the Successful Organizational Downsizing," *Human Resources Management*, 33(2), 1994, pp. 123-146.
8. G. Hall, J. Rosenthal, and J. Wade, "How to Make Reengineering Really Work," *Harvard Business Review*, November-December 1993, pp. 119-131.
9. M. G. Benuvides and P. Rossler, "Reengineering and the Insanity of Right-Sizing," *Engineering Management Journal*, 7(3), June 1995, p. 21.
10. *Ibid.*, p. 21.

11. C. K. Prahalad and G. Hamel, "The Core Competence of the Corporation," *Harvard Business Review*, May-June 1990, pp. 79-93.

12. *Ibid.*, pp. 89-90.

13. Systems by definition are designed to accommodate redundancy and slack resources. Organizations that function on the principles of a systemic mode also rely on such resources to maintain an adaptive posture and ensure competitiveness. The Japanese approach to innovation is such an example. See I. Nonaka, "Redundant, Overlapping Organization: A Japanese Approach to Innovation," *California Management Review*, 32(3), 1990, pp. 27-38. The units that are organized according to these principles would not withstand a rigorous analysis of "core competencies." Their slack resources would be eliminated, thus cutting the very strings that hold the entire operation together. Professor Jan Osterlund from the Royal Institute of Technology in Stockholm, Sweden, has referred me to the theories of M. Bunge regarding systems. He suggested that living systems must fulfill requirements of integration based on cohesion and coordination of the system's component activities. See M. Bunge, "Treatise on Basic Philosophy," in *A World of Systems*, Vol. 4, *Ontology II* (Dordrecht, Holland: D. Riedel, 1983) pp. 32-37.

14. For example, J. D. Duck, "Managing Change: The Art of Balancing," *Harvard Business Review*, November-December 1993, pp. 109-118. The author is a transactional analyst. She suggested that transition management teams should proactive fill the gap and provide employees with relevant information on the change program.

15. Illustrative descriptions of this effect appear in, for example, M. D. Dunnette (ed.), *Handbook of Industrial and Organizational Psychology* (Chicago, IL: Rand McNally, 1976).

16. See E. Mayo, *The Human Problems of Industrial Civilization* (New York: Macmillan, 1933).

17. See, for example, J. T. Whiting, "Reengineering the Corporation: A Historical Perspective and Critique," *Industrial Management*, November-December 1994, pp. 14-16; also see R. Tomsho, "How Greyhound Lines Re-engineered Itself Right into a Deep Hole," *The Wall Street Journal*, October 20, 1994, pp. A1, A4; and G. Plenert, "Process Re-engineering: The Latest Fad Toward Failure," *APICS: The Performance Advantage*, June 1994, pp. 22-24.

18. For example, see W. Casio, "Downsizing: What Do We Know? What Have We Learned?" *Academy of Management Executive*, 7(1), 1993, pp. 95-104; and H. O'Neill, "Restructuring, Reengineering, and Rightsizing: Do the Metaphors Make Sense?" *Academy of Management Executive*, 8(4), 1994, pp. 9-11.

19. Drucker, *op. cit.*, pp. 46-47.

20. The organization and strategy literatures have had many studies reported on this topic. See, for example, D. Crane and Z. Bodie, "Form Follows Function: The Transformation of Banking," *Harvard Business Review*, March-April 1996, pp. 109-119; also see F. Suarez and J. Utterback, "Dominant Designs and the Survival of Firms," *Strategic Management Journal*, 16(6), September 1995, pp. 415-430.

21. This is a case quite similar to that of Greyhound Lines. See Tomsho, *op cit.*

22. *Ibid.*

23. This is a different company from the one described in Chapter 5, in which overzealous attention was given to output performance measures, at the expense of the unit's contribution to the value chain. The company described here in Chapter 6 is currently attempting to reverse the damage caused by reengineering.

24. See, for example, W. Baker, "Bloodletting & Downsizing," *Executive Excellence*, 13(5), May 1986, p. 20; also see J. Witherill, "Is Corporate Re-Engineering Hurting Your Employees?" *Professional Safety*, 41(5), May 1996, pp. 28-32; and M. Davids, "Some Deadly Sins of Reengineering," *Child Executive*, 113, May 1996, p. 56.

25. R. Hall, *Organizations: Structures, Processes, and Outcomes*, 6th ed. (Englewood Cliffs, NJ: Prentice Hall, 1996). Also see M. Manning, C. Jackson, and M. Fusilier, "Occupational Stress, Social Support, and the Costs of Health Care," *Academy of Management Journal*, 39(3), 1996, pp. 738-750.

26. S. Wood and M. Albanese, "Can We Speak of a High Commitment Management on the Shop Floor?," *Journal of Management Studies*, 32(2), 1995, pp. 215-247; also see A. Pettigrew and R. Whipp, *Managers Change for Competitive Success* (Oxford: Blackwell Publishers, 1992); in particular, see D. Gordon, *Fat and Mean: The Corporate Squeeze of Working Americans and the Myth of Managerial Downsizing* (New York: The Free Press, 1996).

27. R. Kaplan and D. Norton, "Using the Balanced Scoreboard As a Strategic Management System," *Harvard Business Review*, 79(1), 1996, pp. 75-87.

28. R. Kaplan and D. Norton, "The Balanced Scorecard—Measures that Drive Performance," *Harvard Business Review*, 70(1), 1992, pp. 71-79.

29. See T. Johnson and R. Kaplan, *Relevance Cost: The Rise and Fall of Management Accounting* (Boston, MA: Harvard Business School Press, 1987).

30. For example, see the case of Compaq Corporation described in E. Lawler, *From the Ground Up: Six Principles for Building the New Logic Corporation* (San Francisco: Jossey-Bass, 1996). In this book Ed Lawler illustrates a company that transferred itself without the unidimensional method of change of reengineering.

31. An example from the software industry is the introduction of the NT operating system by Microsoft in 1993, and its market growth in the middle 1990s. See, R. Cafasso, "NT Enters the Mainstream," *Software Magazine*, August 1996, pp. 24-31.

32. See, for example, G. Duystersand J. Haggerdorn, "Strategic Groups and Inter-Firm Networks in International High-Tech Industries," *Journal of Management Studies*, 32(3), May 1995, pp. 359-382, also see A. Sharma and I. Kerner, "Diversifying Entry: Some Ex Ante Explanations for Post-Entry Survival and Growth," *Academy of Management Journal*, 39(3), 1996, pp. 635-677.

33. See, for example, J. Tidd, "Development of Novel Products Through Interorganizational and Interorganizational Networks: The Case of Home Automation," *The Journal of Product Innovation Management*, 12(4) (September 1995) pp. 323-333.; also see B. Dos Santos and K. Pfeffer, "Rewards to Investors in Innovative Information Technology Applications: First Movers and Early Followers in ATMs," *Organization Science*, 6(3), 1995, pp. 241-259; and Kaplan and Norton, "Using the Balanced Scoreboard," *op. cit.* Although Kaplan and Norton use in their scoreboard such measures as percent of sales from new products, and goals such as technology capability and technology leadership, the measures in the balanced scoreboard fall short of pointing to the deterioration in the technology base of the corporation following intensive BPR.

34. For an indirect criticism of activities that lead to obsolescence and technological caging, see G. Pisano and S. Wheelwright, "The New Logic of High Tech R&D," *Harvard Business Review*, 73(5), 1995, pp. 93-107.

35. For example, see R. Calantone, S. Vickery, and C. Droge, "Business Performance and Strategic New Product Development Activities: An Empirical Investigation," *The Journal of Product Innovation Management*, 12(3), 1995, pp. 214-223. In this paper the authors argue that there is a strong relationship between business performance and specific innovation-related activities. They used the example of the furniture industry and contended that top performers have created a corporate configuration that gives new product development much more responsibility and the capability to avoid the harmful overflow of changes in other parts of the organization.

36. There is a voluminous literature in this and related topics. See, for example, E. Mansfield and J. Rapaport, "The Cost of Industrial Product Innovation," *Management Science*, 21(1), 1975, pp. 1380-1386; also see W. Souder, "Promoting an Effective R&D and Marketing Interface," *Research Management*, 23(4), 1980, pp. 10-15; and Z. Pascal, *Showstopper: The Breakneck Race to Create Windows NT and the Next Generation at Microsoft* (New York: The Free Press, 1994).

37. See, for example, E. Segev and P. Gray, *Business Success: Strategic Unit Comprehensive Computer-Based Expert Support System* (Englewood Cliffs, NJ: Prentice Hall, 1990) and G. Donaldson, "A New Tool for Boards: The Strategic Audit," *Harvard Business Review*, 73(4), 1995, pp. 99-108.

38. The relationship between focus on efficiency (short-term benefits) and effectiveness (longer term) has received some attention in the management literature. See, for example: B. Golany and E. Tamir, "Evaluating Efficiency-Effectiveness-Equality Trade-offs: A Data Envelopment Analysis Approach," *Management Science*, 41(7), 1995, pp. 1172-1184; also see W. Brian Arthur, "Increasing Returns and the New World of Business," *Harvard Business Review*, 74(4), 1996, pp. 100-111; and R. McGrath, M. Tsai, S. Venkataraman, and I. MacMillan, "Innovation, Competitive Advantage and Rent: A Model and Test," *Management Science*, 42(3), 1996, pp. 389-403. In this last paper, the authors argued that in order to capture rents from an innovation, four antecedents are necessary: causal understanding, team proficiency, emergence and mobilization of new competencies, and creation of competitive advantages. This model may be an illustration of a similar model for assessing long-term performance, defined by the authors in terms of economic rents.

39. See, for example, I. Dierickx and K. Cool, "Asset Stock Accumulation and Sustainability of Competitive Advantage," *Management Science*, 35(2), 1989, pp. 1504-1513; and M. Peteraf, "The Cornerstones of Competitive Advantage: A Resource-Based View," *Strategic Management Journal*, 14(4), 1993, pp. 179-192.

40. See, B. Bozeman and J. Melkers (eds.), *Evaluating R&D Methods and Practice* (Boston: Kluwer Academic Publishers, 1993).

41. See, for example, V. Borden and T. Banta, *Using Performance Indicators to Guide Strategic Decision Making* (San Francisco: Jossey-Bass, 1994); also see N. Carter, R. Klein, and P. Day, *How Organizations Measure Success: The Use of Performance Indicators in Government* (London: P. Routledge Publishers, 1992).

42. E. Geisler, "An Integrated Cost-Performance Model of Research and Development Evaluation," *Omega*, 23(3), 1995, pp. 281-294; also see E. Geisler, "Key Output Indicators in Performance Evaluation of Research and Development Organizations," *Technology Forecasting and Social Change*, 47(1), 1994, pp. 189-204.

43. B. Lloyd, "Knowledge Management: The Key to Long Term Organizational Success," *Long Range Planning*, 29(4), 1996, pp. 576-580.

44. E. Geisler, "Measuring the Unquantifiable: Issues in the Use of Indicators in Unstructured Phenomena," *International Journal of Operations and Quantitative Management*, 1(2), 1995, pp. 145-161. The linking of distinct events separated by time and sometimes by concept or design is found in many areas of the social and management sciences. A major body of literature exists on linking various organizational and managerial functions and activities to the strategy of the organization. Some examples are S. Raphuram, "Linking Staffing and Training Practices with Business Strategy: A Theoretical Perspective," *Human Resource Development Quarterly*, Fall 1994, pp. 68-79; also see D. Schroeder, S. Congden, and C. Gopinath, "Linking Competitive Strategy and Manufacturing Process Technology," *Journal of Management Studies*, 32(2), 1995, pp. 163-190; and B. Boar, *The Art of Strategic Planning for Information Technology* (New York: John Wiley, 1993).

45. E. Geisler, "An Empirical Study of a Proposed System for Monitoring Organizational Change in a Federal R&D Laboratory," unpublished doctoral dissertation, Northwestern University, 1979. I also consulted R. Burton and B. Obel, *Strategic Organizational Diagnosis and Design: Developing Theory for Application* (Norwell, MA: Kluwer Academic Publishers, 1995).

46. S. Ackroyd, "On the Structure and Dynamics of Some Small, UK-Based Information Technology Firms," *Journal of Management Studies*, 32(2), 1995, pp. 141-162; also see F. Damanpour, "Organizational Complexity and Innovation: Developing and Testing Multiple Contingency Models," *Management Science*, 42(5), 1996, pp. 693-716.

47. See for example, M. Tushman and E. Romanelli, "Organizational Evolution: A Metamorphosis Model of Convergence and Reorientation," in L. Cummings and B. Staw (eds.), *Research in Organizational Behavior* (Greenwich, CT: JAI Press, 1985).

48. See R. Whittington, T. McNulty, and R. Whipp, "Market-Driven Change in Professional Services: Problems and Processes," *Journal of Management Studies*, 31(1), 1994, pp. 829-846; and B. Bonathy, *Designing Social Systems in a Changing World* (New York: Plenum, 1996).

49. The movements of a flock of birds was instrumental in the development of chaos theory, which has also been applied in some instances to organizational phenomena, such as entrepreneurship.

7

CLEANING-UP:
THE PROCESS OF RESTORING BALANCE

The poet and philosopher Khalil Gibran once wrote: "For a divided house is not a den of thieves, it is only a divided house. And a ship without rudder may wander aimlessly among perilous isles yet sink not to the bottom."[1]

A company that has been reengineered and finds itself in a state of chaos, uncertainty, and confusion need not be discouraged. There are means and ways to restore stability and balance. This chapter begins the process for restoring balance and rebuilding the corporation, which will be continued in the remaining chapters..

BACKGROUND OF THE CLEANING-UP PROCESS

In essence, the cleaning-up process is based on the premise that corporations are facing two converging phenomena. The first, described in the previous chapters, is the lateral damage caused by the application of Business Process Reengineering. In early 1996 there has been an increase in the popular press of pronouncements by academics that reengineering has not fulfilled its promise. Carrie Leana, a professor of business at the University of Pittsburgh, writes:

It is easy for executives to ignore the hidden costs of restructuring because there is an immediate reward: their firms do well in the markets. But not necessarily in the market in which they take their goods and services. . . . Our corporations—the greatest social instruments we have, the source of the wealth of the nation—are in crisis, and it is time to reshape them.[2]

Leana calls for freeing corporations from the shackles of Wall Street, where maximization of short-term performance is the guiding principle. This, she and others claim, affects the corporation's ability to foster a knowledge-based workforce.

Ori Sasson, the CEO of Scopus Technology, a small provider of client-server customer information management systems, wrote about technology companies and their rush to outsource, as an outcome of reengineering: "Conventional wisdom says that reengineering brings businesses closer to their customers. . . . The theory sounds nice, but in the real world things can be painfully different."[3] Sasson contends that some types of outsourcing place a third entity between the company and its customers. This may obscure the flow of information between customers and the company.

A third example is that of Canon, the Japanese electronics manufacturer. Ikujiro Nonaka and Martin Kenney have discussed the different philosophy of management employed by Canon to gain a constant flow of innovations.[4] In contrast with Silicon Valley companies (where the authors contend the rule is a chaotic system), Canon's philosophy is that the manager becomes a catalyst, rather than an autocratic type leader whose role is to restructure, thus disregarding the resulting loss of competencies and information—so necessary for a long-term innovation policy.

Therefore, a manager who is committed to reengineering, by definition has the task of re-creating a structure. Hence this manager cannot act as a catalyst and make sense out of chaos through highly developed skills of communications and assistance to the innovation teams. In this example reengineering is so dramatic and radical that it creates chaos rather than be an instrument that creates order and a new and better format for the corporation.

The three illustrative articles cited above show the variety of basic arguments that BPR has created dangerous situations in the corporation, which demand corrective action. Whether it is the damage to the workforce, the philosophy of management, or the threat to customer relations, the systemic failure is a strong phenomenon that calls for a measured yet powerful response for cleanup and restoration of balance.

The second phenomenon is the crisis in management, described in Chapter 3. Managers are suffering from an *overdose of change phenomena*. The quality revolution of the early 1980s continued through the corporate transformation by means of growth, mergers, and acquisitions, and into the 1990s with downsizing and reengineering.

Managers are watching a rapidly changing business environment, while at the same time they are subjected to a torrent of change programs to deal with these changes in their environment. Crises are being generated: "the productivity crisis" and "the world competitiveness crisis" are but two of the crises that bewitch our executives. The messages from consultants and scholars are mixed, and the solutions are overpromising and radical. Who do we believe? In *what* do we believe? What can we, or should we do? This is the *real* crisis.

The coming together of a host of damaging side effects from reengineering—and the bewildered and skeptical managers—is the background on which I construct a cleaning-up process that leads to stability and balance.

THE "SLEEP ANALOGY"

Researchers have long established the fact that people need sleep in order to recover and to recompose damage to the human body. Recent studies have indicated that the common practice of people to cut their sleep short during a workweek and then "recoup" the loss on weekends is not healthy. It usually creates sleep deprivation.

This is an analogy to the recovery and restoration of the damage caused by reengineering to the corporation. If we attempt to ignore the damage by perhaps acting on one aspect of it (in the hope that we can catch up with it later), we are bound to accumulate "sleep loss" and to threaten our corporate health. The corporation thus needs a consistent program of recovery that will concentrate on an overall recovery in a systemic view of the corporation.

Moreover, sleep researchers have concluded that human sleep is a process that occurs in stages. They have also identified stages III and IV as the "slow-wave" sleep, in which the person is most restful, and in which much of the recuperation occurs. In the corporate process of recovery, I am also proposing a stage process, composed of six stages. We can also identify those stages in the corporate recovery process in which the damage is repaired.

CLINICAL CLEANING-UP

What I call in this book the "reengineering intervention" is essentially several activities and actions that cut across units, functions, and workgroups in the corporation. They leave in their wake a diverse and dispersed set of powerful side effects, some immediately noticeable, others hidden in work processes and in the discontent of the workforce.

Any intervention for the purpose of cleaning up and for initiating the restoration process must have seven characteristics, as summarized in Figure 7.1.

"Clinical Approach"

The first characteristic of the cleaning-up process is the "clinical approach," which may be roughly defined as treating the corporation as a wounded or "sick" entity for the purpose of effecting a therapeutic action. In addition, as in medical practice, the cleaning-up process should be such that no additional damage is inflicted on the corporation. In other words, if the cleaning-up process creates a chaotic disturbance that exacerbates the condition of the corporation (before making things better), such an approach would not be acceptable.

Figure 7.1
Characteristics of the Process of Cleaning-Up After Reengineering

• "Clinical Approach:" Repair damage and don't cause any harm
• Salvaging those benefits from previous change programs compatible with the recovery process
• Commitment of senior management
• Clear and well-defined objectives
• Identifiable stages of the process
• Commitment from the workforce
• Affordable in resources and time constraints

The clinical approach also provides for a reasoned intervention, in that the cleaning-up process is designed to improve the condition of the corporation by bringing it back to stability (or what can be defined as "health").

Salvaging Benefits from Previous Change

Unlike reengineering, the cleaning-up process does not obliterate everything that preceded it. Change programs (including reengineering) leave a trail of benefits alongside the harmful side effects. In fact, we would not be naming these side effects were it not for the main effect of the change program. As I describe in this book, the inability to succeed is inherent in reengineering and its premises. However, there are benefits that accrue from the application of this change program.

Ironically, these benefits occur because reengineering is usually misdirected and implemented in a piecemeal mode. This means that reengineering becomes a program of selected improvements in the efficiency of work processes. In this environment the reengineering intervention does produce some beneficial effects—primarily improvements in work flow and their efficiency.

There is no reason to discard these benefits, if and only if they are compatible with the recovery process. Thus, we don't discard them just because they are the product of reengineering, and we don't keep them just because they are improvements. These are salvaged when they can be incorporated into the recovery program.

Commitment of Senior Management

The process of cleaning-up and restoring balance must have the support of senior management. This will require their understanding of the crisis they face, the issues involved, and what cleaning-up will do for their corporation. Here we run into the problem of skeptical executives who "have heard it all". What would the cleaning-up program do for the corporation more than reengineering?

It is important to note, as I have consistently done in this book, that cleaning-up is *not* a surrogate for reengineering, nor is it promising to do more or less than reengineering. It is presented to senior management in exactly the form that it is: a program that corrects the errors, repairs the damage, and restores stability. The cleaning-up program does not promise improved performance nor more efficient workflows, although it is assumed that when the corporation repairs the damage caused by reengineering, it will be on the way to recovery and to success.

Clear and Well-Defined Objectives

Robert Quinn, in his book on rational management, has described the "competing values model," which contains such competing elements as internal versus external focus.[5] In essence, the model suggests that rationalization (emphasis on productivity, planning, and efficiency) is competing with the human relations model (cohesion, innate value of human resources), as well as the open system and internal processes models. All of these models have their own values, which are different from one another and some are even in conflict.

Quinn proposed an overall model in which effective organizations are able to balance out the conflicting values by emphasizing some (at the expense of others), in accordance with the stages of the life of the organization.

Inherent in Quinn's overall effectiveness model is the premise that managers are able to adapt to these changes in the "values portfolio arrangement" to accommodate the changing focus.

Quinn's model exemplifies the idea behind clear and well-defined objectives of the cleaning-up program. These objectives are at once limited to what the program promises to achieve, and different enough to create a change in focus: from reengineering to restoring balance. That is, from radical change to restoration of stability.

Yet different corporate objectives, as implied in Quinn's model, are not necessarily mutually exclusive nor even in conflict. Different objectives may reside peacefully together when they define the constraints of a space or domain that the corporation is pursuing. For example, the Honda motto, pronounced by the founder of the automaker is: to make the best possible vehicle for its price. This objective sets the constraints, although it may sound as maximizing one domain ("best").

The objectives of the cleaning-up program thus should define the constraints and the domain of the program. Although some may be different from one another, they coexist by mutually defining domains that are overlapping. For instance, one objective states that the program will restore stability, while another states that benefits generated by reengineering will be maintained (although they may be part of what caused the damage in the first place).

Clearly, the objectives must be well-defined in order to allow managers and employees of the corporation to gain full understanding of what the program is about, and what is about to happen. One of the inherent problems with BPR was the fuzziness of its operational objectives, beyond the overall restructuring and performance enhancement goal.[6]

Identifiable Stages of the Process

Any program of change or any kind of organizational intervention must be clearly defined as to what it constitutes. This allows for better planning as well as telling the people and units involved what they should expect, and also what is coming next.

Since the cleaning-up program is shown as a process, it must have clearly identifiable and distinct stages, into which resources can get allocated, a time frame assigned, and measurable outcomes that can be computed.

Commitment from the Workforce

In addition to commitment from senior management, the cleaning-up program requires commitment from the workforce. All employees in the corporation have been exposed to BPR and many bear the mark of frustration and skepticism. They should comprehend the necessity for cleanup operations, thus providing commitment to the program. Commitment is usually along a dimension running between no reaction at all (yet also no resentment nor active opposition) to actively supporting the program. The more we can approach the active support, the better the chances of the cleaning-up for success.[7]

Affordable in Resources and Time Constraints

The corporation at this point is drained of its slack resources, downsized, and painfully wounded. Therefore, the cleaning-up program should possess the characteristic of being affordable. A major redesign of the corporation for the purpose of cleaning-up would be an unfortunate choice, because it will be beyond the financial means and will of the company. Yet moderation should be accom-panied by a program that has enough muscle to indeed perform the cleaning-up necessary to restore stability.

CONCEPTUAL BASIS FOR CLEANING-UP

What are the antecedents for cleaning-up? What are the conceptual bases we now possess for a program of damage control and revitalization of the corporation? The applicable questions are much more prosaic: (1) Can we do such a restoration of balance at all (once BPR happened and the damage ensued)? and (2) Do we know enough to attempt such a program?

As I already mentioned, a program for cleaning-up should be comprehensive (organization-wide) as well as focused on each unit or function. This leads to an operational problem which is essentially a conceptual issue in the organization and management sciences. The operational problem is limited to the ability to conduct both a comprehensive and a localized effort to restore balance. The issues that seem to arise are the ability of the cleaning-up team to do both, general and specific, within a rationalized and matched framework. If the emphasis on the comprehensive redesign is much more powerful than the focus on units and functions, the cleaning-up team may commit errors similar to those of BPR—namely, lack of coordination and creation of unbalanced components of the organization. Figure 7.2 summarizes these issues.

The first of the conceptual issues related to this problem is very intensive and is deeply rooted in the persistent dichotomy between general and specific.

The Great Schism

In studies of organizations and their management, scholars have identified the duality between the concepts of efficiency and effectiveness, between strategic and tactical, between general and specific or localized. As I extend this discussion (which began earlier in the book), there emerges a question of how much do we really know about this schism, and how much can we use in our design of a cleaning-up program?

Figure 7.2
Issues in the Conceptual Basis for Cleaning-Up Intervention

❋ **Great Schism**
  • Linking overall, organization-wide design with localized, specific units
    and functions
❋ **Organizational Learning**
  • Organizational routines and organizational memory
  • Organizational cognitions, mindsets, cognitive maps and modeling
❋ **Managers' Search for Quantitative Data**
  • Availability
  • Accessibility
  • Cost
  • Readability
  • Validity
  • Interpretation
  • Cognition and Quantitative Data
❋ **Issues in Unobtrusive Measurement**
  • Accessibility of archives
  • Vulnerability of archival data
  • Continuity of records and methods of recording
  • Privacy and proprietorship
  • Data transformation: readability and meaning
  • Interpretation
  • Data paucity and embellishment
  • "True" description of reality?

The duality of these two concepts goes beyond a continuum. There is a schism that separates the concepts, thus making it very difficult to bridge the gap and to find common mechanisms, in concept and practice.

What we have here is the gap between exercising changes in processes and work design at the level of the unit, *versus* the broader picture of the direction the company is taking, why it does so, and how to achieve it in the context of the company within its industry. This is what I referred to as the link between strategy and its application in the corporation—usually wrought with a gap in translation, interpretation, and a shared direction.[8] Another debate in the literature related to this issue is the study of organizational effectiveness.[9] Defining effectiveness in the broadest sense also includes internal processes. But this mixed definition encounters difficulties when implemented, due to sharp differences between the conceptual framework and the frame of mind of people who apply them on both sides of the schism.

Repairing the damage caused by BPR becomes a difficult task because reengineering affects both sides of the schism. Any program for cleaning-up must therefore be linked to both ends, the general and the specific. It also must ensure that there are no threatening conflicts between repairing the overall direction of the company (e.g., the "vision") and individual units and functions.

How do we secure an effort which will bridge the gap and allow for a coordinated program across the schism? The knowledge base we currently possess can be found primarily in the strategic management literature, and the research on the link between senior management's thinking and action, and the lower echelons of the organization.

In the strategic management knowledge base it is becoming evident that there are strong correlations between specific activities and the overall strategy of the firm. For example, a positive relation between manufacturing and overall corporate strategy has been shown to exist.[10] Recently, J. Dean and S. Snell have concluded that "there is enough evidence now to suggest that IM and manufacturing strategy are potentially synergetic—and clearly some of the firms we studied are using them synergetically."[11] Yet, in the more "professional" units, such as R&D and information systems, there is a consistent failure to create synergy with senior management.

Nevertheless, if we assume that BPR's most devastating effects are primarily in work processes which lend themselves to synergy with senior management, there is potential for a cleaning-up effort that could bridge the great schism.[12] So, if BPR affected the work processes by redesigning them and by impacting their efficiency and productivity, it is therefore possible to deal with the widespread lateral damage *and* link it to revitalization through strategic redesign at the senior management level. This *is* a strong statement and a major promise, but I believe that such linkage is possible, while always keeping in mind that the schism exists and that the differences inherent in it may, at any time, disrupt any honest attempt to clean up and to restore stability.[13]

Organizational Learning

A different dimension of the conceptual basis for cleaning-up is organizational learning. This dimension is both a presumed facilitator for cleaning-up and a problematic barrier.

The importance of learning (in the context of the organization) to cleaning-up is primarily in the fact that the cleaning-up effort is an evolutionary process. As I outline in this book, the cleaning-up effort is not a revolutionary approach designed to counteract BPR's effects—revolution versus revolution. Rather, it is based on a compilation of existing knowledge in management and organization sciences.

As a program of change, the cleaning-up effort relies on the learning abilities of organizational members and perhaps also on the learning ability of units and the organization. A crucial portion of this change program is the ability of members to understand the damage inflicted by BPR, to draw conclusions from the history of that intervention, and by so learning, to implement and appreciate the benefits of a cleaning-up intervention.

Can organizations learn? Here is a stream in the management literature that focuses on the phenomenon they describe as organizational learning.[14] The answer to the question posed above may be crucial to our ability to design and implement the cleaning-up program, because of two main reasons: managers' search for quantitative and measurable information, and the difficulties associated with unobtrusive measures.[15]

Managers' Search for Quantitative Data

I am not an advocate for the concept of organizational learning. I believe that people learn and their collective knowledge base thus accumulated becomes an organizational asset—if it is properly and adequately maintained, recorded, and used. Essentially, the knowledge base involved with learning is made up of two types: quantitative and qualitative data. The latter are the feelings, attitudes, and sentiments of the organizational players. Managers have always searched for quantitative data to better understand the patterns of their corporation's behavior and those of their external environment.

This search for quantitative data is hardly a capricious exercise by corporate executives. Rather, it is an essential need for information that would allow these managers to better perform their duties. A company cannot be managed by feelings and attitudes alone.

Here's the problem: the search for quantitative data is a very difficult endeavor because the data in question (as shown in Figure 7.2) pose difficulties in availability, accessibility, cost, readability, validity, and interpretation.

Quantitative data are, in many instances, *unavailable*. Management scholars have struggled with this fact in the conduct of their studies of corporations and in designing their models of how organizations behave. For example, models of competitive strategies, developed in the 1970s, 1980s, and early 1990s, are derived from analyses that are based on quantitative data. M. Porter's generic value chain, a similar model developed by McKinsey and Company, and the modeling of the company's competitive position in its industry (developed by the Boston Consulting Group, McKinsey, and Andersen Consulting, among others) are illustrations of the heavy reliance on quantitative measures. Some of these measures include market share, cost data, speed of delivery of goods to market, reliability of supplies, quality data, profitability, economies of scale, and cyclical data.[16] These and other data elements are not always available in the corporation or in the marketplace. If available, they may not be *accessible* to the managers at the point in time when they are most needed.

Cost is another criterion in the search for such data. I have consulted for a mid-size company that was preparing a bid for supplying the government of a West African nation. The information it needed for preparation of the bid was largely unavailable and unaccessible. Those data items deemed accessible turned out to be very expensive to obtain. The exaggerated cost also included a long time frame for obtaining such data. Owing to these considerations, the company decided to withdraw its bid.

Readability of the quantitative data is also a difficulty in the quest for such knowledge. This means that many times the data appear in a form that is hard to decipher and to read. *Validity* of the data that exist in the organization and particularly in its environment is another difficulty for managers. In their own organizations managers have a degree of control over how data are obtained, how valid they are, and how reliable. Marketplace data and data on vendors, competitors, and customers are beyond their control, hence there is a limit to how reliable and valid such data are. Can managers trust the data on their external environment? Even in the United States, where we place much trust in statistical data generated by private and public organizations, some data are produced for political and other reasons, and may thus reflect the interests of those who generate them. As the economy becomes global, the validity and reliability of data generated in other countries is problematic.

Finally, the *interpretation* of the data requires an analysis which produces results that need to be condensed and made into recommendations, policies, and courses of action. This activity is ruled by cultural biases, level and sophistication of the skills of the analysts, and what managers "really" wish to read into the data.

Cognition and Quantitative Data

James Walsh of the University of Michigan recently reviewed the literature on cognition in organizations.[17] He has compiled the types of measures used through self-reporting in organizations, and classified them into such categories as repertory grid, means-ends analyses, object-sorting, and self-Q techniques.

Among the measures in Walsh's list are folk theories, frames of reference, organizational prototypes, perceptions, mental models, implicit theories, belief structures, and causal maps.

Many of these data elements are not quantitative, yet seem essential to the manager's understanding of how and why the organization behaves the way it does. In the search for quantitative data, managers and researchers alike seem to discount the enormous value of this cognitive pool of crucial information. Walsh has brilliantly tackled this issue:

Our understanding of managerial and organizational cognition is limited because we have been held captive by the computer metaphor of information processing. If our research is to have strong external validity, we must consider the emotional basis of work and its relationship to the cognitive questions that we have been asking. Shrivastava et al. (1987) are virtually alone in their call for such work (p. 307).

This conclusion and the problems associated with quantitative data show that organizational learning will be incomplete (if it exists at all), crippled by our inability to combine the individual and the organizational levels of cognition and knowledge. What holds them together and what makes them "truly" organizational?

I will summarize this discussion later in this chapter, but let me insert this conclusion at this point. The problems with quantitative data and the multilevel existence of cognition and knowledge structures in the organization lead to the need to carefully examine the kind of change program we would select to clean up after reengineering. Such a program will have to take into account that it should rely on proven and current knowledge, and avoid reliance on too many new and quantitative measures specifically created for this task.

Issues in Unobtrusive Measurement

Generally speaking, then, observational and trace methods are indicated as supplementary or primary when language may serve as a poor medium of information—either because of its differential use, its absolute capacity for transfer, or when significant elements of the research population are silent.

This quote is from a seminal monograph by E. Webb, D. Campbell, R. Schwartz, and L. Sechrest.[18] Unobtrusive measures and primarily archival and other records have been artfully discussed in their book, and are of extreme interest to this chapter.

By developing a program to restore stability and to undo the damage caused by reengineering, we may be faced with a situation where many, perhaps most, of the key players in the design and implementation of BPR are no longer with the corporation. In order to understand what "really" happened, so that we may gain an adequate appraisal of the damage inflicted by BPR, we may have to resort principally to archival information.

How good, complete, reliable, and useful is archival information? Webb and his colleagues were pioneers in exploring these issues, and I continued their trend of research in my doctoral studies more than a decade after the publication of their pathbreaking book. The issues are summarized in Figure 7.2.

By unobtrusive measures, I refer primarily to archival information—that which is found in records of the organization, its members, and records of its stakeholders (suppliers, customers, regulators, researchers who studied them, and even competitors).

At the outset it seems that archival data are the "best" sources for reliable and meaningful information. The modern organization has been known for abundantly, orderly, and overwhelmingly recording every transaction, communication, and activity that occurs within and without its boundaries. The hierarchical and bureaucratic structure of the modern corporation requires such means for control and communication among its units and various levels of managers, both vertically and horizontally. Therefore it would stand to reason that following a major change program such as BPR, there will be massive data waiting to be collected, analyzed, and interpreted.

The problems with records in organizations are many, as summarized in Figure 7.2. This is true with any records and physical trace measures,[19] but particularly so with the aftermath of BPR. The essence of reengineering (as I reiterate in this book) is to obliterate the existing and to create a new reality. By so doing much of the existing records and trace data are probably discarded or lose their significance.

But the problems I discuss here are inherent in the nature of archival data and trace measures. These problems should be taken into account when we select a program for cleaning-up that would rely to some or to a large extent on archival sources of data.

The first issue is *accessibility*. Archival data are of various types, located throughout the organization. Their *classification* modes and criteria may be, and usually are, very different from those of the person searching for these data. For example, in a study I conducted at a National Aeronautics and Space Administration

(NASA) installation, personnel records existed in no fewer than 12 different units. Even with the ubiquitousness of computers, some archives were decentralized, making accessibility very difficult.

A subissue are those records which do exist, yet are essentially inaccessible for other reasons. In the early 1990s I interviewed a technical manager in a large manufacturing company who maintained extensive records of performance of different machines and other systems in the company's inventory. The manager made such data inaccessible because of the role that these records played in determining his power base. Not even his superiors had knowledge of the enormous potential and excellent coverage and comprehensivenss of his database.[20]

The second issue is the *vulnerability* of archival data. Records are routinely destroyed, modified, and transcribed, so as to lose much or all of their usefulness post-factum.

A third issue is *continuity* of archival records and the methods of recording them. This may also be considered a subissue of the vulnerability of such form of data recording. Continuity of records may be divided into two categories. The first is continuity of the recorder. People in organizations leave, are transferred, change jobs, and retire. The new organizational actors usually change the way activities are recorded. Managers also tend to change such aspects of data recording as topics of relevance, length and coverage of data to be recorded, and the timing and frequency of recording. A key prerogative of a parvenu manager is control over data recording and distribution. This creates discontinuities in the time-series of the data.

The second issue of continuity is the mode of recording, both the physical method and mode of storage. Excellent examples of such problems are the technological advances in information storage, recording, and accessing. Data recorded on computer "punched cards" are obsolete today, and there are few, if any, machines capable of accessing such data. At one time eight-track tapes recorded music, yet the average consumer cannot listen to this music.

Privacy and *proprietorship* are issues in the management of unobtrusive, archival measures. With the advent of electronic mail, important data are exchanged with the use of ciphers and passwords. This makes accessibility and usage by others almost impossible.

In addition, information deemed private is well safeguarded in the corporation. Access is usually denied even to authorized personnel. As a management consultant I am well aware of the common practice among middle managers to safeguard certain information, even though I am authorized total access by instructions from senior management.[21]

Another issue is *data transformation*, readability, and meaning. When archival information is created and stored, the data are transformed, adapted, and compressed so that they will be ready and applicable for recording and storage. Thus data are transformed, making them difficult to read and to interpret. Moreover, these data are collected for reasons that are different from those of the people who prepare them for archival storage.

Interpretation is a separate issue. It concerns the ability of the user of archival data to understand the meaning of the data. This is a problem researchers usually face with archival data. Unlike data obtained from organizational members, archival data are cold, limited, and precise words, pictures, and other representations of reality—as inserted into the archive by those who recorded them. These data lack the expression in the face of the key informant. They lack the intonations in the voice of the storyteller (which is more revealing in person than on tape, when combined with facial features and hand movements). They also lack the capacity for *interactivity*, so that the user of the data is thus unable to ask questions and request clarification.

In a consulting project for a large division of a multinational manufacturing company, I was confronted by a document produced by a former project manager, who had left the firm the previous year. The document described the R&D project, its origins, and its progress in the first 18 months. Upon interviews with the current manager and several members of the project team, I was able to arrive at *four* different views of what the document intended to portray: (1) a project doomed from the start; (2) a project with great potential and very poor management; (3) a project with great technical potential, excellent management, and corporate politics that derailed it; and (4) a document that was unintelligible—just some conflicting statement without a coherent story or picture of what really happened.

Data paucity is a difficult issue, and data *embellishment* is a serious issue in archival information. Data paucity refers to the instances when there is not enough information in the archives that satisfactorily describe a phenomenon or an occurrence. Too few facts are recorded, or too few observations and explanations are added to recorded facts.

Conversely, sometimes data are embellished so that the user of the information is faced with a "tall tale" of what happened, or of what the depositor of the information, or the collector of it, believe or say is what happened. Corporate reports are an especially excellent source for both paucity and embellishment of information. Managers need to protect their turf, their sources, and their careers, so they manipulate the data to suit their needs.

Finally, as shown in Figure 7.2, the issue of "true" description is inherent in all archival data. To what extent does archival information describe reality? Since the data recorded are so selective, transformed, manipulated, poor, and embellished—how much is left to "truly" describe what actually happened, what are the "true" facts?

There is a popular belief that if the information is archival—recorded and "written" or in any way made into a permanent record—then it is useful and a good description of the facts. As the discussion above shows, this is far from the truth. Archival information should not be accepted on its face value (simply because it is archival) but with the same skepticism and doubts usually reserved to survey data and the "memories" of people we question, debrief, and interview.

Relevance to Cleaning-Up

Why is all this information about issues in unobtrusive data management relevant to the cleaning-up intervention? In our search for a systemic approach to restore stability and to clean up in the aftermath of reengineering, one of the critical steps will be the collection of data on the damage done to the corporation.[22] We assume that many of the preengineering actors (who may serve as key informants) have been downsized in the wake of BPR, so that we would rely on existing records they (and those actors who are still with the organization) have left behind in corporate records. Therefore, special attention must be given to the validity and reliability of these records, per the issues described in Figure 7.2. Much of the weight of the criteria we would use to accept these data will be on faith—corroborated by interviews with the current members of the organization.

Role of Information Technology in Data Collection and Analysis

D. H. Lawrence perhaps felt contempt mixed with pity when he wrote about his generation who endured the experiences of the First World War: "All the great words were cancelled out for that generation."[23]

Information technology brought about a transformation in the way we deal with data. What, then, is its role in the collection and analysis of the data we will be collecting for the cleaning-up effort?

An initial glance would probably conclude that the issues I raised in Figure 7.2 will be completely resolved by proper application of relevant technology. James Champy, one of the founders of BPR and his colleagues at CSC index (their consulting company), have recently described the marvels of the World Wide Web in the consumer markets.[24] Information technology may indeed provide a revolutionary means of data manipulation, transformation, storage, and retrieval—but it cannot influence or ameliorate the *content* of the data nor its utility to a user such as the one responsible for cleaning-up after BPR.

Whatever goes into the network, comes out of it. Whatever data enter the archives of the corporation will be accessed for cleaning-up purposes. IT could not greatly facilitate nor carry BPR, nor does it offer much hope for successful cleaning-up, unless the data set is powerful enough. IT in this case remains simply the messenger, whereas the quality and utility of the message are what really counts.

IT may help in accumulating archival data and in allowing for more comfortable accessing and retrieval. Reports on the radical change to which corporate units were exposed may be compressed in electronic form, hence used later for the analysis that leads to cleaning-up operations. Computer-based decision and simulation models may be useful in analysis and interpretation of the mass of data thus accumulated. But the fact remains that the choice of a cleaning-up model and techniques will depend on the content of the data we are able to find and to utilize.

WHICH SYSTEM TO CHOOSE?

Cleaning-up is itself a change process. As an example, let me compare the choice we are about to make with the current debate on the nature of personal computers. There are two distinct philosophies, systems, or versions of what the personal computer (PC) of the future will be.

Larry Ellison, CEO of Oracle Corporation, has argued: "You need 90 percent penetration to have a true information age, and we'll never know that with the PC because they're too complex and too expensive."[25] Ellison is advocating Oracle's network PC, as a low-cost and easy-to-use machine. The difference is that his machine will have little intelligence built in. Like a telephone, it will rely on intelligence from an external location into which it will be linked. The present PC concept has all the intelligence needed for operations built into the machine (operating systems).

Similarly, the choice of the cleaning-up system or concept would be between a totally new and complex system which will incorporate as much knowledge as possible about radical change *and* the focal corporation, or a more simplistic system with enough knowledge to be a generic tool for cleaning-up.[26]

There is a difference between the *system* to be chosen and the *approach* within such a system. In the following section "Choosing the Cleaning-Up Approach" I explore the various approaches, such as "triage" and "systems." But both approaches are variants of the overall system of cleaning-up to be chosen.

In essence, the choice of the system also depends on the availability of data which need to be incorporated into the complex and knowledge-based option. As I argued above, the aftermath of reengineering may have produced a vast quantity of data of all types, but perhaps not enough data which is relevant to the cleaning-up operation. There are data that will show damage within the units and between the units (in the linkages), as well as overall in the corporation. In these instances archival data may be incomplete, unavailable, or even misleading, since much of the damage is cumulative and will not easily be recorded in routine processes and documents.[27]

The "Serpent Curve"

Choosing a system for cleaning-up after BPR follows a rationale that is very similar to that used by organization scientists in their analysis of organizations. The idea is to go from the segmented to the general and back. Data generated at the segmented version (levels of the unit) are generalized to the level of the organization, whereas data at the broader level of the corporation are projected to the segments. Organization scientists distinguish between two aspects of organization, which I may generically call "mechanistic" and "organic," following the nomenclature of J. Burns and G. Stalker.[28] These aspects delineate the degree of rigidity in the organization (extent of control, centralization, formalization, and the like)—going from the more rigid and formal (mechanistic) to the less rigid (organic).

Thus, when the dimensions of rigidity and level of analysis are compared, we have the contingency table shown in Figure 7.3. The figure shows a "serpent curve," in which the organization starts as an amorphous and generalized entity, progresses to segmented and organic, then to a more rigid and formal structure, from a generalized to finally a segmented version.[29] Although the serpent curve indicates a temporal and stagewise direction and progression, data (particularly archival) may be found in organizational records in all four cells or types of any given time.

Figure 7.3
Evolution of Organizational Format and Organizational Data as Function of Structural Rigidity and Level of Analysis

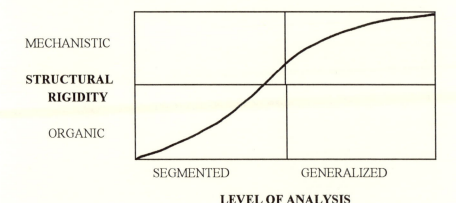

MECHANISTIC

STRUCTURAL RIGIDITY

ORGANIC

SEGMENTED   GENERALIZED

LEVEL OF ANALYSIS

The relevance to the choice of the system is in the choice of the levels at which the data collection and analysis—and finally the cleaning-up—should be undertaken. This is then a choice along the continua of level of analysis and level of structural rigidity.

Several alternatives for action thus emerge. They are summarized in Figure 7.4. Cleaning-up after BPR should be divided toward both the total organization *and* the level of the unit. Hence the data collected should be at these levels. The more rigid the organization (mechanistic), the more archival data will probably be available, due to the high degree of control exercised in such a format. The more organic the structure, the more one has to rely on subjective assessments by members.[30]

The Choice

Based on the limitations and strengths discussed in the foregoing sections, the choice of a model or system for cleaning-up must be a generic system. This means a system that has enough intelligence built into it to accommodate data that can be collected at the various levels of rigidity and analysis. The principal criterion seems to be that of enough flexibility in the model to allow for freedom of movement along the continua of Figure 7.3 and among the alternatives of Figure 7.4.

Hence the system would be a model of change that would best deal with the aftermath of *radical* change, with all its consequences at the level of the unit as well as the larger organization. We do possess today sufficient knowledge on turning-around corporations that had been hard hit by restructuring. A detailed description of available options and approaches follows in the next section.

Figure 7.4
Alternatives for Data Collection and Analysis on Damage from BPR

• Collect data on the broader aspects of the organization • Collect data at the level of the unit • Analyze data at level of the organization • Analyze data at level of unit • Relate data from units to total organization • Analyze data in relation to level of structural rigidity (Mechanistic = larger volume of archival data Organic = reliance on interviews with members)

CHOOSING THE CLEANING-UP APPROACH

The dictionary defines the word "approach" as "the taking of preliminary steps toward a particular purpose."[31] In the case of cleaning-up, what approach should we select to bring about the recovery of the corporation. There are two main avenues of action: triage and systems. For each of these approaches there are two main modes of cleaning-up: surgical and strategic. The approaches and potential modes are summarized in Figure 7.5.

The Triage Approach

The dictionary defines "triage" as "the sorting of and allocation of treatment to patients and especially battle and disaster victims according to a system of priorities designed to maximize the number of survivors."[32]

Figure 7.5
Approaches and Modes of Cleaning-Up after Reengineering

	POSSIBLE APPROACHES	
POSSIBLE MODES	**TRIAGE**	**SYSTEMS**
SURGICAL	**Scenario A:** *limited* *focused* *intervention*	**Scenario C:** *focused* *intervention*
STRATEGIC	**Scenario B:** *limited* *broad* *intervention*	**Scenario D:** *broad* *intervention*

The operational word in the definition is "priorities." In the case of the cleaning-up process, the triage approach means that certain parts of the organization will be treated first, so that the damage they suffered may be repaired in a short time period. This choice of approach does not preclude any further action on *other* parts and units of the organization. It also does not preclude the abandonment of the treated part or unit of the corporation if recovery is determined to be impossible.

Triage is simply the approach that singles out one or more particular units in which the *immediate* attention of the cleaning-up process will probably maximize their chance of recovery. The triage approach is necessary when resources for cleaning-up are scarce, and when the damage caused by reengineering was so widespread as to require prioritizing the targets for recovery operation.

There are two potential modes of action for the triage approach. The first is a surgical mode. In Figure 7.5 we see the intersection of "triage" and "surgical mode" as Scenario A, which I call *limited focused intervention*.

In this scenario the aim is at a limited intervention in one or more units, selected for cleaning-up and recovery. For example, a work process that had been damaged by reengineering in another unit in its value chain would be targeted for cleaning-up and recovery in a way that limits the intervention to the workflow itself.

A different mode within triage is a strategic mode. The intersection shown in Figure 7.5 between triage and the strategic mode produces Scenario B, *limited broad intervention*. This is a scenario in which a choice is made of selected units, and the recovery process takes into account the overall impact of the recovered unit (or workflow) on the value chain or the entire corporation.

The Systems Approach

As seen in Figure 7.5, the systems approach also has two possibilities. The first is the intersection between the systems approach and the surgical mode. The resultant Scenario C is *focused intervention*.

For example, I recently consulted for a large consumer-products company in the range of Fortune 200. The company had reengineered its marketing and production units. Three plants had been the target of the reengineering program, as well as the marketing contingent of over 800 employees. Side effects and lateral damage were widespread. In its initial attempt at recovery, the company chose to treat all the units that had been reengineered, thus to repair the damage done *to these units*. There was little interest in treating lateral damage to other units, or to discover and then treat any effects that the recovery process might have on the corporation. The motto seemed to have been: "If people are unhappy and/or performance is down in Unit A, let's repair it, clean it up, and restore it to health." Our recovery efforts are still in place at this company.

Another scenario is the result of the interaction between the systems approach and a strategic mode of operation. This Scenario D is *broad intervention*, and it is the scenario that I advocate in this book and my other writings. This scenario D consists of intervention in all units that had suffered damage, either simultaneously or in sequence. While assuming that even if carried out in sequence the program encompasses all units, this scenario in effect considers the entire corporation. The program in this scenario is aimed at achieving overall corporate balance and overall recovery, without additional side effects from the cleaning-up process itself.

Moreover, this scenario for a cleaning-up program also offers the advantage of allowing the corporation to include the program within its effort to reinvent itself. This is facilitated by the use of a strategic mode of operation. What is reinvention, and how does it relate to cleaning-up after a reengineering program?

CLEANING-UP AND REINVENTING THE CORPORATION

Reinvention of the corporation is *not* reengineering. The two concepts are totally different, in principle as well as in their operational implementation.[33]

In a compelling article published in the *Harvard Business Review* in late 1993, Tracy Goss, Richard Pascale, and Anthony Athos suggested that re-invention of the company is a "sink or swim" proposition.[34] They defined reinvention as "not changing what is, but creating what isn't." Yet, although their discussion of the topic is similar to the reengineering concept of Hammer and Champy (in that they call for creating something totally new), their examples of such companies as Honda, Nordstrom and Häagen-Dazs are illustrations of reinvention that resembles strategic choice rather than total redesign of the corporation.

As I see it, reinvention is a strategic choice that radically differs from where the corporation is now and where it was heading before the choice was made. Strategic choices involve the road to be taken by the company as it competes in its industry and its markets. Clearly, this is a top-to-bottom process, in that a strategic decision involves the entire corporation as a competitive player in its environment—leading to a matching structure and its processes. In other words, when a company decides on a strategic direction, it needs to adjust its work processes, work flows, structure, and climate to match or to "fit" the new direction. Reinvention therefore includes *both* the strategic choice and the top-to-bottom "fit" and adjustment.

The Case of Hughes Electronics

Take for example the case of Hughes Electronics and its chairman, Michael Armstrong.[35] An executive with IBM, Armstrong took over the $15 billion Hughes Electronics Corporation in 1992. The company was primarily a defense contractor and had undergone some radical downsizing. The previous chairman, Malcolm Currie, had downsized the company by over 9,000 jobs. Earnings of the company in the early 1990s were sliding, as two-thirds of the business was defense oriented.

Armstrong revamped the company by doing precisely what I described above: strategic redirection, and internal matching and adaptation. In the strategic redirection Armstrong emphasized the commercial business of the company while consolidating and focusing the defense side of the business. Under his leadership, Hughes invaded several new markets by transferring the knowledge and product lines from defense to commercial applications.

Simultaneously, Armstrong revamped the internal corporate scene to match and support the strategic redirection. He continued the downsizing by reducing the workforce by 25%, but in the newly opened markets he initiated the hiring of new knowledge workers. Armstrong also revamped Hughes' R&D laboratories by making them more responsive to the commercial units of the corporation. Since the company dealt primarily with defense agencies, the culture had to be changed so it would fit a primarily commercial new set of customers.

Hughes is an example of redirection. There was no workflow redesign. Rather, there was a "fit" between the new direction that the company was taking and the planned redesign of structure and processes by marketing the requirements of a commercial rather than a defense contractor company. Much of Hughes' existing capabilities and competencies had adapted to the new exigencies. There was no need to obliterate, merely to change and redirect. Those units, processes, and people who could not or would not adjust and adapt had to go. This is the advantage and the result of a top-to-bottom process.

Requirements for Reinvention

In many respects reinventing the company is similar to the program of cleaning-up after reengineering. In my view there are six basic requirements for a successful effort to reinvent the corporation, as summarized in Figure 7.6.

These requirements are similar to the basic preconditions for the cleaning-up change program. In choosing scenario D, we are promoting a recovery program that not only repairs the damage caused by reengineering but also redirects the company toward a systemic recovery that is very similar to reinvention. In particular, the focus of the cleaning-up program is on structure, processes, human resources, *and* the corporate culture. The direction of the company in the cleaning-up program is toward stability and balance.

Yet the cleaning-up program is versatile enough to be fully incorporated in any reinvention effort. A program such as that implemented by Armstrong at Hughes can be mounted on top of a cleaning-up after a reengineering operation. In fact, it would soundly benefit from the outcomes of the cleaning-up program, primarily because once stability is achieved, redirection can be initiated with minimal disruption

WHO NEEDS CLEANING-UP

The organizations who need cleaning-up are a strange mix of those who have undergone intensive BPR, and those who mildly experimented with it. When all these organizations wake up to the aftermath of restructuring—however mild the experience—they are usually stricken with inaction.

The historian Arthur M. Schlesinger, Jr. used a marvelous array of words when he narrated President Franklin D. Roosevelt's hesitation in the early 1930s.

Figure 7.6
Basic Requirements for Reinventing the Corporation

- Have a clearly defined and operationally feasible strategic outlook
- Understand the "fit" between strategic redirection and internal structuring
- Have a feasible and logical program of internal restructuring to match and support the strategic redirection
- Obtain the support and commitment from middle managers and the workforce
- Be prepared and willing to endure the reinvention through a long period of adaptation and changes before positive results appear
- Act on structure, processes, human resources, *and* corporate climate in an integrated program of change

He badly needed to be on the crest of the wave . . . the basic reason for his inaction was that he was simply unprepared to act. . . . It was that the inscrutable processes of decision were moving all too slowly within. He could not lead until he knew where he wanted to go.[36]

It is precisely this type of inaction that has embraced so many of the corporations following the wave of unbridled restructuring. Among the torrent of mergers and acquisitions which is still going on in the late 1990s, there are so many instances of yet another downsizing—some large scale such as AT&T or IBM, others barely make the news. In August 1996, Campbell Soup Co. cut 650 jobs in its American operations (1.5% of its workforce). TRW, even Hewlett-Packard, and the megabanks such as Chase and Chemical are all trimming their "fat." As I have repeatedly argued in this book, there is a leakage of talent, hemorrhaging the basic skills of these industries.

The popular and some professional magazines are replete with predictions of the huge prospects for an unimaginable bright future for many industries.[37] Perhaps such predictions will come true in the next century, but at present many companies are in dire need of restoration of balance to even be able to join the next wave of prosperity—let alone compete within it.

Who needs cleaning-up? Any company or organization that had undergone some form of radical restructuring. If a company trims its production department because of the introduction of new machinery or efficiency measures—this is hardly cause for cleaning-up intervention. But BPR and other major restructuring programs, which emanate from senior management and have applications across units and functions, are natural candidates for cleaning-up, although many times they are unaware of any damage brought about by the restructuring program.[38]

In summary, BPR (or any radical restructuring program) can shake a successful company that doesn't really need it—but it can destroy a shaky company that badly needs restructuring.

In addition, because of the massive effects on people from BPR and similar programs, there is a feeling in the economy that the rising tide is not lifting all boats anymore. People feel that the game is somehow rigged—although the game is extremely complex and there are no "bad guys" that can be clearly identified.

Nevertheless, these sentiments may lead to questioning the practice of corporations to attenuate the rise in earnings through the squeeze on labor costs. In this BPR cannot and has not helped. As I reiterated above, BPR lacks a clear idea of a substitute system, therefore it inevitably ends up squeezing labor costs through restructuring the human component of corporate processes. It is a natural flow. It is where "fat" and redundancies obviously reside. The current context of market conditions is a strange combination of the globalization of the economy, rapid movement of plants and skills, flexibility fostered by IT, weakness of unions, and the frenzy to restructure. The net effect is a rush to reengineer. The long-term effects on corporate performance and the health and support of financial markets is threatened and in need of assessment. In Europe such pressures are already operational.

What needs cleaning-up? Virtually every company that participated in the managerial magic of the 1990s: reengineering, restructuring, and striving to be better, leaner, and meaner.

THE STAGES OF CLEANING-UP AFTER REENGINEERING

When I refer to the cleaning-up effort I use the terms "process" and "program" interchangeably. In fact, cleaning-up is both a program of change and a process. It is a program in that it comprises a reasoned effort to repair the damage caused by reengineering and to restore balance. It is also a process inasmuch as it is composed of several logical stages that are sequential and have distinguishable content.

The seven stages of the cleaning-up process are summarized in Figure 7.7. These stages are elements of a process. They describe specific actions that senior management needs to execute in their effort to clean up after reengineering.

At a glance it seems that these stages in Figure 7.7 are merely steps in a process, and are essentially devoid of real content. This has been my main criticism of the BPR concept: "A shell devoid of content."

Yet the stages in Figure 7.7 are also components of a *program of change*. That is, they include specific activities, their purposes, and their implementation in specific situations and for specific lateral damage.

Figure 7.7
The Stages of the Process of Cleaning-Up after Reengineering

- Announce restoration of stability
- Empower a champion
- Assess the damage
- Co-opt middle managers
- Establish resources
- Introduce localized changes
- Refreeze

It's time to clean up and to restore balance and stability. Therefore, the following chapters are selectively dedicated to the stages in the program for cleaning-up and restoration of balance. The chapters clearly and methodically describe the activities that senior management should undertake, the reasoning behind these activities, and their effect when activated within the overall program.

NOTES

1.   Khalil Gibran, *The Prophet* (New York: Alfred A. Knopf, 1982) p. 64.

2.   Carrie R. Leana, "Why Downsizing Won't Work," *Chicago Tribune Magazine*, April 14, 1996, pp. 16-18.

3.   Ori Sasson, "Reengineering Can Be Hazardous to a Company," *Upside*, May 1996, p. 20.

4.   Ikujiro Nonaka and Martin Kenney, "Towards a New Theory of Innovation Management," *Journal of Engineering and Technology Management*, 8, 1991, pp. 67-83.

5.   Robert E. Quinn, *Beyond Rational Management* (San Francisco: Jossey-Bass, 1988).

6.   See, for example, J. Boyett, *Beyond Workplace 2000: Essential Strategies for the New American Corporation* (New York: Penguin, 1996); also see Bill Gates, *The Road Ahead* (New York: Viking, 1996).

7.   See, for example, R. Goodman and M. Lawless, *Technology and Strategy: Conceptual Models and Diagnosis* (New York: Oxford University Press, 1994); and R. Kanter, *World Class* (New York: Simon & Schuster, 1995); also see C. Handy, *The Age of Paradox* (Boston: Harvard Business School Press, 1995).

8.   This issue is similar to that of implementation woes, but goes much beyond it. The gap includes differences in the frames of mind of those working on the general versus the specific, their tools, their time horizon, their problems, and their criteria for success. See, for example, V. Barabba, *Meeting of the Minds* (Boston, MA: Harvard Business School Press, 1995).

9.   See, for example, K. Cameron, "Effectiveness as Paradox: Consensus and Conflict in Conceptions of Organizational Effectiveness," *Management Science*, 32(2), 1986, pp. 539-553; also see H. Mintzbey, *The Rise and Fall of Strategic Planning* (New York: The Free Press, 1994); and A. Tsui, S. Ashford, L. St. Clair, and K. Xin, "Dealing with Discrepant Expectations: Response Strategies and Managerial Effectiveness," *Academy of Management Journal*, 38(6), 1995, pp. 1515-1543.

10.   J. Dean and S. Snell, "The Strategic Use of Integrated Manufacturing: An Empirical Examination," *Strategic Management Journal*, 17(6), 1996, pp. 459-480.

11.   *Ibid.*, p. 476.

12.   In the same study, Dean and Snell have suggested that many firms find it difficult to establish a bridge across this schism. They commented that "organizations that become so enamored of particular tools that they lose sight of their overall strategic missions—or that use a tool in the context of a strategy to which it is ill suited—are unlikely to reap the competitive rewards the tool offers" (p. 476).

13.   See, for example: D. Boje, R. Gephart, and T. Joseph (eds.), *Postmodern Management and Organization Theory* (Thousand Oaks, CA: Sage Publications, 1995); also see H. Thomas, D. O'Neil, and J. Kelly (eds.), *Strategic Renaissance and Business Transformation* (New York: John Wiley, 1995); and P. Grindley, *Standards, Strategy, and Policy* (New York: Oxford University Press, 1995).

14. There is a growing segment of the relevant literature devoted to organizational learning and cognition. For example, an early text is C. Argyris and D. Schon, *Organizational Learning* (Reading, MA: Addison Wesley, 1978); also see B. Levitt and J. March, "Organizational Learning," *Annual Review of Sociology*, 14(3), 1988, pp. 319-340. More recently, see C. M. Fiol, "Consensus, Diversity, and Learning in Organizations," *Organization Science*, 5(3), 1994, pp. 403-420; J. Lant and S. Mezias, "An Organizational Learning Model of Convergence and Reorientation," *Organization Science*, 3(1), 1992, pp. 47-71; and M. Cohen and P. Bacclayan, "Organizational Routines are Stored as Procedural Memory: Evidence From a Laboratory Study," *Organization Science*, 5(4), 1994, pp. 554-568. Other scholars have used the organizational learning and research framework to investigate the relationships between selected organizational phenomena and learning. For example, see B. Virany, M. Tushman, and E. Romanelli, "Executive Succession and Organizational Outcomes in Turbulent Environments: An Organizational Learning Approach," *Organizational Science* 31(1), 1992, pp. 72-91; M. FIol and M. Lyles, "Organizational Learning," *Academy of Management Review*, 10(4), 1985, pp. 803-813; B. Hedberg, "How Organizations Learn and Unlearn," in N. Nystrom and W. Starbuck (eds.), *Handbook of Organizational Design*, Vol. 1 (Oxford: Oxford University Press, 1981); and A. McCartt and J. Rohrbaugh, "Learning to Change: An Information Perspective on Learning in the Organization," *Organization Science*, 6(5), 1995, pp. 569-584. Finally, a paper that summarizes the relevant literature is G. Huber, "Organizational Learning: The Contributing Processes and the Literature," *Organization Science*, 2(1), 1991, pp. 88-115.

15. Within the relevant literature, see, for example, M. Jones, *Studying Organizational Symbolism: What, How, Why?* (Thousand Oaks, CA: Sage Publications, 1996); J. Meindl, C. Stubbert, and J. Brac, *Cognition Within and Between Organizations* (Thousand Oaks, CA: Sage Publications, 1996); and R. Hirschheim, H. Klein, and L. Lyytinen, "Exploring the Intellectual Structures of Information Systems Development: A Social Action Theoretic Analysis," *Accounting, Management and Information Technologies*, 6(1-2), 1996, pp. 1-64.

16. For descriptive examples of these models, see J. Barney, *Gaining and Sustaining Competitive Advantage, op. cit.*; M. Porter, *Competitive Advantage* (New York: The Free Press, 1985); P. Nayyar, "On the Measurement of Corporate Diversification Strategy: Evidence from Large U.S. Service Firms," *Strategic Management Journal*, 13(3), 1992, pp. 219-235; M. Lubatkin and R. Shriever, "Toward Reconciliation of Market Performance Measures to Strategic Management Research," *Academy of Management Review*, 11(4), 1986, pp. 497-512; and S. Clegg and G. Polmer, *Producing Management Knowledge* (Thousand Oaks, CA: Sage Publications, 1996).

17. J. Walsh, "Managerial and Organizational Cognition: Notes from a Trip Down Memory Lane," *Organization Science*, 6(3), 1995, pp. 280-321; especially see Table 4, pp. 309-310.

18. E. Webb, D. Campbell, R. Schwartz, and L. Schrest, *Unobtrusive Measures: Nonreactive Research in the Social Sciences* (Chicago: Rand McNally College Publishing, 1966), p 168.

19. Trace measures are physical and other evidence that may be collected by a trained or alert observer. For example, a visit to an organization may culminate with a host of archival data on productivity and investments in human resources and in the work environment. Yet an alert or trained visitor may experience a depressing work environment, lack of minimal comforts for the organizational workers, and a general atmosphere of malaise and discontent shown in the faces and in the behavior of employees.

20. Research in related areas has alluded to issues such as those of unobtrusive quantitative measures and their sources. See, for example, E. Hirschman (ed.), *Interpretative*

Consumer Research (Provo, UT: Association for Consumer Research, 1989); and S. Hurt, "On the Rhetoric of Qualitative Methods: Towards Historically Informed Argumentation in Management Inquiry," *Journal of Management Inquiry*, 3(3), 1994, pp. 221-234.

21. Privacy and proprietorship of information in the age of electronics have been widely discussed in the literature in the past several years. See, for example, A. H. Rubenstein and H. Schwartzel (eds.), *Intelligent Workstations for Professionals* (Berlin: Springer-Verlag, 1992); also see J. Foley, "Data Dilemma," *Information Week*, June 10, 1996, pp. 14-16.

22. The same rationale also applies to collection of data on the *benefits* accrued to the organization from a radical change program such as BPR. This is true for the collection of data for any evaluative purpose. I hasten to add that there are other issues involved in evaluation such as "corruption" of the data and statistical errors. See the seminal work of Donald Campbell in this respect, and other scholars who followed.   D. Campbell, "From Description to Experimentation: Interpreting Trends as Quasi-Experiments," in C. W. Harris (ed.), *Problems in Measuring Change* (Madison, WI: University of Wisconsin Press, 1963), pp. 212-242; D. T. Campbell and D. Fiske, "Convergent and Discriminant Validation of the Multitrait-Multimethod Matrix," *Psychological Bulletin*, 56(1), 1959, pp. 81-105; R. Quinn and K. Cameron, *Paradox and Transformation: Toward a Theory of Change in Organization and Management* (Cambridge, MA: Ballinger Books, 1988); and R. Reger and T. Palmer, "Managerial Categorization of Competitors: Using Old Maps to Navigate New Environments," *Organization Science*, 7(1), 1996, pp. 22-39.

23. Quoted by Barbara Tuchman in her monumental work on World War I: *The Guns of August* (New York: Bantam Books, 1962, 4th printing, 1980), p. 489.

24. J. Champy, R. Buday, and N. Nohria, "Creating the Electronic Community," *Information Week*, June 10, 1996, pp. 57-64.

25. Quoted in Tim Jones, "Hyping the Network Computer," *Chicago Tribune*, September 7, 1996, Section 2, p. 1.

26. In this regard, see an interesting interview with Lee Alberthal, CEO of Electronic Data Systems, in *Upside*, October 1996, pp. 84-98.

27. See, for example, P. Shoemaker, "Scenario Planning: A Tool for Strategic Thinking," *Sloan Management Review*, 36(2), Winter 1995, pp. 25-40; also see R. Kaplan and D. Norton, "Putting the Balanced Scoreboard to Work," *Harvard Business Review*, 71(5), 1993, pp. 134-142.

28. J. Burns and G. Stalker, *The Management of Innovation* (London: Tavistock Institute, 1962).

29. The source of the figure is E. Geisler, "Technology and Organization," manuscript in preparation.

30. The organization science literature has dealt profusely with this and related topics. For example, C.. Markides and P. Williamson, "Corporate Diversification and Organization Structure: A Resource-Based View," *Academy of Management Journal*, 39(2), 1996, pp. 340-367; T. Amburgey and T. Dacin, "As the Left Foot Follows the Right? The Dynamics of Strategic and Structural Change," *Academy of Management Journal*, 37(6), 1994, pp. 1427-1452; D. Collis and C. Montgomery, *Corporate Strategy: Resources and the Scope of the Firm* (Burr Ridge, IL: Irwin, 1996); and D. Tccce, R. Rumelt, R. Dosi, and S. Winter, "Understanding Corporate Coherenece: Theory and Evidence," *Journal of Economic Behavior and Organization*, 23(1), 1994, pp. 1-30.

31. *Webster's New Collegiate Dictionary* (Springfield, MA: G&C Merriam Company, 1977), pp. 56.

32. *Ibid.*, p. 1246.

33. Reinventing the business enterprise has been the topic of several books recently published. For example, Roy Harmon, *Reinventing the Business* (New York: The Free Press,

1996); Russell Ackoff, *The Democratic Corporation: A Radical Prescription for Recreating Corporate America and Rediscovering Success* (New York: Oxford University Press, 1994). In the public sector, an excellent account of reinventing public schools in Minnesota is Nancy Roberts and Paula King, *Transforming Public Policy: Dynamics of Policy Entrepreneurship and Innovation* (San Francisco: Jossey-Bass Publishers, 1996).

 34. Tracy Goss, Richard Pascale, and Anthony Athos, "The Reinvention Roller Coaster: Risking the Present for a Powerful Future," *Harvard Business Review*, November-December 1993, pp. 97-108.

 35. The story is told in Eric Schine, "Liftoff," *Business Week*, April 27, 1996, pp. 136-147.

 36. A. M. Schlesinger, Jr., *The Politics of Upheaval* (Boston: Houghton-Mifflin, 1960), p. 11.

 37. See H. Psaraftis, "Countdown to 2004: Greek Coastal Shipping Prepares for Deregulation and Colossal Changes," *OR/MS Today*, 22(3), June 1996, pp. 30-35.

 38. To a large extent many organizations are unaware of the need for any correction as they are enveloped by the presumed success and benefits from restructuring. There are some recent books and publications that illustrate this viewpoint. See, for example, M. Malhotra, V. Grover, and M. Desilvio, "Reengineering the New Product Development Process: A Framework for Innovation and Flexibility in High Technology Firms," *Omega*, 24(4), 1996, pp. 425-441; and D. Gertz and J. Baptista, *Grow to be Great: Breaking the Downsizing Cycle* (New York: The Free Press, 1995).

8

ANNOUNCING RESTORATION
OF STABILITY

LIFE CYCLE AND ECOCYCLE

D. Hurst and B. Zimmerman have introduced the conceptual framework of the ecocycle to complement the long-standing idea of the life cycle of organizations.[1] They have argued that the life cycle approach is not entirely systemic, and does not explain how corporations move between stages or skip stages in times of hardship. As they put it: "the ecocycle incorporates the conventional life cycle and illustrates how mature organizations may become systematically vulnerable to catastrophe. The ecocycle also deals explicitly with what happens after complex systems die and how and in what sense they may be thought of as being renewed."[2]

The ecocycle approach or model compares the corporation to a forest. There are four basic stages: exploitation, conservation, creative destruction, and renewal. As a complex system, both forests and corporations seem to follow a similar pattern of development along similar basic stages.

These ideas stem from the ecology model of organizational growth and survival. Although useful in explaining large-scale changes of entire industries, this approach would help us here to describe the *renewal* and recovery of corporations that have suffered side effects from reengineering.

More specifically, as Hurst and Zimmerman have indicated, the move from the stage of creative destruction to renewal is a process in which the weak interconnections begin to solidify in a systemic mode.[3] This is a movement designed to counteract the previous stage in which the systemic connections between parts of the organization have collapsed or dissipated. Hurst and Zimmerman have summarized this dynamic in the following way:

In organizational renewal, then, in the absence of visionary genius, the challenge is not just to make things happen but to first create the conditions under which the "things" are allowed to happen: to manage the organization's change ability rather than change. Creating the conditions includes a variety of processes, such as changing the measuring yardstick as in GE [General Electric] or changing the formal structure or performance evaluation policies.[4]

This model of renewal is useful in understanding the overall pattern of corporate change, and in focusing attention on the stages or steps in the reversal of lateral damage from reengineering.[5]

As we move to the first stage of the process of cleaning-up, there is a need to make the process a systemic enterprise. It is not enough to keep it a top-down mode, in which senior management decides on renewal and cleaning-up and things yet done. There is an urgent need to propagate the news and the purpose of the cleaning-up process throughout the corporation.

The reengineering intervention left in its wake much uncertainty that affects managers and all employees. Following the downsizing effort, those who remain in the corporation are highly skeptical and very weary of any additional maneuvers to change the existing conditions—however poor they may be.

Therefore there is a need to enlist support from the workforce by letting everybody know what is going to be done next. Operationally, this means to annouce the purpose of the forthcoming activities, the activities in the program, and to promote confidence in the corporate destiny.

Announce Purpose of Forthcoming Activities

Senior management should make the announcement through all channels, by officially contacting middle managers, and by providing overall "policy" announcements. The word must go down that cleaning-up is designed to restore stability, and that it is done *throughout the corporation*. The case must be made for reinstituting stability and balance.

The announcement of the purpose of cleaning-up should not be a one-shot occurrence. It should be a program of communication which reiterates on a periodic basis the purpose of the activities. It is therefore a continuing program of reminders to the corporation that cleaning-up operations are being conducted, and that their purpose is to *restore stability*. Again, it should also be emphasized that stability is not synonymous with slowdown, cutting, or inability to adapt and change. Stability should be defined as restoration of a systemic meaning and balance to the corporation, so that the benefits from previous change programs (reengineering and downsizing) can be absorbed and stability restored. The purpose is to repair the damage, thus to strengthen the organization.

Announce Activities in the Program

In addition to announcing and periodically reminding the workforce of the purpose of cleaning-up, there is also a need to publicize the various activities that are going to be carried out. This means that senior management through middle management should specify that the activities would include repairing damage and restoring stability.

However, the activities are more than just repair of the damage. They are intended to promote a systemic approach, along the lines described above of the renewal of the corporation as a strong and balanced unit. This means that activities will include reengineering the workforce and bringing about some additional changes.

Thus, the program should be outlined for the workforce as including the following major activities:

- Analysis of the damage and assessment of what went wrong and what can be repaired, reformulated, and reestablished.

- Creating and instituting linkages, units, and/or functions to strengthen the corporation as a whole.

- Introducing necessary changes, including cuts and other transformations to arrive at a stronger and more balanced organization.

It should be emphasized that these activities are geared toward the purpose of restoration of balance and stability and not toward radical changes that would bring about immediate improvements in efficiency or performance. These are activities geared toward longer term survival of the company. They should reflect the *confidence* of senior and middle managers in the future of the company.

Promote Confidence in Corporate Destiny

The announcement of the cleaning-up and recovery should emphasize and promote the confidence of senior management *and* middle management in the future of the company. This is similar to the renewal action described by ecology scientists, so that the corporation is at a stage where recovery is possible and renewal quite feasible.

In the larger picture within its industry, the corporation is thus taking a step toward its destiny to be a renewed, stronger, and more balanced organization. There must be a diffusion of such beliefs from senior management to the corporation. It is a belief in the company and its destiny and its confidence in what the company is doing and how it intends to do it.

Alternatively, this promotion of confidence does not necessarily imply that a "vision" is needed in these announcements. The program of cleaning-up may or may not be tied to a visionary outlook, but its success is not dependent on the existence nor operationalization of such a "vision."

In fact, it is more productive for senior management to promote a cleaning-up operation with a sense of renewal and ultimate stability, rather than a visionary "call to arms," as some radical change programs profess to do. In this manner, this *low-key approach* provides a workable atmosphere that promotes confidence but does not create a climate of radicalness and major changes. The main idea is not to reconfigure or redesign the corporation but rather to repair the damage and to promote renewal through a planned move toward stability.[6]

NOTES

1.   D. Hurst and B. Zimmerman, "From Life Cycle to Ecocycle: A New Perspective on the Growth, Maturity, Destruction and Renewal of Complex Systems," *Journal of Management Inquiry*, 3(4), 1994, pp. 339-354.

2.   *Ibid.*, p. 340.

3.   *Ibid.*, p. 348.

4.   *Ibid.*, p. 351.

5.   For additional reading, see M. Waldrop, *Complexity: The Emerging Science at the Edge of Order and Chaos* (New York: Simon & Schuster, 1992); also see Garth Morgan, *Images of Organization* (Beverly Hills, CA: Sage Publications, 1986).

6.   See, for example, W. Pasmore, *Designing Effective Organizations: The Sociotechnical System Perspective* (New York: John Wiley, 1988). This and other such books provide the reader with a view that organizations can be redesigned without radical changes by employing perspectives that emphasize balance as a final outcome.

9

EMPOWERING A CHAMPION

In a masterful account of the state of the art, Warner Burke summarized the topic of organizational change. He focused on eight areas, including the process of change, leadership, structure, training and development, and organizational performance.[1]

In his description of "what we need to know," Burke emphasized the issues of chaos during transition and communication. With regard to the first, he commented: "We can at a minimum help in at least two ways. One is to convince organization members that a sense of chaos during the transition state is not unusual—in fact, it is rather normal—and that it will last for quite some time."[2] The topic of communication was also discussed. Burke suggested that *timing* of the message and the *amount of information* are critical variables.

But Burke clearly emphasized the role that competent leadership plays in corporate change. He concluded:

Leading the visionary process, ensuring that the organization's purpose and mission are established and articulated, developing multiple programs and initiatives that are clearly linked to values that will help to guide the implementing of the change, and communicating all of these are some of the primary leadership acts that are necessary to bring about organization change.[3]

Therefore, there is clearly therefore a need to establish early on the leadership of the cleaning-up program. This should be done by senior management who empower a champion.

ATTRIBUTES OF A CHAMPION

There is a vast and prolific literature on leadership; many models and theories have emerged in the past several decades.[4] The prevalent view is that leaders have a given style that should be matched against the situation they are put into and the people or units they are supposed to lead.

In the case of a champion for the cleaning-up program, the general attributes of such a leader, summarized in Fig. 9.1, would be preferred.

Figure 9.1
Attributes of a Champion-Leader

- Senior manager
- Able to devote all, if not most, of his/her time
- Profound knowledge of the organization
- Known and respected throughout the company
- Shares the values (vision) of senior management
- Has no specific "hidden agenda" or "ax to grind"

Senior Manager

The champion should be a senior manager, preferably a former CEO, perhaps a retired CEO. The reasons are clear. This is a task which requires a total corporate view, access, and action. The champion must be an executive who can freely and fluently deal with the top managers of the corporation, and be perceived by the workforce as having the clout and the empowerment to proceed with the task of cleaning-up and restoring of balance. The champion will be empowered with much authority, hence he or she should be at an executive level where such authority is normal.

The mistake practiced by many companies that reengineered themselves was to assign the task to a not-so-senior executive, or to an outside consultant. In the case of the cleaning-up program, only a senior executive (as high as possible in the hierarchy) should be empowered to lead this program.

Able to Devote Time

The champion-leader of this program should be an executive who can and will devote most, if not all, of his or her time to this program. Part-time management is unacceptable and will not be effective. The champion-leader cannot be someone who takes this task as an extra job, in addition to one's basic routine and administrative burden.

This task requires the full attention and time of the executive in charge. The company's future and well-being depend on a sound discharge of this challenging task. Therefore the executive selected should devote not only time but also thoughts, analysis, and ideas. All of these need time to brew and to mature in a person's head. Focused attention thus becomes crucial. This is not an *added* task for a busy executive, but a full-time position for an executive who can totally devote skills and attention to this job.[5]

Corporation of Cincinnati, Ohio.[8] As owner-manager, Frey described his experience: "A manager has to force change. My role was to make people change at a faster pace than they would ever have chosen. . . . I wouldn't take no for an answer. Once I had made my two great pronouncements, I was determined to press ahead and make them come true."[9]

Although Frey opted to bring about change in the form of empowering his employees and sharing responsibility, profits, and risks with them, he nevertheless was able to induce such change because as owner he had the authority and the power to do so.

So, when a champion is selected, such power and authority should be delegated to him or her, if the job is to be successfully carried out.

NOTES

1. W. Warner Burke, "Organization Change: What We Know, What We Need to Know," *Journal of Management Inquiry*,. 4(2), 1995, pp. 158-171.

2. *Ibid.*, p. 160.

3. *Ibid.*, p. 161.

4. See, for example, J. Burns, *Leadership* (New York: Harper & Row, 1978); also see F. Fiedler, *A Theory of Leadership Effectiveness* (New York: McGraw-Hill, 1967). The predominant model nowadays is that leadership is contingent upon the situation, and that certain types of leaders are appropriate for certain types of situations. Another view contends that leadership exists only as a perception (attribution theory). In this respect, see, for example, B. Caedes, "An Attribution Theory of Leadership," in B. Shaw and G. Salancik (eds.), *"New Directions in Organizational Behavior* (Chicago: St. Clair Press, 1977), pp. 179-204.

5. See, for example, R. Campbell, U. Sessa, and J. Taylor, "Choosing Top Leaders: Learning to Do Better," *Issues and Observations*, Center for Creative Leadership, 15(4), 1995, pp. 1-3.

6. "Desert Storms: The 1996 Upside Technology Summit," *Upside*, May 1996, p. 73.

7. See, for example, C. Hampden-Turner, *Charting the Corporate Mind* (New York: The Free Press, 1990).

8. Robert Frey, "Empowerment or Else," *Harvard Business Review*, September-October 1993, pp. 80-94.

9. *Ibid.*, p. 88.

Profound Knowledge of the Organization

A common mistake of senior managers when they choose an executive to run a change program is to select a manager from outside the company. In many instances the choice is a consultant. This is the wrong approach.

In this case of a champion-leader, the choice must be an insider. The champion must be someone who knows the organization very well. The reason for this is the need to be able to act quickly and to conduct rapid analyses of the organization, assess the damage, and most of all *understand* the company—where it has been and where it is going.

Even an executive from the same industry will not be an effective champion. The choice must be an *internal* candidate, with experience and knowledge in the corporation, preferably in a high-level position.

Examples abound of such choices, some successful, other doubtful. Apple Computers hired John Scully to be its CEO; he came from Pepsi and was well versed with consumer products and the marketing of products to individual consumers. Yet Scully failed to understand the computer industry, its intricacies, and its pattern of development. In 1996 Michael Dell, CEO of Dell Computer Corporation, commented: "The problems at Apple are both strategic and operational. I don't know that the brightest minds in the world could change its long-term course. Its fate has been sealed."[6] This may not be entirely the legacy of Scully at Apple, but one lesson to be learned is the value of industrial insights versus functional knowledge—that is, selecting a top executive because he or she has knowledge in the type of product or market or production leaves much to be desired. In essence, it leaves out the knowledge of the specific industry and the corporation.

Some may even argue that IBM is more like General Electric than Dell Computer Corporation, not only because of its size, but also because it markets to both industrial and individual markets. Yet the computer industry has very strong bonds of attributes, trends, and idiosyncrasies that are shared by all companies in this industry.

Known and Respected

The champion-leader should also be well-known and well-respected throughout the corporation. This cannot be a job for an executive who is being "punished" for some lack of performance or because of personality problems. This task should be given to an executive who has earned the respect of the workforce, and who has a relatively "clean slate" with the corporation.

This position of champion-leader should not be viewed as the "purgatory," the "Siberia" of assignments, or the "Devil's Island" of jobs. The executive selected should not only be highly respected but also be willing to undertake this job and to successfully execute it.

Shared Values of Senior Management

Precisely what I had indicated above is also evident in this attribute, namely that willingness to undertake this job should also mean that the executive selected shares the values of senior management.[7]

This is not a trivial requirement. Sometimes a senior executive, particularly when such an executive may have retired or now be involved in another task, does not share the vision and the values of his or her colleagues. It is therefore crucial that the executive selected will be at least in agreement with what senior management desires for the corporation in the postreengineering period.

No Specific "Ax to Grind"

In many instances executives selected for sensitive and highly responsible jobs find themselves in conflict when they have a specific "hidden agenda" or an "ax to grind." Such executives may be pursuing their own agendas in order, for example, to advance their careers or to use such jobs as stepping stones to other positions or companies.

It is therefore very important to select an executive who is not going to use this position for a personal interest. A very senior executive or a former CEO would be a good choice. The golden rule should be that the executive brings more to the position than the position can give to him or her.

Clearly it is impossible to totally avoid any kind of hidden agenda. Even when an executive agrees with the vision of the corporation and has no covert ax to grind, the executive will put his or her personal stamp on the position. This means that biases, feelings, preferences, strengths, and weaknesses will be an integral part of the job that will be created and executed. But this is the individual mark that any and all executives bring to a job. The selection of the champion-leader should be such that this mark is highly beneficial, educated, and experienced.

EMPOWERING THE CHAMPION

The champion-leader should be entrusted with the power and authority to carry out the cleaning-up program. This entails a clear pronouncement from senior management that the champion has the authority to lead, manage, and execute the program. It should also be clearly stipulated that the champion has the full support of senior management and the authority to act as their change agent.

This pronouncement should be communicated with all possible speed and through all possible means of communication within the company, not only internally but also externally.

Full support, a clear mandate, and the specific areas of responsibility and authority should be the charter given to the champion by senior management. This is a CEO-sponsored program and it should so be advertised.

An excellent example of the need for top-level support and empowerment is found in an article by Robert Frey, who told the story of his company, the Cin-Made

10

ASSESSING THE DAMAGE

How does one assess the damage caused by reengineering? In essence, there are two dimensions to this question. The first is: What damage should be assessed—that is, what are the *categories* of damage. Second, what methods and techniques could one apply to assess the damage? This chapter is designed to answer the two dimensions of this question.

CATEGORIES OF DAMAGE

The categories of lateral damage caused by reengineering have already been listed in Chapter 6. Here I am rearranging and regrouping these categories into three basic types of damage: (1) damage to people, (2) damage to structure, and (3) damage to strategic position.

Damage to People

This is by far the most publicized type of damage, widely discussed in the academic as well as the popular literature. As I showed in Chapter 6, the damage to people is both much more noticeable to senior management and much more harmful in the short run.

There are two main aspects of lateral damage to people following reengineering. They are both grouped under low morale in Figure 6.1: low morale and motivation, and its effects on productivity and the climate in the corporation.

Low Morale and Motivation

The first aspects of damage are *low morale* and *motivation*. These are hard to assess although there have been many instances in which researchers measured morale and motivation operationally. This is done through two converging sets of indicators. They are summarized in Figure 10.1 which shows some of the indicators, objectively

Figure 10.1
Indicators Used in Assessing Morale and Motivation

Objective Indicators	Subjective Indicators
Morale • Rate of absenteeism • Pronounced dissatisfaction • Rate of turnover • Rate of complaints	*Morale* • Overall malaise • Perceived loss of control over one's environment • Decline in loyalty • Perceived alienation
Motivation • Rate of willingness to participate in tasks, workgroup, and other functions • Rate of verbal and physical outburst and abuse in workplace and in home life	*Motivation* • Expectancy/valence theory instruments • Self-assessment instruments

and subjectively measured, that help to assess the changes in the levels of the constructs of motivation and morale. The figure is by no means exhaustive. The reason I am listing these indicators is not to engage in a specific analysis of this type of damages, but rather to illustrate that there are means to conduct such assessment.[1]

In a concise article in 1995, R. Manganelli and S. Raspa emphasized the need to reorient individuals when companies implement reengineering programs.[2] They used the example of AT&T Capital Leasing Services and argued that individual workers should receive equal attention to that given by reengineering teams to restructuring and process redesign. New career paths, cross-training, and new compensation criteria are some of the elements of reorientation that they have argued for inclusion in the reengineering effort.

These elements of redesign are very similar to the indicators used in subjective methods of measuring motivation. Expectancy theories are based on the assessment of perceived expectations and outcomes, which are influenced by perceptions of career opportunities and compensation structures.

All of this clearly leads, as had been advocated by many, to steps to be taken during the *implementation* of reengineering. Here I list these indicators as a powerful tool in assessing the damage caused to people *after* reengineering had been implemented. It is possible to measure such damage to morale and motivation.

For example, as Figure 10.1 shows, some objective indicators are known to emerge and become recognizable to middle and senior managers even without careful analysis. This may happen through isolated yet highly visible and stirring cases. In a Fortune 200 company with whom a colleague had consulted, the rate of absenteeism in one department climbed dramatically, whereas other employees manifested their dissatisfaction with anonymous complaints on bulletin boards and in discussions on the Internet. It was very difficult for both middle and senior management not to observe and register such anomalies. In addition, my colleague reported that there was a pervasive sense of fear and uncertainty, which was revealed to him through his interviews with workers and managers. In one case, an engineer, 47 years of age with 12 years of service in the company, commented:

I know that my job is relatively more secure than others in this department, but I'm telling you that if I could I'd leave. Everybody is upset, at least everybody that I know in my network here . . . I just don't understand any more what kind of division we are and where this place is supposed to go . . . I'm telling you that everybody is looking at the future and it's quite bleak.

Senior management must be able to assess this type of damage by using all the tools and methods at its disposal. On the one hand there are effective techniques to measure objective and subjective indicators; on the other hand, there is the old method of "gut feeling" that managers have that something is wrong. People are unhappy, they are not as enthusiastic, not as loyal, and they avoid added responsibilities. Although many workers will hide their distaste and unhappiness for fear of losing their jobs, the overall effect tends to be quite clear and it permeates the organization.

The indicators and methods for assessment of the damage are given here in order to show the feasibility of assessing this phenomenon. Corporate executives should not discount their "gut feelings" or their intuition in perceiving that the workforce is restless and unhappy. The best of all worlds is a combination of actual measures (such as rates of absenteeism, notes of complaints, and a deterioration in the working climate) with the intuitive perceptions of executives and middle managers.

Effects on Productivity

In addition to the impact on how employees feel and negatively react to reengineering, there is also the impact on the productivity levels of both individuals and units.

Organization scientists have discovered several reasons why employees tend to restrict, curtail, or otherwise lower their work productivity. Among the many such reasons are negative forces. I can list five basic indicators: (1) unsatisfactory rewards, (2) weak linkage between rewards and performance, (3) distrust of management, (4) control over the job environment, and (5) lack of job involvement.[3]

All five factors are usually influenced or impacted by the effects of the reengineering program. Rewards are generally not commensurate with the changes incurred after reengineering. Workers commonly complain about additional workload, longer hours, and less recognition for work well done. The second factor is also very prevalent in the corporations that my colleagues and I visited and for whom we consulted. There seem to be inequities between rewards and outcomes that are perceived by the workforce. Not only are the rewards inadequate but they are also, in many instances, not tied to the performance or outcome measures that had emerged following the reengineering program. This is true not only in units that had been radically transformed or severely downsized, but also in other units linked to these by virtue of the value chain.[4]

Another factor is the distrust of management, which seems to exist in the post-reengineering era. One company's experience is that of a service corporation in the health care industry, providing services to large chains of hospitals. This company was a participant in a study of hospitals and medical centers that my colleague, Ori Heller, M.D., and I conducted in 1995 in an effort to explore aspects of the management of medical technology. Following the participation of the company in the study, I was asked to help with its reengineering program which was close to completion. Already we could observe indications of distrust of management. An internal survey had exposed the following quotes from middle managers:

There was hardly any downsizing in my department, but for the life of me, I don't know what Mr. ___ (CEO) wants done. I think he wants to sell the company and parachute with a golden treasure.

This company is going to hell in a handbasket.

It's all lies. We didn't have to reengineer. They told us it will improve our performance. Where? How? Nothing, nada.

Distrust of management may take several forms, most of which are internalized by workers and usually can be detected through focused interviews.

The distrust of management leads to uncertainty about the intentions of senior managers. Therefore, middle managers as well as the rank and file tend to create an elaborate world of a virtual situation and to tailor their performances to this reality. Usually it results in lower than desired levels of productivity, enough to satisfy the minimum, but below what reengineering would have predicted. Productivity is kept at a level that defies criticism but still far from merit and high accomplishment. Entrepreneurship and enthusiasm are kept to a minimum. Innovation is used only to avoid punishment, criticism, and any new directions from above.

Lack of control over one's job environment is a powerful factor in curtailing productivity. The way it works is usually through defensive behavior in view of perceived loss of control which is promoted by reengineering. People feel that the changes in the work processes (normally toward more efficiency and rationalization) have taken away some of their freedoms and some of their relative control over their jobs—*what* they do and *how* they do it.

Additionally, the movement toward increased usage of information technology has diminished the role that actual contacts had in the relations and the communication patterns among people. For example, in the health care services company, one employee, a manager in charge of a large department, had this to say:

I used to have meetings with my staff and with others in ____ department and with the comptroller's office. Now I mostly communicate by e-mail, but I and many here feel that we can't influence anybody anymore. They can choose not to respond to your messages or to take their sweet time and let things cool off. It's terribly frustrating. When you can't discuss things face to face you can't get things done.

The relative isolation and anonymity of electronic communications, coupled with incomprehensible changes in work processes and job descriptions, cause a perceived loss of control that employees have, or wish to have, over their jobs. Thus, the behavioral response is to create barriers, fences, and other protective devices through slack resources and a lower rate of productivity. These allow for better manipulation of resources such as time, people, equipment, and activities. The slack in productivity offers the opportunity to increase or decrease performance at the command of the employees rather than senior management or an established automated system.[5]

Finally, lack of job involvement will have similar effects on productivity as the perceived loss of control. Workers will show their displeasure with the job they are assigned or with changes in it after reengineering was implemented by manipulating productivity levels. Usually by-products will be increased alienation, withdrawal, and absenteeism. The effects on productivity may not be clearly discernable at first. However, when a combination of the factors listed above takes effect, the impact cannot be missed, both in reduced productivity and in the increase in the cost of human resources.

Why should senior management be concerned with these phenomena? Some would suggest that such decline in productivity and the factors causing it are "natural" consequences of radical change and as the changes are established, they will improve and their effects will be neutralized. This is hardly the case. The factors described in this chapter not only have a life of their own, but they seem to build upon each other and to multiply or snowball the general impact on performance. As I indicated in chapters six and seven, the effect also intensifies when it is transferred from unit to unit.

Thus, senior management must be aware of these effects on productivity and must be able and willing to assess them and to determine the level of their severity and permanence over time. Most of all, senior management must *understand* the criticality of the impact of these phenomena and the value added in knowing what they are by assessing them throughout the corporation.

To summarize, the damage to people is in the form of the combined effects of decline in morale and motivation and the manipulation and decline in productivity. People who are affected (or perceived to be affected) by the reengineering upheaval will behave defensively, thus leading to a climate of unhappiness, fear, and decline in productivity. At best, people will not achieve their potential. At worst, the defensive behavior will lead to a severely crippled workforce: unhappy and unproductive.

Damage to Structure

Dominant Designs

This category of damage is perhaps the least understood and the hardest to assess. In recent years, organization scientists have introduced the concept of dominant designs. In this context, P. Anderson and M. Tushman suggested in 1990 that "a breakthrough innovation inaugurates an era of ferment in which competition among variations of the original breakthrough culminates in the selection of a single dominant configuration of the new technology."[6]

They defined dominant design as "a single architecture that establishes dominance in a product class."[7] They also concluded that "dominant designs permit firms to design standardized and interchangeable parts and to optimize organizational processes for volume and efficiency."[8]

The concept of dominant design has proven useful in modeling technological evolution. This concept can also be transported to the area of changes in the structure and processes of the corporation as a result of reengineering. The analogy is possible by borrowing the concept to indicate a dominant design of the structure of the corporation, following the ferment caused by reengineering. In doing so, let us consider two converging phenomena in the corporation.

The first is the tendency of executives to encourage activities and structures that work, and to institutionalize them. This practice makes new excursions into management practices quite difficult. On the other hand we also have changes that are imposed on the corporation, such as reengineering, which bring about new forms of organization and conducting the work. The convergence of these two phenomena and their integration into an acceptable format gives birth to what we might call a dominant design. Out of the many possibilities, one format emerges which incorporates both these features that have proven to be workable, and the features of the change program. In striving for such congruence, the dominant design will also bring in its wake a plethora of damaging situations and phenomena.

What is the dominant design? It can be defined as the nonephemeral structural arrangement of the corporation after reengineering. It is composed of the arrangement of formal units (divisions, departments, etc.); the functions of the corporation and each unit (marketing, manufacturing, legal, R&D, etc.), and the processes that are set to accomplish the workflow. Such arrangement is normally the product of an evolutionary process, imbedded with compromise, social and organizational requirements, and a large dose of executive biases, ability, and success in putting this together. The dominant design, rather than being the redesigned or reinvented format (as articulated by BPR), is a woven tapestry of what has worked, what seems to work, and what we hope and pray will work.

Nevertheless, a common side effect of the emergence of the dominant structural design is the disturbed and weakened network of liaison functions, coupled with the misuse of the concept of core competencies. These phenomena were described in Chapter 5. Here I again bring them to the fore because they should be assessed, because of their negative impact on unit performance and on the systemic performance of the corporation.

Liaison Functions

The road map for senior management in assessing structural damage is to look for the reduction in liaison functions and the impact that this causes on the ability of the corporation to be flexible and adaptive.

The dominant structural design sometimes tends to veer toward what we hope will work, at the expense of the proven ability of liaison units and functions. When the desire to conserve resources and to dramatically increase efficiency overpowers the experiences of the success in the past—then the dominant design emerges without adequate liaison functions.[9]

Assessment procedures of the damage should first evaluate the number and range of activities of liaison units and their functions. Next, an evaluation of "snowballing"—this combined effect of the remaining liaison units—should be undertaken. This will provide a measure of the isolation of structural units and their inability to communicate.[10]

As an illustration, consider the case of a computer company that underwent reengineering and ended up with a dominant design to match its existing technology. Let's remember that BPR is a change program aimed at the redesign of work processes. The technological makeup is not disturbed. The dominant structural design that emerges—if lacking the elements of flexibility and adaptability such as adequate liaison functions—will be unable to deal with massive technological innovation. In order to exploit the new technology, the corporation has to adapt or totally transform itself. If it does the latter, it is already at a disadvantage vis-à-vis other, more flexible competitors who are able to adapt the technology and to run with it.

Damage to Strategic Position

Samuel Butler once said: "Life is the art of drawing sufficient conclusions from insufficient premises." In essence, this is what we do when we embark on assessing damage to the strategic position of the firm following the reengineering program.[11] We assess the potential harm to the competitive position of the corporation by evaluating the ability of the emerging "dominant design" to carry the company forward in a densely competitive market. This means that, in addition to damage to people and structure, we are now looking at the total corporation, as a system, and its competitive potential.

In Chapter 6 I gave the example of a pharmaceutical company which was reengineered with the focus on product development at the expense of R&D and other functions. This is a strategic decision. Manganelli and Raspa[12] suggested that "poorly conceived and executed reengineering projects are becoming a by-word in American Business . . . . Experts believe it is because reengineering has been deployed tactically rather than strategically."[13]

How does one measure damage to the strategic or competitive position? Mostly by implementing a *strategic* analysis of competencies and needs in a turbulent external environment. For example, S. Hart and C. Banbury have concluded that "firms with high process capability—the simultaneous use of multiple strategy-making process modes—outperform single mode or less process-capable organizations.[14] They have also concluded that "the *process* through which strategy is made holds the potential for competitive advantage and requires purposeful design and management attention."[15]

The strategic management literature is replete with models and mechanisms that link the resources, managerial processes, and existence of strategic directions to the success or failure of the corporation in its markets.

Assessment of damage to strategy can benefit from these techniques. The ultimate goal is to make sure that senior management has a clear idea of any discrepancy between what reengineering generated and the strategic demands of the company in its competitive environment.[16]

DIRECT AND LATERAL DAMAGE

In an excellent study of ten newly appointed top managers, Robert Simons, a Harvard Business School professor, concluded: "In situations of strategic change, control systems are used by top managers to formalize beliefs, set boundaries on acceptable strategic behavior, define and measure critical performance variables, and motivate debate and discussion about strategic uncertainties."[17]

In addition, he also suggested that "finally, management control systems appear to be vitally important in building credibility and selling a new strategy to various constituents . . . . New top managers are consistent in the way they used management control system targets to communicate direction and create credibility with both superiors and subordinates." Any such control and communication in the period following radical (strategic) change requires a basic understanding of the effects such change has created.

A good way of classifying such damage is by using the military notions of direct and lateral (or collateral) damage. Although in chapter six I asserted that the nature of postreengineering damage is primarily lateral damage, this is merely a matter of definition. Some damage may easily be classified as direct, when the impacts of radical change, such as reengineering, affect the ability of a unit or a function to continue its usual activities, and when such effect is relatively immediate.

In this I refer to Simons' finding that new managers create credibility and are engaged in selling their new strategy. Assessing the damage in an effective manner is thus crucial to building credibility and becomes the essence of the message that top managers send across the organization.

In addition to the classification of damage by the broad categories of who and what was impacted, the effects of radical change may also be categorized by the *degree of damage*, the *functions affected*, and the *proneness to measurement*.[18]

Degree of Damage

Direct and lateral damage usually differ along two dimensions. The first is the time dimension, where direct damage occurs within a short period of time. Occurrence means that the damage inflicted is discernable and leads to complications and problems that negatively impact the performance and even the functioning of a unit or members of the organization. Lateral damage takes longer to brew and tends to appear at a later time, although clearly its consequences may be as severe as direct damage and perhaps even stronger and more damaging.

In this sense, direct damage is the more visible of the two types. In a company that has been downsized due to reengineering, some of the consequences will be observed in employees' negative behavior and deteriorating attitudes. This is partly direct damage on the workforce. The resultant decline in morale and commitment would appear later and would be best defined as lateral damage. There is, of course, some causal link between direct and lateral damage along the time dimension. Strong direct damage will produce subsequent lateral damage in other directions. Such is a "snowballing" effect,[19] and it is very similar to the effects of *planned* change on *organic* changes which I have previously discussed in chapter six.

In general, we may propose that the stronger and more damaging the direct damage, the stronger will be the shock waves and the subsequent lateral damage to the organization—providing that management is incapable of detecting direct damage and dealing with it before it spreads.

In an excellent article on such a process, *The Economist* summarized what I have consistently argued in this book.[20] The magazine commented on U.S. firms that are now concerned about corporate America, brought about by reengineering and downsizing. Corporate memory is badly hurt, weakened, and even distorted when informal social networks, in which relationships flow and memories are kept, are dismantled by radical changes.

Moreover, as I have argued, *The Economist* also suggests that information technology cannot protect the company against the loss of its memories and those of its people.

The phenomenon of corporate amnesia is an illustration of the link between direct and lateral damage. Direct damage affects the corporate workforce, disrupts social networks and communication hubs among employees. This, in turn, leads down the road to loss of memories which affect key functions such as new product development and marketing.[21]

Biomedi (not its real name) is a biotechnology company, one of the many that emerged during the frenzy of the late 1980s. Formed by two researchers who worked for large pharmaceutical companies, and happened to be working on similar topics, Biomedi received a generous venture capital push to become one of three leaders in the research and potential manufacturing of a potent and highly desirable genetically transformed compound. In late 1994 the company hired consultants who advocated reengineering the scientific as well as administrative branches. One of the cofounders objected to what he called "commercial tactics that interfere with science." Despite his protests the company was reengineered. The objective was to create a leaner and more aggressive corporation and to reduce the time to market of the compound. Internal processes were redesigned, duplication was eliminated, and personnel were cut by over 20 percent.

In mid-1996, when I had a conversation with the cofounder who objected to the reengineering effort, we learned that the time to market was not shortened. Rather, the company found itself mired in a disaster. Two groups had been working in parallel on the same problem using a methodology which another group, under the cofounder, had already tried and discounted. As the cofounder put it: "We lost almost 20 months of Sisyphean work. Very good people working on something they should have known wouldn't work! We didn't know that on top of people being unhappy about cuts, they also stopped talking to each other!"[22]

Biomedi is an example of the effects that the degree of damage has on the corporation. When BPR creates strong direct damage, the consequences for lateral damage may be devastating downstream.

Functions Affected

Earlier in this chapter I argued that damage from BPR may happen to liaison functions and to dominant designs in the structure of the organization. Perhaps more harmful are effects on some key functions, which then reverberate throughout the affected organization, like brushfire in the California landscape.

BPR is usually deployed in the most crucial and the busiest functions in the organization. In order to be reengineered, the function must have an important role in productivity and efficiency, and must lend itself to relatively easy manipulation. Thus we have the operational concepts of "streamlining," "redesign," "transforming," "restructuring," and "reorganization" as terms used to describe the radical changes implemented in a corporate function. Among the common functions that have undergone reengineering are those that rely on a flow of activities or a process of various administrative and managerial stages. For example, financial functions and their units and processes, administrative functions such as human resources (HR) departments, and specialized functions such as credit departments are optimal candidates for reengineering.[23] However, some observers of the BPR experience have already noticed the weaknesses inherent in the trend to zero-in on such functions. The more the function lends itself to reengineering, the more the people aspect becomes problematic. R. Dawe explored business logistics as a target for reengineering.[24] He explained:

Although information systems help BPR succeed, a dearth of people power guarantees its failure. The people aspect of BPR is usually the weakest part of the BPR project, as it is not designed to run concurrently with systems and process design. This delayed approach to people reengineering normally leads to the forcing in of new systems and processes to see who will rise to the challenge and who will not.

When functions are reengineered, the emphasis is on redesign and streamlining the activities, the tasks, and the flow. The direct damage is usually in the systemic linkages (as I explained earlier), but the more consistent and lingering damage is the lateral damage. This is normally brought about by reactions of people in the organization.

Note that the emphasis on people as the element that spreads the ills of reengineering is not a malicious attempt by me or other writers who made such comments to purposely single out people over systems. The problem with lateral damage is that it spreads in various directions, generally following each organization's unique dynamics. So the way things work is that direct damage to a function is then taken by people-steps forward to become lateral damage in other parts of the corporation. People are purveyors of lateral damage. Why? Because although the direct damage is inflicted on functions and selected units, people are the link of these functions to the rest of the organization. Structures and systems don't change by themselves. People change them as a result of reengineering and the damage done to the functions and units it has changed.

BPR concentrated (at least in practice) on high-potential functions such as finance, logistics, transportation, supporting activities, and administration. These functions had the potential to improve and to change. Yet, as such changes have occurred, the people impacted by this have extended the damage to their linkages and to their involvement with other parts of the company. The more they were involved, the more the lateral damage. Clearly, the more the function was a key activity, the more its people were involved. So the more key functions were targeted for reengineering, the higher the probability that the accumulating lateral damage down the road increased.[25]

How, then, can we assess such damage? It is essential to identify the patterns that occur in the move from direct to lateral damage. In a manner similar to the move from planned change to organic changes that result from it, lateral damage follows direct damage along several different venues in the corporation.

Organization science is currently at a stage where we have sufficient understanding of these processes and an adequate basis to offer some direction on what general pattern the damage will assume.

While assisting a telecommunications company on another matter, we assessed the development of lateral damage from a reengineered human resources department. Interviews with key managers and employees revealed a pattern of strong commitment formation toward an artificial unit that was substituting a unit dismantled by the change process. In other words, some key employees by the HR department created their own informal entity which began to influence other functions linked to HR. They created an informal network for communication, as well as evaluation of on-going activities and people.[26]

How to Obtain the Data?

But even if we identify such evolving patterns, how do we obtain the data to assess the damage? In chapters six and seven I discussed the issues in measurement, and the role that archival and survey methodologies play in this process. When assessing damage (direct and lateral) to functions and units, a combination of using archival and interview data is recommended.

The main problems with interviews are:

- People are no longer there, so the memories are erased, distorted, or irrelevant.

- People don't like to talk about hardships and the shortcuts they take to overcome them. In fact, much of what we learn from these interviews comes hidden between the lines. We need all the knowledge at our disposal on how organizations and people in them function to distill the interviews and to get at the desired patterns.

- People simply don't know why they do what they do. Many times they react instinctively and are hard-pressed to describe motives and to point to a logical succession of steps they had taken.

In all, although there are problems in obtaining information from those involved, the patterns of lateral damage in corporate functions after BPR can be adequately assessed.

Proneness to Measurement

The proclivity of certain functions and units to be measured makes the task of assessment more plausible. A difficulty arises when the damage from BPR is *hidden among the benefits*. This is particularly the case where functions are showing noticeable improvements such as costs being cut, increased efficiency and productivity, and specific savings in selected processes. These are relatively easy to measure, and as I have noted in chapter four, fondly used to describe BPR's undoubted benefits.

Yet the idea behind measuring such direct and lateral damage from BPR is to recognize the wolves among the sheep.[27] In the Watergate scandal the journalists Bob Woodward and Carl Bernstein were told by their confidential source: "Follow the money." In assessing such hidden damage, the motto should be: "Follow the people." In addition to measurement of the outcomes of units and functions, it is the people who spread and transport the hidden damage and who are the "carriers" for dormant damage that will ultimately result in lateral damage down the road.

The starting point for senior management and the team assigned to assess the damage is to commence with those activities, units, outcomes, and functions that are more prone to measurement. There are two reasons why this is advisable.

1. These measurements will produce rapid results that may be easily detected and quickly analyzed. They also provide encouragement to the intervention team conducting the measurement that outcomes are feasible.

2. These measurements *do* uncover damage and they provide an added set of clues to follow for those functions and units where measurement may be a harder task.

Some units and functions untroubled by BPR may still be at the mercy of damages transported to them from units and functions that have undergone the radical changes. Therefore, senior management should not ignore these functions, although they are difficult to measure and had been spared by BPR.[28]

SUMMARY

This chapter looked at the assessment of the damage to the corporation following reengineering. The damage categories varied from the clearly identifiable to the highly conceptual. Yet the main idea is for senior managers to take the pulse of the type and the amount of damage that has been caused. Very few top executives have done so, and fewer to the extent that this book advocates.

Senior managers must gain an *understanding* of what damage has been inflicted and the potential harm it can cause in the short as well as the long term. Awareness of the phenomenon will then give way to action on their part—such action to be planned, measured, and decisive.

Cleaning-up and the return to stability can succeed only when senior managers have obtained an excellent grasp of the lateral damage and its importance to the future of the corporation.

NOTES

1.   For a discussion of these and other indicators of morale and motivation, see for example, R. Steers and J. Stewart Black, *Organizational Behavior*, 5th ed. (New York:Harper-Collins, 1994); also see B. Staw, "Motivation in Organizations: Towards Synthesis and Redirection," in B. Staw and G. Salancik (eds.), *New Directions in Organizational Behavior* (Chicago: St. Clair Press, 1977), pp. 55-96.

2.   R. Manganelli and S. Raspa, "Why Reengineering Has Failed," *Management Review*, July 1995, pp. 39-43.

3.   These are listed in Steers and Black, *op cit.*, p. 166.

4.   This phenomenon is reminiscent of the "Hawthorne Effect" which was described in chapter four.

5.   There are various accounts of this phenomenon in the management literature. See, for example. Chris Argyris, *Overcoming Organizational Defenses: Facilitating Organizational Learning* (Needham, MA: Allyn & Bacon, 1990); also R. Kilmann and T. Covin and Associates, *Corporate Transformation: Revitalizing Organizations for a Competitive World* (San Francisco: Jossey-Bass, 1988).

6.   P. Anderson and M. Tushman, "Technological Discontinuities and Dominant Designs: A Cyclical Model of Technological Change," *Administrative Science Quarterly*, 35(4), 1990, p. 606.

7.   *Ibid.*, p. 613.

8.   *Ibid.*, p. 614.

9.   Successes in the past may be ignored because they cannot be easily measured, as they tend to be in the background of corporate occurrences. This is usually the case with liaison units and functions. Their contribution to success is seldom emphasized. Only when they are eliminated or curtailed, and when they are not adequately replaced by information technology, then they may be responsible for transforming potential success into catastrophic failure.

10.   There is a substantial literature on this and related topics. See, for example, N. Nohria and R. G. Eccles (eds.), *Networks and Organizations* (Boston: Harvard Business School Press, 1992); also see, P. Nayak and J. Ketteringham, *Breakthroughs* (New York: Arthur D. Little, 1987).

11.   Wang Laboratories comes to mind as an example, although clearly there were other factors that led to its declaring chapter 11 bankruptcy, and it wasn't a result of BPR.

12. Manganelli and Raspa, *op. cit.*

13. *Ibid.*, p. 40.

14. S. Hart and C. Banbury, "How Strategy Making Processes Can Make a Difference," *Strategic Management Journal*, 15, 1994, pp. 251-269.

15. *Ibid.*, p. 266.

16. See, for example, R. Priem and D. Harrison, "Exploring Strategic Judgment: Methods for Testing the Assumptions of Prescriptive Contingency Theories," *Strategic Management Journal*, 15(4), 1994, pp. 311-324; also see W. Finnie, *Hands-On Strategy: The Guide to Crafting Your Company's Future* (New York: John Wiley, 1995).

17. R. Simons, "How New Top Managers Use Control Systems as Levers of Strategic Renewal," *Strategic Management Journal*, 15(3), 1994, pp. 169-190 (quotes from pp. 169 and 187).

18. Some recent voices in the literature have begun to address these issues and have pointed, to some degree, to such damage categories. See, for example, K. Branco, "Bubble Bursting," *Executive Excellence*, 13(5), May 1996, p. 19; also see, J. Queenan, "What They Don't Tell You in Reengineering School," *Chief Executive*, 113(3), May 1996, pp. 61-62; E. Mumford and R. Hendricks, "Business Process Reengineering RIP," *Personnel Management*, 2(9), 1996, pp. 22-29; and W. Friedel, "Reevaluate Risks when Reengineering," *Best's Review*, 96(1), 1996, pp. 74-78; and W. Neil and P. Wood, "When You are Profitable But Not Competitive," *ABA Banking Journal*, 88(2), 1996, pp. 99-102.

19. Some writers have recently recognized this effect and have included it in their broader assessments of BPR. See, for example, D. Carr and H. Johansson, *Best Practices in Reengineering. What Works and What Doesn't in the Reengineering Process* (New York: McGraw Hill, 1995); B. Harrison, *Lean and Mean: The Changing Landscape in the Age of Flexibility* (New York: Basic Books, 1994); and G. Donaldson, *Corporate Restructuring: Managing the Change Process from Within* (Boston: Harvard Business School Press, 1994).

20. Editorial Staff, "Fire and Forget?" *The Economist*, Vol. 339, April 20, 1996, pp. 51-52.

21. See, for example, J. Want, *Managing Radical Change: Beyond Survival in the New Business Age* (New York: John Wiley, 1995); also see U. S. Department of Labor, *Economic Competition: Restructuring, and Worker Dislocations (Washington, D.C., 1995),* Office of Policy and Research, Employment and Training Administration; and T. MacTaggart, *Restructuring Higher Education: What Works and What Doesn't in Reorganizing Governing Systems* (San Francisco: Jossey-Bass, 1996).

22. Although in late 1996 the cuts in human resources in many corporations have leveled off or have been reduced from the highs of previous years, there are still continuing cuts in many corporations. In August 1996, Campbell Soup embarked on a major reorganization with layoffs at its headquarters in New Jersey. In September 1996, Miller Brewing Company eliminated 18.5% of its salaried workforce. American TransAir also eliminated 15% of its workforce in 1996. In the first nine months of 1996, over 2,000 jobs a day were eliminated in corporate America. Many companies are continuing the reduction in force, so that the cumulative effects over a period of several years are yet to unfold.

23. See, for example, J. Fitz-Enz, "On the Edge of Oblivion (the Departments Need to Reengineer Their Own Staff to Survive), *HR Magazine*, 41(2), 1996, pp. 84-88; and A. Horowitz, "Bean Zapping (Re-reengineering the Finance Department)," *Computer World*, 30(12), April 27, 1996, p. 72; also see W. Parker, "Real World Reengineering: Supporting Organizational Change at Premier Bank," *National Productivity Review*, 15(5), 1996, pp. 67-80; R. Angus, A. Goodman, and P. Pfund, "Reengineering for Revenue Growth," *Research/Technology Management*, 39(3), 1996, pp. 26-31; and D. Strischek and R. Cross,

"Reengineering the Credit Approval Process," *Journal of Lending & Credit Risk Management*, 78(1), 1996, pp. 19-34.

24. R. Dawe, "Systems Are People Too. Information Systems and Business Logistics Process Reengineering," *Transportation and Distribution*, 37(1), 1996, pp. 86-87.

25. M. Klein, "Tips for Aspiring Reengineers," *Planning Review*, 24(1) 1996, pp. 40-41. Also see B. Fisher, "Reengineering Your Business Process," *Journal of Systems Management*, 47(1), 1996, pp. 46-51; and especially see L. Zucker and M. Darby, "Costly Information in Firm Transformation, Exit, or Persistent Failure," *American Behavioral Scientist*, 39(8), 1996, pp. 386-394.

26. See, for example, the 1996 Optiman Award winner for managing change, which went to Siemens-Rolm of Santa Clara, California, for its effort to reengineer its HR department. "HR's Advances Reengineer a Restructuring," *Personnel Journal*, 75(1), 1996, pp. 60-61; also see T. Callaghan, "Riding the Tide of the '90s (Reengineering and Running the Credit Department), *Business Credit*, 98(2), 1996, pp. 46-48; and J. Chandler, P. Prashant, and J. Thompson, "The Orion Project: Staged BPR at FedEx," *Communications of the ACM*, 39(1), 1996, pp. 99-107. In this paper the authors described the Optically Recorded Information Online Network (Orion) project at FedEx. Designed to handle documentation worldwide for almost 100,000 employees, the project redesigned the way the company disseminates, processes, stores, and retrieves HR documentation. This is an example of a highly targeted BPR project in which the change was primarily technical, by changing the way records are handled. The case did not describe organizational or managerial implications from this change.

27. Some authors have recently alluded to this phenomenon, although indirectly and with little focus. See, for example, R. Pascale, *Managing on the Edge: How the Smartest Companies Use Conflict to Stay Ahead* (New York: Simon & Schuster, 1996); and F. Hilmer and L. Donaldson, *Management Redeemed: Debunking the Fads that Undermine Our Corporations* (New York: The Free Press, 1996); R. Harmon, *Reinventing the Business* (New York: The Free Press, 1996); and D. Lombardi and T. Miner, "Reengineering in the Food-Service Industry: Is It "Rightsizing"? *The Cornell Hotel and Restaurant Administration Quarterly*, 36(4), 1995, pp. 43-47.

28. Illustrative examples of such damage among the benefits in hard-to-measure functions can be found in, for example, T. Quelette, "Good Medicine for Re-Engineering," *Computerworld*, 29(6), December 18, 1995, pp. 51-53; C. Gillis and R. Mottley, "Rebooting a Supply Chain: Torrent of Worldwide Product Orders Forces Three Computer Giants to Re-Engineer Logistics," *American Shipper*, 37(4), December 1995, pp. 52-59; Arthur P. Little, "Reengineering your Reengineering," *Datamation*, 41(12), December 1, 1995, pp. 15-16.; and Y. Pollalis, "A Systemic Approach to Change Management: Integrating IS Planning, BPR and TQM," *Information Systems Management*, 13(3), 1996, pp. 19-25. Other examples in the field of education include C. Hutchison, "Concept Reading: A Process for Reengineering Processes," *Performance and Instruction*, 34(9), 1995, pp. 12-22; and G. Chesley, "The Engineering of Reconstructuring: What Do We Do and How Do We Do It?" *NASSP Bulletin*, 78(3), 1994, pp. 21-27.

11

CO-OPTING MIDDLE MANAGERS

Cleaning up and restoring balance are the key punctuating elements in a program of stabilizing the corporation. It is also a program of change that requires the support of middle managers.

ROLE OF MIDDLE MANAGERS

The group of executives known as "middle" or "general" managers can be defined as "organizational mentors who (1) supervise other organizational members, (2) have authority over an organizational unit, (3) have discretion over resources, and (4) are not members of the executive group reporting directly to the Chief Executive Officer of the organization."[1] This definition includes general managers as well as managers of professional units who have control over small, highly specialized units.

In his 1988 article and in other writings, Peter Drucker predicted the transformation of the new organization into an "information-based" format, where the hierarchy is flattened, with the disappearance of layers of middle managers.[2] Other management scholars predicted the arrival of the m-form of organization, which is a looser form of the multidivisional organization. It would also be amorphous and knowledge-based, promoting mobility, flexibility, and entrepreneurial behavior.[3] Yet this prediction has only been partly fulfilled. Although much of the downsizing has been inflicted on middle managers, and many corporations have indeed become more "flat" by eliminating levels of management, the average company still depends on and enjoys the services of a large contingent of general managers.

In his excellent book on general managers, Francis Aguilar defined them by the broad categories of tasks that compose the job.[4] Although he also included the CEO or president of a corporation in his definition, nevertheless the characteristics of the job are certainly those of a middle manager.[5] Aguilar's six tasks are: "1) creating and maintaining organizational values and norms; 2) setting strategic objectives and direction; 3) negotiating with stakeholders; 4) marshaling, developing, and allocating people and other resources; 5) organizing the work; 6) attending to ongoing operations."[6]   He also suggested that *unpredictability* and *disorderliness* are characteristics of the general manager's job.

Middle managers usually find themselves squeezed between the senior executives and their own subordinates. They are charged with communicating policy and strategic direction from the top to the bottom, and with carrying out the feedback from the company upward to senior management. They are therefore "stuck," as one manager put it, "between the rock and the hard place."

Most important, middle managers are the key to instituting any change program. The history of such programs has shown that without the complete and enthusiastic support of middle managers, the change program will fail. This was seen in technology applications (such as automation), in Total Quality Management and, most recently, in reengineering. Middle managers are also responsible for motivating their subordinates and for maintaining the innovation process. They do so by forging the intrapreneurial process and by making sure that valuable ideas are implemented.[7]

Another crucial role played by middle managers concerns their functional ability to handle the communication needs in the organization. Perhaps based on this quality of middle managers, Drucker and others have suggested that with information technology becoming more diffused and ubiquitous, this may be the time to replace middle managers with technology.

My view differs, in that communication is only one function that middle managers perform, as are control and coordination. All three functions may be done to some extent by direct communication between senior managers and the rest of the organization. However, the role that middle managers play in the company is much more complex and includes technical as well as social, functional, and psychological aspects of managing people and other resources.

In recent years organization scientists have uncovered the role that middle managers play in the implementation of strategic decisions in the corporation.[8] This role is of critical importance to the corporation, because if strategies are to be implemented, they can be adequately and successfully achieved only through the active cooperation of middle managers. They are charged not only with seeing to it that strategies are implemented, but also with the role of interpreting the strategy and the allocation of the various tasks needed for implementation.[9]

Thus, middle managers are essentially the administrative and managerial skeleton of the corporation. They make things happen, make information flow, and see that decisions are carried out. Clearly, they may also impinge negatively upon the organization by creating bottlenecks and by thwarting information, or by accumulating unnecessary slack resources in the making of "miniempires." But, on the whole, middle managers are indispensable, particularly where there is a need to call the organization to arms, to gather support for a change program, and to carry out this program. This is exactly the situation we find ourselves in with the cleaning-up after reengineering effort.

Figure 11.1
Strategies for Co-optation of Middle Managers

• Evoking a Crisis Mode
• Transferring Information
• Providing Advantages
• Promoting Challenges and Responsibilitiesz

STRATEGIES FOR CO-OPTATION

The dictionary defines co-optation as taking into a group by means of absorption or assimilation. The origin of the verb is the Latin verb to choose.[10] Therefore, co-opting middle managers should be an act that allows them to *choose* to be an active part of the cleaning-up program. The co-optation should be carried out by the champion, with the full support from senior management.[11] The strategies for co-optation may be divided into four categories summarized in Figure 11.1.

Evoking a Crisis Mode

The first strategy for co-optation of middle managers is the action by which the champion evokes a crisis mode. Middle managers must be aware of the fact that cleaning-up after reengineering is a vital activity at this time, and that restoration of balance is crucial to the continued well-being of the corporation.

Moreover, middle managers must be made cognizant of the fact that failure to clean up will result in the permanency of the damage and its possible ramifications into other parts of the organization. People in organizations tend to react and to cooperate in radical programs when they believe that a crisis is upon the organization, and that their support and actions are critical. Middle managers are no exception. They will co-opt, cooperate, and actively support the cleaning-up program when they perceive the situation as grave and critical in the life of the organization.

Transferring Information

As part of the crisis mode, and for the general edification of middle managers, the champion should transfer to these managers information regarding the forthcoming cleaning-up program, its objectives, and its mode of operation.

The more middle managers know about the program, the more they will actively cooperate. Information includes the statements that the cleaning-up program will replace fear with planning, tension with a climate of stability, and uncertainty with a program designed to reenergize the organization on the road to balanced growth.

In addition, the information transferred to middle managers includes their role in the program, from assessment of the damage to devising ways to neutralize and solve these problematic situations. The criticality of their role in getting the program done should be consistently emphasized. Also, if possible, a blueprint for action in the various units that have been damaged and are slated for change should be given to middle managers. Clearly, their participation in setting up the cleaning-up program should be encouraged.

Providing Advantages

"What's in it for me?" is the perennial question that organization members routinely ask when called upon to partake in unusual endeavors. In the case of middle managers the champion's co-optation strategy should clarify the advantages that will accrue to middle managers who participate in the cleaning-up program.

For example, middle managers should be advised that they will have a central role in shaping the program for cleaning-up and restoring stability. By doing so, they will have the advantage of weaving their needs and addressing their concerns into the framework of changes envisioned by the champion. In essence, the mere knowledge they are receiving and the information provided them *prior* to the change program are already tremendous advantages. It becomes a situation where they *cannot afford not to* partake in this endeavor. The champion must underline and emphasize the advantages, and let the middle managers "mull them over" and make their own decisions.[12]

Promoting Challenges and Responsibilities

Finally, middle managers should become aware of the challenges involved with this program of cleaning-up and restoring of balance. This should be done in conjunction with an array of responsibilities that are to be assigned by the champion to middle managers. Responsibilities include their normal skills and organizational functions, plus other tasks and special skills they would need to accomplish their job in the cleaning-up program. Middle managers are responsible for the diffusion of the message that cleaning-up operations are under way. They are charged with the propagation of this message by all means of communications that are open to them.

Second, middle managers are responsible for coordination and linkage among units and functions in the corporation. Middle managers are the cornerstone of the *systemic approach* to cleaning-up and restoring of balance. They act as a liaison among units, thus ensuring the integrity of the corporation as a system. Their actions protect against biases that create preferences of units or processes—at the expense of the corporation.

Furthermore, they are the glue that holds together the fragments of reengineering debris, in the form of units, subunits, processes, and activities. They understand the operational minutiae of these processes and structural units, thus they are able to identify damage as well as to act upon them in a corrective mode.

But it is not enough for the champion to know and to recognize all this. The champion must advertise his or her recognition to middle managers, by building their self-esteem and their pride in their crucial role in the program ahead—thus gaining their uninhibited support and enthusiastic co-optation.

SUMMARY

Co-optation is a difficult task, particularly in the postreengineering period, when middle managers are suspicious of any new overtures from senior management, and when they tend to be skeptical, confused, uncertain, and scared.

Some middle managers may not cooperate, and choose to remain on the sidelines. This is a normal occurrence and should not be perceived by the champion as a failure to bring *all* managers to the fold. Additional effort should be expended to co-opt as many middle managers as possible and to persuade those who are "sitting on the fence" that their services are very much needed. In other cases, where middle managers are unwilling or unable to cooperate or refuse to be actively co-opted, personnel changes are recommended. The champion should work with divisional and other executives (who are cooperating in the program) to execute these personnel actions.

Overall, the co-optation activity will be vastly successful when the co-opted middle managers are well informed and highly motivated.

NOTES

1. E. Geisler, "Middle Managers as Internal Corporate Entrepreneurs: An Unfolding Agenda," *Interfaces*, 23(6) 1993, p. 55.
2. Peter Drucker, "The Coming of the New Organization," *Harvard Business Review*, January-February, 1988, pp. 45-53.
3. For example, J. Mahoney, "The Adoption of the Multidivisional Form of Organization: A Contingency Model," *Journal of Management Studies*, 29(1), 1992, pp. 49-72.
4. Francis Joseph Aguilar, *General Managers in Action: Policies and Strategies* (New York: Oxford University Press, 1992).
5. Beginning with this chapter and for the remainder of the book I use the terms "general manager" and "middle manager" interchangeably, although some authors have pointed out some operational and hierarchical differences between the terms.
6. Aguilar, *op. cit.,* p. 12.
7. See, for example, L. Fulop, "Middle Managers: Victims or Vanguards of the Entrepreneurial Movement," *Journal of Management Studies*, 28(1), 1991, pp. 25-44. In this article Fulop emphasizes the professional as well as administrative skills of middle managers. She concludes that their role is critical yet not fully recognized by corporations.
8. Illustrative studies include Paul Nutt, "Strategic Decisions Made by Top Executives and Middle Managers with Data and Process Dominant Styles," *Journal of Management Studies*, 27(2), 1990, pp. 173-194; and F. Westley, "Middle Managers and Strategy. Microdynamics of Inclusion," *Strategic Management Journal*, 11(5), 1990, pp. 337-351.
9. S. Floyd and W. Woolridge, "Middle Management Involvement in Strategy and its Association with Strategic Type: A Research Note," *Strategic Management Journal*, 13(3), 1992, pp. 153-167.
10. Webster's New Collegiate Dictionary (Springfield, MA: Merriam Co., 1977).
11. At this point the champion has the leadership position and the authority to enter into contacts with middle managers. The champion now enjoys the full support of the senior executive (CEO) of the company.
12. M. Brousrine and Y. Guerrier, *Surviving As a Middle Manager* (London: Croom Helm, 1983).

12

ESTABLISHING RESOURCES

A fundamental action in commencing a change process is to establish the resources necessary for the process to succeed. A recurrent problem encountered in many organizations that are promoting change programs is downplaying the need for adequate resources. There is a feeling among senior executives that a change program, once planned (by internal people or external consultants), will be executed on a shoestring. This notion is well illustrated in the case of the establishment of information technology systems.

THE EXAMPLE OF INFORMATION TECHNOLOGY

A large midwestern bank was a participant in a study which I conducted in the early 1990s on the link between strategic management and the management of information technology in the service industry.[1] The bank had installed a new information system at a cost of millions of dollars. In my interviews with the executive vice-president in charge of this project, it became apparent that a gross misjudgment had occurred. The project team had assessed the total cost for the information technology at about $10 million, including in this projection both the hardware and software.

However, the project team left out of their computations the costs of other components of the implementation, such as adaptation of the software to the bank's environment, training, maintenance of the software, and updating the system. When these costs were finally added to the project, the total cost had more than doubled and had produced an unpleasant response from the CEO and the bank's management committee.

In the postproject analyses, the bank's personnel arrived at the correct conclusion that there were two basic elements of costing such a project that they had overlooked: (1) the life cycle approach to resources allocation, and (2) the systemic approach to resources allocation. These elements are also the building blocks of the allocation of resources for a change program such as cleaning-up after reengineering.

LIFE CYCLE APPROACH

A change program is a long-term project, with effects that linger in the corporation long after the change agents have completed their tasks. In the case of the cleaning-up after a reengineering program, the life cycle approach means that the program extends beyond the application of change, into the adaptation stage which includes training and additional minor adaptations to the changes introduced.

In his excellent book on change, Paul Nutt conceived a stage model of planned change.[2] In this model there are five stages: (1) formulation, (2) concept development, (3) detailing, (4) evaluation, and (5) implementation. The detailing stage includes techniques such as PERT diagrams to assess the time and cost resources necessary for the planned change.[3]

Clearly, the resources thus computed must take into account the entire life cycle of the change program, from its initiation to its conclusion. This includes adaptation and training.

Adaptation: Examples from Manufacturing

The concept is clear: The life cycle of any change implementation includes the process of adaptation of people and organizational units to the change. This means time and financial resources expended with the objective of getting accustomed to the change and learning how to live with it—successfully!

An excellent example is the introduction of production automation technology and information technology into manufacturing companies. In the period 1970-1990 such introductions were quite common and a series of studies documented what happened. Adoption of new technologies, such as flexible manufacturing systems, had posed long-term difficulties of adaptation, learning, and customization: for example, Belz Gold's studies in the steel industry;[4] E. Von Hippel's studies in the equipment making industry;[5] and a series of studies by Harvard University researchers led by R. Jaikumar in various manufacturing industries.[6] All these studies have found that any program of change (in these cases technological changes) requires extended periods of adjustment, adaptation, and a long learning curve.

In the case of organizational changes, such as the program of cleaning-up after reengineering, the adaptation period may be as long and perhaps even longer. Therefore, when resources are allocated to the change program, senior management must appreciate the entire life of the change program—until all the changes have been incorporated into the organization.[7]

Stages of the Life Cycle

Essentially, there are three basic stages of the implementation life cycle of a change program: (1) adoption, (2) adaptation, (3) maintenance and updating.

The *adoption* stage includes the actual change implementation, as I describe it in the next chapter. When changes are made in selected units and processes of the corporation, they are forced upon the people and the structural units, even when there is participation on the part of the employees and management. These changes now need to be *incorporated* into the structure and processes, some to the extent that they replace structural elements and part or whole of the work processes.

Yet incorporation is only the first step in a long and difficult procedure aimed at making the adoption of the change a successful endeavor. The resources to be expended here are usually capital intensive (when the change involves equipment), or are massive expenditures on "getting the change on board." This means that the adoption stage incurs the first outpouring of resources to make the change happen.

One example in the medical field is the introduction of computerized axial tomography (CAT) scanners into two large hospitals that we were studying in early 1996. The hospitals allocated resources for the adoption of the scanners several years earlier, including resources for training physicians and technicians. One hospital had stopped at this step, and did not allocate any funding for adaptation and maintenance. The second hospital considered the entire life cycle of the change.

The *adaptation* stage of the change process in the case of the CAT scanners included linkage of the scanners to other systems in the hospital. This linkage was composed of on-line data transfer and analysis and the education of other units and functions in the hospital as to the role of the scanner in clinical health care delivery.

In the first hospital no provisions were accounted for this stage. The hospital director was confronted with a series of "crises" of adapting the CAT scanners to the routine of the hospital. In our interviews, he commented: "I thought this was a type of innovation technology that you plug-in, have your people go through some training, and you're on. I was wrong; it was a hell of an experience, nothing worked the way it was supposed to." These statements are not an unusual reaction to technological innovation, but they are also encountered in other types of change programs.

In the case of a large chemicals supply company, the billing system had been changed over a period of two weeks. The change involved the elimination of some paperwork in charging customers for shipments. In addition, performance criteria for the order-taking and shipping department had been modified to accommodate these changes. There were no provisions made for the adaptation of the new billing system with other processes in the order and shipping units.

Hence, when the changes accrued as performance measures, both units went on the defensive, creating havoc by instituting a monstrous web of paperwork to guarantee their performance appraisal. This was simply adaptation "on the spot," without the benefit of overall planning and a systemic outlook.

The *maintenance and updating* stage in the life cycle is a longer term view of the change process. As we evaluate the outcomes of the change process, updating and various correction activities may be required. The idea is to make sure that monitoring the change does not cease with the adoption or adaptation stages.

Maintenance and updating are not limited to change programs that emphasize technological or capital expenditures. Corrective action and updating are essential also in changes of work processes, even without technical change.

A case in point is a cruise line which had modified the reporting of customer complaints. The new system had changes in the definitions of complaints, their degree of severity, and their resolution. Senior management neglected to follow up and to "maintain and update" the new system. Monitoring of the system was considered part of the accounting function, which did not waste any time in relegating it to an activity that "we'll do it tomorrow—if we get to it."

Passengers kept complaining until several lawsuits had been filed, and a nationwide television program had picked up the seemingly pitiful condition of the cruise line. Sales dropped, travel agents cancelled reservations, and the order of the day at corporate headquarters was to save the company from disaster.

Lack of monitoring may create a situation similar to what I just described, where functions and activities fall "between the chairs." Lines of responsibility are unclear, and signals get mixed.[8]

The main lesson to senior management is to assure the allocation of resources for the entire life cycle of the change program. In the case of cleaning up after reengineering, it is not enough to simply create and implement the program. It is necessary to allocate resources (time, money, and people) to the entire life cycle, including monitoring and maintenance down the line.

SYSTEMIC APPROACH

The basic idea behind bringing up the issue of systems is that senior management must allocate resources for the cleaning-up program with an eye on its ramifications throughout the corporation. Every change program creates aftershocks and waves that extend to other parts of the corporation, regardless of whether they were participants in the change program.[9]

Thus, when we institute the cleaning-up, program resources must be allocated and targeted to effectively handle any such side effects on other units in the corporate system. Such allocation of resources should be closely linked to a subprogram of evaluation of the outcomes from the cleaning-up program. Based on the evaluation, resources will then be deployed to deal with any damage or unplanned changes—*anywhere in the corporation.*

A systemic approach does not necessarily imply additional resources that would make the whole program untenable and too costly. Far from it, the systemic perspective is based on the premise that early detection and planned intervention will be adequate prevention of major (and costly) events which might be caused by the cleaning-up program.

In essence, the systemic approach is a reminder to senior management that cleaning-up after reengineering, by virtue of its being a curative measure, still requires awareness of what might happen when change is implemented. Even programs that are designed to "make things right" are in themselves interventions in the organization, so they should be carefully executed, tightly monitored, and any side effects they cause should be addressed. For this, resources must be allocated and planned.[10]

HOW MUCH IS ENOUGH?

Now that I have detailed where resources should be allocated and at which stages they should be targeted, the question is: How many and what types of resources are enough to carry out an acceptable program of cleaning-up after reengineering?

Clearly the answer depends on the individual corporation, its needs, its condition, and the amount of damage sustained. The champion and leader would be able to ascertain the resources needed to accomplish the program. My discussion will be limited to an overall appraisal of standard resources that might be needed.

If the champion decides to *outsource* the program, the cost of the program would depend on the consultants hired, and the gravity of the situation they encounter.

If, however, the champion opts for an *internal* project, the resources are roughly of three types: (1) time, (2) people, and (3) skills.

Time

A program of cleaning-up after reengineering, in its immediate stages of adoption and adaptation, normally will take 6-12 months. Other downstream stages would extend beyond this time horizon. All depends on the individual company and its characteristics.

People

The champion must gather a project team of managers who are able to analyze the condition of corporate units and processes, and to recommend—as well as execute—corrective measures.

Based on my previous description of the kinds of damage that a corporation may sustain from reengineering, the team assembled by the champion must have managers from various specialties and functions of the corporation. It is recommended that a mix of insiders and outsiders be used in the composition of the team. Insiders provide legitimacy and quick learning of the situation at hand based on sharing culture and experience. Outsiders provide a measure of objectivity and the experiences and lessons from other corporations. The ideal size of the team is a compact unit of 6-12 individuals, with adequate clerical and administrative support.

In a large company in the consumer products industry, we encountered a cleaning-up team of six highly proficient managers. Under the direction of a former vice-president of marketing, the team was considered to be "lean and mean," yet the team members were able to form a "supportive environment" in which units and people in the corporation had *trust*, leading to a good measure of cooperation between the units and the team.

Skills

There are two categories of skills that members of the project team must possess: people skills and professionalism.

People skills is a term that has become quite a cliché. Here I am using it in the generic sense, meaning the ability to create and sustain interventions. This means that some, if not all, of the project team members must be able to interact with other employees and corporate managers to exchange information and to assist and consult with them.

By no means am I advocating "leadership tests" or other such techniques to identify people-oriented personalities. My argument is much simpler and more prosaic. The champion should select the members of the team with an eye on their ability to interact with coworkers. They don't have to be psychologists. But they cannot be individuals who are intensely disliked in the corporation, or who have been isolated and perhaps on the verge of being terminated.

The project team should not be a haven for malcontents or people that the corporation wants to discard or to move somewhere else—"where they can do the least harm." As we know from experience, managers tend to hold back their best people, and to assign to projects their second- and third-rate people.[11]

The champion's job is to see to it that first-rate people are assigned to the program. As a good project manager, the champion should ask, trade, cajole, insist, threaten, advertise, embellish—do all that is necessary. With all of the above, the champion must always use the clout and the support from the CEO as an ultimate tool to gain the best possible team.

Professionalism can be defined here as the knowledge and expertise that the team members have in the various functions and activities of the corporation.

In one example, a large bank was instituting a change program and had assembled a team to implement the program and oversee it. All but one of the members of the team were accountants from one division of the bank. They lacked the breadth of professional understanding of the various banking functions and activities. Needless to say, the program failed.

Breadth of expertise allows the team to perform in a corporate and systemic manner. If highly specialized expertise is needed, it can be imported. The members of the team must be able to grasp the totality of what the individual unit and the corporation do, and to be able to ask the right questions. They must be able to know when they need other specialized expertise, and where they can get it. A team composed of only or mainly economists, or lawyers, or accountants, or engineers, is bound to fail. The secret is a mix, a variety of professional experts working together, and cognizant of their value to the team, to the champion, and to the future of the corporation.

NOTES

1.   Some of the findings have been reported in E. Geisler and A. Rubenstein, "The Role of Information Technology in the Operating Effectiveness of Service Sector Firms," in David Bowen and Richard Chase (eds.), *Service Management Effectiveness* (San Francisco: Jossey-Bass, 1990).

2.   Paul C. Nutt, *Managing Planned Change* (New York: MacMillan, 1992).

3.   *Ibid.*, pp. 383-390.

4.   Bela Gold (ed.), *Technological Change: Economic, Management and Environment* (New York: Pergamon Press, 1975).

5.   E. Von Hippel, "Transferring Process Equipment Innovations from User Innovations to Equipment Manufacturing Firms," *R&D Management*, 8(1), 1977, pp. 13-22.

6.   R. Jaikumar, *Flexible Manufacturing Systems: A Managerial Perspective* (Boston: Harvard Business School, Division of Research, January 1984).

7.   For example, in a study of the adoption of software technology, it was found that when managers support the adoption process "before, during and after the implementation" the adoption process is more successful. See E. Geisler and A. Rubenstein, "The Successful Implementation of Applications Software in New Production Systems," *Interfaces*, 17(3), 1987, pp. 18-24.

8.   There is a rich literature on this and related topics. Some examples are R. Grant, "A Resource-Based Perspective of Competitive Advantage," *California Management Review*, 33, 1991, pp. 114-135; M. Best, *The New Industrial Competition* (Cambridge, MA: Harvard University Press, 1990); and J. R. Ernshoff, *Managerial Breakthroughs: Action Techniques for Strategic Change* (New York: AMA-AMACOM, 1980.

9.   An excellent illustration can be found in D. G. Fryback, D. H. Gustafson, and D. E. Detmer, "Local Priorities for Allocation of Resources: Comparison with the IMU," *Inquiry*, 15, 1978, pp. 265-274.

10.   A good example for further reading is E. S. Quade and W. I. Boucher (eds.), *System Analysis and Policy Planning* (New York: Elsevier Publications, 1968).

11.   The literature on project management has many descriptions of this phenomenon. For example, A. Shtub, J. Bard, and S. Globerson, *Project Management: Engineering, Technology and Implementation* (Englewood Cliffs, NJ: Prentice-Hall, 1994).

13

INTRODUCING LOCALIZED CHANGES

This chapter is the heart of the application of the program to the clean up after reengineering. It describes the actual activities and actions that are needed to implement the cleaning-up effort. The chapter focuses on localized changes as the means to bring the corporation from uncertainty to stability. Finally, this chapter also describes the ways by which the cleaned-up corporation can proceed to reinvent itself.

This chapter and the program I describe here are not just another recipe for change. It is a program specifically designed to intervene in those parts of the organization where such intervention is most beneficial and where it can assist in the move toward balance, stability, and reinvention.

In writing this and the following chapter, I was doubly concerned with utilizing the current knowledge in organizational change research, but in a manner that adopts this knowledge to the particular circumstances of the cleaning-up program.

WHY LOCALIZED CHANGES?

The changes to be introduced in the cleaning-up program will be primarily of a strategic mode and with a systems approach, as described in Figure 7.2. The scenario that emerges calls for broad interventions throughout the corporation, but these are still targeted at specific units and processes that were negatively affected by reengineering.

The use of broad interventions does not preclude the inclusion of other scenarios in the cleaning-up program. In fact, scenario B (limited broad interventions) and scenario C (focused intervention) are also in the portfolio of changes in the cleaning-up program.

The issue of localization of the changes is essential for the clarification of the program of cleaning-up. Contrary to reengineering—which relies on *total* redesign and redeployment of resources—the cleaning-up program is composed of changes that are well targeted, yet with a shared purpose of recuperation, healing, balancing, and reinvention. Therefore, the objective of the cleaning-up program is to achieve a systemic recovery of the organization via a concerted set of interventions in critical parts of the organization—with a dedicated group of parameters, subjugated to an overall purpose. As Figure 7.1 clearly exposes them, the characteristics of the process of cleaning-up include well-defined objectives and a "clinical approach," which emphasizes *repair* activities rather than substantial redesign and restructuring.

In an excellent collection of essays, James March and Roger Weissinger-Baylor introduced in 1986 the perspective of the "garbage-can" models of organizational decision making in the context of military decision situations.[1] In this volume, Philip Bromley discussed some issues in the planning activity in large organizations.[2] He reinforces my advocacy in this book of a systemic approach to localized changes, as elements of a well-coordinated effort at stabilization. Bromley commented:

In addition, the stability in a system lies in the organization not in the individuals. . . . That is, to understand the operations of the macroplanning system, we should be able to build on the units that participate rather than the individuals within these units. Of course, we address average behavior while recognizing that idiosyncratic behavior does occur.[3]

The garbage-can model proposed by these and other scholars combines the following building blocks for decision making in organizations: (1) choice situations, (2) participants (organizational units), (3) problems, and (4) solutions. This model, as was defined by Michael Cohen *et al.* in 1972,[4] and again by J. March and J. Olsen,[5] suggests that the four elements listed above "are independent, exogenous streams flowing through a system."[6] Also "they are linked in a manner determined by their arrival and departure times and any structural constraints on the access of problems, solutions and decision makers to choice opportunities."[7]

In essence, this model of action in organizations proposes that situations in complex organizations are dealt with in accordance with their timing and the load of problems and resources that are allocated to them at a given point in time. Rather than be subjected to a strict regimen of orderly structure, complex organizations may be more effective in resolving problems and acting upon required choices through a myriad of parameters such as timing, interconnection of problems, or belief structure and existing normative duties.

The localized changes in the cleaning-up program follow a pattern which may be captured by a garbage-can model of organizational action. The choices made and and changes implemented are not deterministically ordered by a unified action structure, rather they are designed to provide the best possible effort that meets the requirements of the unit or process affected by reengineering. One localized change may differ from another localized change, while the systemic effect on neighboring units and the value chain are strictly monitored. Here, as well, solutions to dislocations in the value chain may differ from unit to unit.[8]

CATEGORIES OF LOCALIZED CHANGES

The categories of localized changes are the intersection between the possible approaches to cleaning up (described in Figure 7.2) and the targets of the program (which were described in Chapter 10). The targets are people, structural units, and processes. Figure 13.1 summarizes the approaches and the targets.

Figure 13.1
Categories of Localized Changes

	Possible Approaches	
Targets of Cleaning-up Program	Scenario C: Focused Intervention	Scenario D: Broad Intervention
1. **People** •Morale •Motivation •Cost •Decline in productivity	C1	D1
2. **Structural Units** •Performance •Systemic breakdown •Threats to competition	C2	D2
3. **Processes** •Value-chain integrity •Maintenance of efficiency	C3	D3

Figure 13.1 has produced six possible sets of interventions, C1-C3, and D1-D3. In the figure I have utilized only those scenarios from Figure 7.2 that describe systemic activities, because they are the more complex and more comprehensive. Also, the sets of interventions generated by Figure 13.1 are essentially a road map or a blueprint to the program of cleaning-up after reengineering. In fact, they provide a plan of action which is detailed down to the level of activities and their operationalization.

Scenarios C1 and D1: Cleaning-Up Damage to People

Scenarios C1 and D1 are lumped together because they are quite similar, in that they target the system while they differ only in being either "surgical" or "strategic." Yet their similarities are stronger than their differences.

In the action on people, the scenarios include those changes that are aimed at morale, motivation, and cost of human resources. Figure 13.2 shows the types of changes/interventions for the *people* target.

The changes shown in Figure 13.2 are subprograms designed to correct and repair the damage done to people. The champion/leader and his or her team have four such subprograms to which I have given descriptive titles. Each subprogram is essentially a set of activities aimed at restoring balance through a concerted impact on a specific type of damage.[9]

Figure 13.2
Types of Changes/interventions Aimed at Damage to People

Damage to People	Scenarios C1 and D1: Focused and Broad Interventions (Subprograms for Change)
•Decline in Morale	•Boosting Confidence
•Decline in Motivation	•Supportive Environment
•Cost of Human Resources	•Allowing Defensive Mechanisms
•Decline in Productivity	•Control and Compensation

Boosting Confidence

The German philosopher Friedrich Wilhelm Nietzsche's aphorism declared "that which does not kill me makes me stronger." This is not the case in the situation in which damage has been inflicted by reengineering to the human side of the corporation. In fact, to paraphrase Nietzsche: In the case of the damage from reengineering, that which does not kill you now, will severely weaken you and possibly kill you later.

The champion/leader in charge of the cleaning-up program can embark on a program that relies on the change scenarios listed in Figure 13.2. These scenarios need not be applied sequentially but their application, *as a set*, is likely to achieve a magnified rate of success.

Boosting confidence is the first scenario that is aimed at the phenomenon of decline in morale. What does it mean to boost confidence?

In an interesting article in the *Harvard Business Review*, the veteran organization psychologist Karl Weick compared the effort to fight forest fires with fighting crises in today's organizations.[10] Weick proposes that fires should be fought with fires—in the forest as well as in organizations. He also advocates a larger measure of improvization and the allowance of a flexible structure in small work groups.

In essence, boosting confidence is the antidote to sagging morale. It is similar to fighting fire with fire. The basic principle is to counteract the indications that show decline in morale and motivation. As Figure 10.1 has shown, there are several objective and subjective indicators for this decline. They all boil down to people in the organization showing varying degrees of unhappiness, dissatisfaction, and a sense of alienation.

Boosting confidence is targeted specifically at the decline in morale. It is a mini-program of activities on the part of the champion/leader and the cleaning-up team to reverse the decline and to recharge the organization. This they do in three main tactical approaches: (1) regrouping, (2) reformulating objectives, and (3) redefining identity.

Regrouping is the action taken by the cleaning-up team to bring to the affected personnel a renewed sense of unit pride and organizational spirit. Regrouping means approaching the people in the units affected, and reintroducing them to the tenets of the spirit of the "new" organization and the redesigned corporation. It is primarily the advocacy (in pronouncements as well as directives, seminars, and other means of diffusion of ideas) of the emergence of a redesigned corporation and the adherence of the remaining personnel to its new focus. It is a call to regroup *as a unit*, to regain confidence and pride in the new organization. It is the pride of rebuilding, of starting almost anew, of joining a winning combination of a more powerful and certainly more experienced group of people. Regrouping is the call to arms in a reestablished environment that is designed to win and to excel.

A marvelous example of lack of regrouping is the case of Philips Electronics, the giant manufacturing company in the Netherlands, as told by Paul Strebel.[11] The case revolved, according to Strebel, on the inability of Philips' managers in the late 1980s to institute widespread corporate change due to lack of support from Philips' employees. Strebel suggests that the company did not revise nor articulate what he calls "personal compacts," which are agreements or "organizational contracts" between corporations and their employees.

To a large extent, regrouping is the revision of the contract between the redesigned company and employer, leading to a boost in trust, confidence, and hence, subsequently, commitment. If I use Strebel's terms, regrouping involves the redefinition of the contract with the employees. It now becomes clear that the corporation wishes the remaining employees to join forces with it in order to marshall the challenges ahead. Regrouping calls for "partnership" under a new arrangement of a redesigned and "meaner" company and its workforce. The company is more precise as to what it desires from its employees. It is up to the champion/leader and the cleaning-up team to instill these new principles and the resounding call to arms for a renewed company and a renewed workforce.

Reformulating objectives is the second type of activity that the cleaning-up team should exercise. It is aimed at reversing the effects of lower morale by making it crystal clear to affected employees that the objectives of the company, their own unit, and what is expected of them have changed. This is the ultimate rewriting of the organizational contract between employees and the corporation.

The corporate as well as unit objectives are reformulated so that input from employees can be added to them. After establishing that the challenges ahead are a joint effort between the organization and its workforce (the outcome of "regrouping"), the cleaning-up team now must establish the parameters of this new reality by reformulating objectives, so that employees can relate to the new objectives, thus also being able to tailor their needs, goals, challenges, and aspirations to where the corporation is heading. Reformulation of objectives means a much stronger degree of understanding of what the change program was about and the sincere will of the company to reenergize itself with the *help, support,* and *understanding* of its workforce.

How is all this done? Primarily by carefully phrased documents, meetings with small groups of employees and their informal (as well as formal) leaders and managers. It is an appeal, in a concerted manner, to both the reasoning of the employees and to their emotions.

The idea is to diffuse, propagate, and clearly establish a message that the new objectives are inclusive of the desires of the workforce, and that employees (and their managers) are a deliberate and essential partner in the new enterprise. The emphasis is on "new," "partnership," and "welcome" to the redesigned organization.

The case of the acquisition of Legent by Computer Associates is an example of actions designed to bring about a message of positive changes. When Charles Wang, CEO of Computer Associates (a $4 billion systems and network management company), acquired Legent in 1995 for $1.7 billion, the almost 2,000 employees of Legent feared that the merger/acquisition would mean a leaner company with many pink-slips distributed indiscriminantly.[12] Although Computer Associates continually reassured its contingent of new Legent employees, almost 1,800 employees (about 90%) had either been dismissed or voluntarily left the new company. The message, however, did work on those who remained and they wholeheartedly joined the renewed corporation.

In the case of the company after reengineering, the message is similar to that given the acquired company's personnel. It must be a message of hope, revitalization, and improved confidence. It is also a message of *inclusion* and of partnership. Many of Legent's employees and managers who chose to leave did so because they failed to listen to the message or because the message itself was not resounding nor convincing enough.

Therefore, the champion/leader must reiterate the message of the regrouping and reformulation of objectives through continuous appeals to the workforce. Computer Associates convened sales managers from Legent to a Chicago hotel to a seminar/conference for the delivery of its message. This is not enough. A one-day conference with the "bigwigs" of senior management delivering exciting speeches is not the way to reach employees who are experiencing declined morale and a sense of alienation. The cleaning-up team must provide the message in a continuous, repetitive, and resounding manner, by using all forms of diffusion and communication.

Redefining identity is the third and, to some extent, the most potent of the three main tactical approaches. The redefinition of identity means that the redesigned company is changing its appeal by announcing a cultural awakening, or a change in the corporate identity—particularly with its relationship to its workforce.

The company had undergone reengineering, redesign, and downsizing. These experiences clearly left a taste of uneasiness in the workforce, as well as the workers' perception of the company and its senior management as "greedy," "insensitive," and "uncaring." These attributes must be revised, so that in the minds of the workers the organization is once again (or even perhaps for the first time), a worker-oriented corporation. Again, as in the reformulating of objectives, the principle is one of inclusion, of embracing employees as equally crucial partners. It is a change in the platform of the culture of the corporation. As the corporate president of a midwestern financial company told me when we reviewed his corporation's cleaning-up formula:

We are still a mighty competitive outfit, but we are more open towards our people. I haven't changed the *way* I do business, but I did change the way I manage my employees. I give them more value and more say, and, what I think you'll find fascinating, I make sure that they know this. And I do it over and over, and all my managers are part of the deal. It's not enough to tell or act in some new way—you must publicize it as much as humanly possible in your company.

Redefining identity is an internal action that does not necessarily reflect on the image that the company wishes to create in its external environment. However, in at least two companies with whom I have consulted, this action was made privy to outsiders, in an effort do announce the change in the company's approach to prospective employees and other stakeholders.

Altogether redefining the identity is clearly the means by which a new cultural reality is heralded by the cleaning-up team. It is done systemically throughout the corporation, with an emphasis on those units and people who were affected by the reengineering program.

Supportive Environment

Supportive environment is the second scenario (subprogram for change) that is specifically designed to counteract the decline in motivation. Figure 10.1 lists among the indicators used in assessing motivation the rate of willingness to participate in tasks, and rates of verbal and physical outbursts. Motivation is a complex concept, but put simply, its decline denotes a situation in which workers are less likely to volunteer, to participate, and to produce effectively. It is a symptom of employees who tend to increase their alienation from corporate challenges and to increase the rate of introvertness.

A supportive environment is principally an attempt by the cleaning-up team to plan a more supportive climate. This is done through actual activities and policies directed at the improved welfare of the workforce. The theme is quite simple: "This is a redesigned company with fewer employees and a more responsive workforce. Therefore, additional resources and a large measure of goodwill will be expended to make this new lean and mean corporation more responsive, accommodating, and friendly to its workforce."

Illustrations of this approach can be found in several companies that are consistently singled out as "worker-friendly." Their practices may be used as operational examples to the cleaning-up team which plans a new and supportive environment.

For example, Fel-Pro is a privately held company located in Skokie, Illinois. Fel-Pro manufactures sealants and lubricants for the automotive industry. Its sales approached $400 million in 1995. The company is well known for its elaborate system of comforts for its employees, including a day-care center, flexible times, profit-sharing policies, and educational scholarships for children of its employees.[13]

The principle behind the scenario of the supportive environment is that improvement in motivation means increased commitment on the part of the employees. This also means more trust and willingness to sacrifice for the company. However, this is a two-way street. Commitment and motivation from the workforce are usually a response to the same attributes dispersed by corporate management. Hence, the champion/leader and the cleaning-up team must offer some concrete and tangible programs of corporate support. After all, the workforce that has remained after the upheaval of reengineering is supposedly the best and the most skilled (as well as resilient) of the employees and managers. Therefore they deserve improved treatment—also as the means to reverse the psychological damage of downsizing and reengineering.

The changes in the working environment do not have to equal those practiced by Fel-Pro. But it is essential that tangible actions are put in place and that employees are not only aware of them but have had the opportunity to experience them. This is meant to avoid the mere semblance of change or the installation of some changes for a very short period of time. This supportive environment is clearly a long-term program. It may include: (1) assistance to working mothers, such as a day-care facility and some flexible work times; (2) "listening devices" such as an employee-relations officer who is proactive and assists employees who need help in the matters of substance abuse, mental health, and family problems (many employees are candidates for such difficulties, owing to pressures form the downsizing and the reengineering effort); (3) support to employees and managers in the form of better educational and training prospects.

All of the above need to be part of a concise policy that should be advertised broadly in the company and meticulously practiced to ensure continuity and credibility. Also, the supportive environment is a multistage program, in that the installation of the employee assistance projects should be bolstered by changes in the environment for managers. The climate for managers' input should be emphasized as a receptive environment. Motivated employees are not as effective as when they are led by motivated managers.

In summary, the supportive environment is a combination of programs and structures that stimulate employee participation and commitment by demonstrating support for what employees and managers find to be problems in need of solutions. Each company needs to assess its own set of solutions that would be appropriate for its workforce. What I have illustrated in this chapter is a basic set of potential actions, almost generic in kind. It is up to the individual company to create its own basket of "goodies" that would qualify as items that both boost confidence and foster a supportive environment. Again, the key ingredient in a successful implementation of this portion of the cleaning-up program is a widespread diffusion of the news that this is being done—throughout the company.

Allowing Defensive Mechanisms

One of the more problematic effects of reengineering that tends to continue over a long period of time is the rise in the cost of human resources. To clean up after this effect, I recommend the installation of defensive mechanisms for middle managers.

The cost of human resources tends to surge because middle managers are usually eager to protect themselves, their units, and their turf, by creating slack resources. They manipulate positions, tasks, and the allocation of people so that the work is being done by more people than necessary and in such a way that skills are being imported into their units as a measure of protection of turf.

Resistance to the incorporation of just in time in Japanese companies outside Japan is an excellent example of worker and managerial behavior that is similar to the defensive mechanism approach.

In a study of a Japanese manufacturing company in the United Kingdom of about 1,000 workers, Rick Delbridge documented several deeds of "misbehavior" of employees who would not accept the rigid implementation of Japanese rules and procedures.[14] Delbridge particularly lists symbolic distancing, refusal to engage in discretionary activities, and avoiding overtime. By targeting overt behavior patterns, Delbridge overlooked the more subtle behavior, especially by middle managers, in which resistance takes the form of reallocation of human resources to match the general needs of the manager. This is usually in contrast with the company's needs and objectives, therefore leading to an overall rise in costs.

Types of Commitment

Before I proceed to describe such a case in a company with which I consulted, it is essential that I restate some developments in the theory and study of commitment. A study of 231 managers and 339 subordinates concluded that "managers make inferences about employees' commitment . . . that are distinct from organizational citizenship and job performance."[15] The authors also distinguished between "continuance commitment" (when employees are committed owing to such factors as tenure, seniority, and fringe-benefits) and "affective commitment" (when employees are committed because of their identification with the organization or its objectives). The authors of the study have found that affective commitment is viewed in a positive light by both managers and subordinates and that continuance commitment is viewed by them in a more negative light. They offer an explanation that the organization prefers employees who are able to leave the organization (because of low continuance commitment) but opt to stay because they have high levels of affective commitment (that is, they are emotionally committed to what the organization stands for and is trying to achieve).

What is the relation between these findings and the creation by managers of defensive mechanisms? L. M. Shore, K. Barksdale, and T. H. Shore have suggested that previous research on commitment focused on observable behavior, whereas they ocused on perceptions of managers. In the second case, managers who view employees as committed to the objectives of the company and the unit will favor these employees, at the expense of those who work because of benefits they have in the company. This phenomenon is exacerbated in the case of highly trained and professional employees. These employees receive the majority of their professional "kudos" from outside the corporation and essentially use the corporation as a "workplace" to discharge their professional activities.

Managers are now caught in the dilemma of dealing with downsizing and reengineering. The ratio of employees who are committed to the company owing to "continuance" to those who are "affective" may have shifted. In order to preserve the unit's boundaries and to continue a high level of productivity, middle managers need to rely on highly committed employees. Yet reengineering increases alienation and detracts more from the effectiveness of those employees who are not "affectively" committed. Therefore, middle managers are compelled to increase the ranks of the "affective" employees and to install boundary roles that are filled with talented employees who are *also* committed emotionally to the unit and the company.

What Can the Cleaning-Up Team Do?

Allowing defensive mechanisms means providing middle managers with at least two avenues of action. The first is to provide them with more flexibility in choosing and keeping the employees they wish to maintain in the unit. The second is to allow middle managers the staffing of what organization scientists call "boundary spanning roles." These are essentially positions that form linkages with other units.

Not only is it important to allow middle managers to increase their relations with other units, but the cleaning-up team should promote exchange of personnel among the units, and allow middle managers a voice in selecting the people who will be exchanged. This phenomenon received additional coverage in the book by R. Ashkenas *et al.*, who discussed the ways to bypass the limitations of hierarchy and turf.[16]

The cleaning-up team thus boosts the position of middle managers so that they see less need to create defensive activities. In the course of these actions the cost of human resources will be kept in check.

The Case of Chemicals Inc.

Chemicals Inc. (a pseudonym) is a large company in the Fortune 200 range. Its plants in the Midwest and West Coast had undergone severe downsizing, and its corporate organization was undergoing some form of reengineering when I visited the company to interview senior and middle managers.

Following a series of interviews, it became abundantly clear to me that some middle managers at divisional levels, and at several functional positions, had been creating defensive actions. One manager established a unit with 12 employees which he called "control and quality assessment," although a quality control apparatus already existed. The role of this unit was unclear and its mandate vague. Another created a task group of 18 professionals under the title: "Information Retrieval and Analysis." This "IRA" unit, as it was called, had as its primary objective the collection of intelligence on what the remainder of the division was doing, by generating reports of trends, logistical flows, and possible future scenarios. A third manager hired six employees who had been downsized, as part-time consultants, reporting directly to him.

All of these actions at Chemicals Inc. led me to recommend that the corporation make use of the resources, rather than abruptly and indiscriminantly order the managers to dismantle the units.

Control and Compensation

This scenario is aimed at the decline in productivity that plagues so many units affected by reengineering. Control is defined here as the establishment of a set of rules that would apply to all the units in the corporation, under the umbrella of increased centralization.

Why increase centralization? Simply because productivity is declining and overall control is needed to measure, monitor, assess, and compensate individual and unit productivity. Therefore, the more effective means is to concentrate the control of productivity assessment and to link compensation to productivity throughout the corporation.

The cleaning-up team is entrusted with introducing the concept of centralized control of productivity assessment, and of making it clear that compensation is linked to it. The uncertainty that follows reengineering is now replaced (in this case) by a clear and strong message of a centralized power that is in charge and is able to lead the organization through the difficult times of post-reengineering.[17]

Scenarios C2 and D2: Cleaning-Up Damage to Structure

Scenarios C2 and D2 refer to the cleaning-up changes that are aimed at repairing damage to the structure of the organization. There are three key subprograms that may be applied by the cleaning-up team. As in the previous case of damage to people, these scenarios are generic, so that individual companies may tailor their interventions in accordance with their needs and available resources. These are shown in Figure 13.3.

Reassessment of Roles and Priorities

The reassessment subprogram is aimed at repairing damage done to unit performance. Owing to the pressures of reengineering and the havoc it tends to generate, selected units find themselves with declining levels of performance.

Figure 13.3
Types of Changes/Interventions Aimed at Damage to Structure

Damage to Structure	Scenarios C2 and D2: Subprograms of Change
Unit Performance	•Reassessment of Roles & Priorities
Systemic Breakdown	•Intensifying Liaisons
Threats to Competitiveness	•Strategic Analysis

In an informal survey of 20 divisions in eight large companies across four industries I found that over 75% had experienced declines in selected unit performance. As I already observed in chapters four and six, the decline was due, among other factors, to the cumulative effects of workers' morale, as well as the effect of downsizing and uncertainty on the skills mix and the clarity of unit functioning.[18]

The most effective countermeasure in the arsenal of the cleaning-up team is a reassessment of roles and priorities. Much of what we read and hear in this regard is usually about the entire corporation, with very little said about specific units within it.

For example, Fidelity Investments of Boston has about 13% of all the mutual funds, with a total in 1995 of about $400 billion assets under management. In a story in *Business Week*, Gerald Knight of Toro Co. has suggested that Fidelity's performance has been slipping because it was not focused.[19] Although Fidelity Investment's problem is not the result of reengineering, its lack of focus is characteristic of operational units in companies that came out of reengineering. The general upheaval, shuffling of resources, severe downsizing, and loss of critical resources invariably lead to, in the very least, changes in focus, and usually to loss of focus. Senior management fails to redirect the unit's redesigned mission, role, and tasks in the reengineered corporation. The result is misdirected role and priorities.

Consumer Inc. (a pseudonym) is a Fortune 400 manufacturer of consumer products. Following ten months of intensive reengineering, downsizing, and redesign, the company was faced with two operational divisions that were experiencing continuous decline in performance. The marketing department of division A and the design department of division B had become almost paralyzed. The performance of the marketing department dropped by over 30%, and that of the design department by 50%. When we approached the department and conducted a series of in-depth interviews, we discovered that the company was facing a postreengineering trauma.

The marketing department in division A had been recently evaluated. Sales personnel received quarterly evaluations that deviated negatively from those of the previous year. The external sales force was doing well, but the internal marketing infrastructure was in a state of confusion. Positions had been widely slashed, some combined and others transferred to other functions in the division. The reengineering team did not provide the department with new guidelines, while the division's expectations dramatically increased. "We are now a lean division, let's go out there and kick" was the motto of divisional senior management. Nevertheless, the internal staff was unable to process sales orders and to rearrange itself in light of the enormous changes that had occurred in its structure.

The design department in division B had been decimated by the reengineering effort. With the introduction of computer-aided design there was a massive change in the department's personnel. In what the workers called "the Massacre of Black Monday," most of the older designers had been downsized—through early retirements, alluring separation packages, and "pink slips." What remained was a contingent of several inexperienced designers whose salaries were much lower, and who (presumably) had expertise with the new CAD system. The upshot of the situation was that these designers produced designs that ignored the basic tenets of the division's product line, requiring a much longer time frame to get the products to production and out the door.

Both departments exemplify the situation that requires reassessment of roles and priorities. After BPR, the units affected are essentially new units—with new problems and a set of new expectations as well as roles and priorities. One manager in division A succinctly said:

What are we supposed to do? We have lost our base, our support, and we are expected to keep sales up and up—with what? Jobs were just thrown up in the air and those of us who remained here had to take them, in addition to what we were already doing. This is crazy—we want direction, we got pressure and more pressure.

The cleaning-up team in these cases acts as an extension to reengineering—doing what BPR usually fails to do: redirect the unit.

Reassessing roles means that the cleaning-up team assists the unit to identify and then agree on the redesigned role of the unit in the new organization. The marketing department in division A had a new role, primarily defined as assuring continuity to the sales function while rearranging itself to accommodate this challenge. The priorities had also changed, with the department concentrating on getting its house in order, rather than a total focus on sales. The shifting of priorities determines the direction that the unit will take in the short run, and the reassessment of the role establishes the *identity* of the new (or redesigned) unit.

Cleaning-up teams work with what they have in the field. Their job is not to totally redesign the unit—rather to assist the unit to achieve its goals to establish its identity, and to reestablish its structural framework.[20]

In summary, reassessment of roles and priorities is done by a joint effort with the affected unit. An analysis of the unit's revised needs and problems is followed by the creation of a design for the new roles and priorities of the unit. Joint effort will produce a short document that outlines the roles and priorities as they had been redefined.

Finally, an important item to remember. Workers in the corporation must be able to understand where the company is heading and to identify with its objectives. This reminds us of the "affective commitment" discussed earlier in this chapter. Therefore, when the cleaning-up team reestablishes the new roles and direction of the unit, in cooperation with the unit, there must be a thorough attempt to provide the unit's employees and its managers with the opportunity to identify with the organization. The message must be clear, and it must be delivered by the cleaning-up team: the new roles, priorities, and direction must be in line with those of the company. Workers and managers also must identify with the corporation's objectives, and so must the role and direction of their units.[21]

Intensifying Liaisons

The intensifying liaisons scenario is designed to assist in repairing the damage to the corporate structure that resulted in systemic breakdown. As I described earlier, systemic breakdown usually occurs when liaison functions are diminished or even eliminated by the reengineering effort.

The cleaning-up team has the task of identifying the lack of liaison functions and to intensify these functions by establishing current positions.

How is this done? There are three basic steps. First, the cleaning-up team identifies the problem as systemic failure due to the lack or weakness of the liaison functions. Units affected by reengineering may seem to be inwardly engaged in internal actions, while neglecting any relations with other units in their value chain. This can be detected easily by a drop in exchanges, meetings, joint ventures, and other forms of communication and mutual interaction.

Clearly, the first and instinctive action would be to *resume* such communication techniques. Yet when these techniques are applied without a substantial activity that reaffirms the role of the liaison positions, the communication effort is likely to fail.[22]

The idea of *networking* the unit with other units is hardly new, but it becomes crucial when the unit seems to abandon its networking function. When several units do that, systemic breakdown is inevitable. This is similar to the entire corporation and its interaction with customers and suppliers. It is widely accepted today that successful companies indeed maintain and foster a plethora of networking/cooperative arrangements with their customers and suppliers. Many even enter into various types of cooperative arrangements with their competitors.[23]

The Case of Pharmaco Inc.

Pharmaco Inc. (a pseudonym) is a Fortune 200 company, manufacturing pharmaceuticals, with plants in five countries and a strong competitive position in a very specific type of prescription medications.

In 1995 the company contacted one of my colleagues to assist in its reengineering effort. He relayed the case, in what he described as "the dismembering of a healthy body."

Reengineering was the overall name given to a series of internal redesign of the company in the early 1990s. A major effort was directed toward the new product development (NPD) division. This unit was the key link between the corporate research laboratories and the commercial side of the corporation. NPD was responsible for pushing the compounds as they emerge from the research laboratories through initial testing, leading to the next stages in which Food and Drug Administration approval is sought by the regulatory processes department.[24]

The reengineering effort eliminated several positions in the NPD, which were in charge of liaison with the laboratories *and* regulatory processes. In addition, positions that (on the books) belonged to regulatory and were found in the NPD were quickly returned to their original "home." Some were eliminated. The main idea was to avoid duplication and to make the entire organization more efficient. Another major goal was to cut the time a compound takes from the laboratory to FDA approval process.

The problem with Pharmaco Inc. was well identified as a deterioration of liaisons, leading to systemic failure. The NPD retreated to its own boundaries. New compounds would be given to NPD only to vanish in its "black hole." Little or no feedback would be routinely given to the laboratory nor to the regulatory processes department regarding forthcoming products. From a facilitator, the unit had become a major barrier in the innovation process. The dismemberment of its "tentacles," those liaison positions that had maintained the interface with its environment, had been a major force in creating this confused and uncooperative unit.

What can the cleaning-up team do? At first, identify the liaison needs, then reinstall liaison functions, as well as intensify existing positions by giving them more authority and leeway. Most of all, the message to senior management must be that to avoid systemic failures, in some positions duplication is a key to success. Exchange of personnel in the long term between NPD and the laboratories is a must, and should be encouraged. The laboratories must keep a permanent presence in the NPD, as also must the regulatory processes department. On its part, NPD must maintain a presence in these units. Interaction should not be confined to a weekly or biweekly meeting, or perhaps exchange of reports. The company (as are most corporations) is a totally interlocked operation, where one part depends on the other.

Intensifying liaisons is a set of activities aimed at making sure that liaison positions are in place and are fully operational (regardless of initial cost).

Strategic Analysis

Finally, in the cleaning-up of damage to structure, strategic analysis is a sub-program of change that is aimed at halting or diminishing the threats to the company and competitiveness. As I have consistently reiterated, the changes implemented by the cleaning-up team are curative in nature. They are not made to redesign the company. They are meant to repair damage and, by so doing, ultimately to reinvent the corporation. This is what strategic analysis is meant to do.

In essence, when BPR is inflicted on the organization, the internal upheaval and redesign also create conditions that affect the competitiveness of the corporation. Its strategic position in the marketplace changes, as critical resources and core competencies it possessed before BPR are now dangerously changed. Although some of these changes are initially quite subtle, they nevertheless grow in importance. They become more visible as the uncertainty increases in the postreengineering period.

A State of Mind Versus Critical Analysis

In one of his books on strategy, Kenichi Ohmae, a director at McKinsey & Company in the 1980s, proposed that "successful business strategies result not from rigorous analysis but from a particular state of mind."[25] He continued to explore the attributes of such a mind, with examples from Japanese business leaders. In his view, a good strategist has drive, insight, and the ability to project into the corporation his intuitive view of where the organization should be, in a bold and decisive manner. However, the work of Christopher Bartlett and Sumanthra Ghoshal added a very strong argument regarding successful strategy of complex organization.[26] They argued that a single strategic focus is no longer sufficient, and that corporations must also possess a structure that supports competition in a global and complex marketplace. More precisely, they argued that successful corporations must have an integrated networking structure, dynamic decision making, adoptive coordination mechanisms, and unique innovation capabilities.

The central argument that I propose in this section calls for the drive of both a strategist *and* the supporting organization, so that bold and imaginative steps can be carried out in the strategic route that senior management selects. This argument is hardly new, and it matches the work on core competencies of the corporation. Yet it becomes doubly important here, because the company that emerges from BPR needs to reexamine itself and essentially to restart its strategic management process.

Therefore what is needed at this point is not a state of mind versus critical strategic analysis, but a state of mind *and* critical analysis. Thus, when the cleaning-up team examines the structure of the units affected by reengineering, it should do so with an eye to the corporation and its strategic positioning in its markets.

Some Points of Action

What can the cleaning-up team do, to provide a broad strategic analysis? With the corporation-wide authority of the champion/leader, the team should first examine the contribution of the core competencies and skills mix of affected units on the competitiveness of the team. This means to take stock of the available critical resources and competencies that make the corporation competitive.

For example, Charles F. Knight, chairman and CEO of Emerson Electric Co., with sales of over $8 billion in 1993, described his company's secrets of consistent profitability and successful strategies in the *Harvard Business Review*.[27] With 40 divisions structured into eight businesses, Emerson Electric is a leading manufacturer of electrical, electromechanical, and electronic products in a highly competitive industry. Knight places a high value on planning and careful analysis. He says:

We want proof that a division is stretching to reach its goals, and we want to see the details of the action division management believes will yield results. . . .The structure and everyday generation of Emerson embodies this basic approach: set tough targets, plan rigorously to meet them, and follow through on the plans.[28]

In a seminal article in the *Harvard Business Review*, Robert Schaeffer and Harvey Thomson argued that activity-centered improvement programs or changes fail when they are not driven by results. They claimed that results-driven changes will achieve what they call "specific measurable operational improvements within a few months."[29]

For the cleaning-up team this means that the secret to a successful intervention in a strategic mode is to take four steps:

1. *Identify the new strategy* of the company following the reengineering effort, and the role that the divisions and/or units affected play in this strategy (results/objectives oriented).

2. *Assess the core competencies* and critical resources (people, skills, equipment, knowledge, products, innovations, etc.) that the division/unit has (after the damage from reengineering).

3. *Compile* the set of *core competencies* and critical resources that the unit will *need to* accomplish its *strategic role*.

4. Finally, *compare what the unit has and what it needs*. The result of this analysis will show the gaps in the strategic role of the unit, and will serve as input to careful planning.[30]

The key to successful cleaning-up in this area is to act in a bold, innovative, and energetic manner. The champion/leader of the cleaning-up team must be able to identify with the renewed strategic direction of the company, and, if necessary, to contribute to the strategy-making process by proposing new directions or course adjustments based on his or her knowledge of the postreengineering corporation. In this way the champion/leader embodies both the mind of a strategist and the careful analysis and planning of initial resources and core competencies needed to achieve strategic results.

Scenarios C3 and D3: Cleaning-Up Damage to Processes

These are the subprograms designed to repair the damage caused to processes in the units affected by reengineering. Figure 13.4 shows the types of interventions/changes that are aimed at processes.

Reestablishing Linkages

Serious damage to value chain integrity usually occurs because of reengineering, accompanied by downsizing, redesign of key processes, and deep changes in the culture of the unit. The role of the cleaning-up team is not only to repair damage to the affected processes, but also to do so with an eye on the integrity of the value chain, so that the curative action will be more than just a Band-Aid. The repair should be able to restore the integrity of the value-chain, in addition to repairing localized damage in the processes of the unit.

What Is the Damage to Processes?

Usually, processes that have undergone steep redesign (as is the case with BPR), are downsized, rerouted, and may even have different venues of culture. This is in addition to the debilitating influence of uncertainty and the damage to the workforce described in previous sections.

Figure 13.4
Types of Changes/Interventions Aimed at Damage to Processes

Damage to Processes	Scenarios C3 and D3: Subprograms of Change
Value Chain Integrity	•Reestablishing Linkages
Maintenance of Efficiency	•Role Analysis

Specifically, the damage can be summarized as the inability of a given process to adequately interact with other processes in its value chain. This is because, although this process may now be more efficient and less costly, it may have lost its "flexibility" or ability to communicate, coordinate, and otherwise interface with other processes.

A problem with many organizations is that they measure the success of redesign by such quantitative measures as less time, less cost, less duplication, less rework, and so on. What they fail to do is to also measure the ability of the process (hence the unit) to still contribute to its value chain in an adequate manner.

To a large extent the type and severity of the damage to the process depend on the type of activities in the process that were reengineered. Not surprisingly, the less crucial the activity and the less dramatic the change, the less damage will be inflicted.

For example, the Marshall Space Flight Center in Huntsville, Alabama, is a NASA laboratory with responsibilities over some aspects of the Spacelab mission. The center streamlined the process of the Spacelab mission requirements flow, resulting in a reduction of the averaged processing time by 60%.[31]

Such improvements can hardly be classified as reengineering. Lisa Watson and Thomas Tytula described the reduction in processing time from an average of 78 days to 31 days. This allows NASA personnel more time to prepare for the mission and spend less time on paperwork.

The truism in all of this is that the more independent the process from other processes in the value chain, and the less comprehensive the change inflicted upon it, the less damage will be accrued. Reducing the amount of paper work is an efficiency intervention, but it can be viewed as a self-contained improvement. Conversely, processes that are more complex and dependent on others will be much more problematic.

The Case of "Logistics"

"Logistics" (a pseudonym) is a department in a very large manufacturing company headquartered in the midwestern United States. The company makes industrial machinery for various industrial uses. The department is charged with moving new materials to the production facilities, maintenance of inventories, and overseeing the movement of finished goods from the plants to the warehousing facilities. This is an entire chain of interlocked activities.

Following a *kaizen*-type approach to inventory control, the company also embarked on reengineering the "Logistics" department, starting with the raw materials phase of production. Inventory levels were significantly slashed, personnel reduced, and the time to the manufacturing plants was sharply cut. The company dealt with this issue as a simple efficiency round, with solutions that were typical industrial engineering/operations research improvements.

The vice-president of manufacturing in one of the company's plants described the resulting situation:

They simply cut the time it took to get materials to the plant, in a way that we do materials management. But nobody was looking at our production schedules and needs. This is unbelievable that they did what they did with total disregard to what we do here. They just wanted to make sure that the materials get here sooner and with less hassle—which is fine by me—but this messed up my schedules and messed up my input to what materials I need. To complicate matters, the computer program they had installed was alien to my software and we could not reconcile the two. It was a mess.

What the cleaning-up team needs to do in cases where the integrity of the value chain becomes compromised, is to reestablish the linking mechanisms along the chain. Such linkages are people and/or computer programs (as in the case of "Logistics").

To do so, the team must identify the value chain and the role that the unit plays in it. Then the team puts back (or installs for the first time) those linkages that will promote and maintain an effective flow.

Multiunit Processes

Another complication for cleaning-up operations is when the reengineered process flows through several units/departments or divisions. Such a situation would have required the BPR team to work with different managers and different cultures. The damage in this case would be especially concentrated in linkages, rather than individual subprocesses. Here again the role of the cleaning-up team is to ensure that the flow is protected by linking mechanisms that connect different units and that facilitate effective flow of people, materials, information, goods, and so on.

Role Analysis

The role analysis intervention is aimed at maintaining the efficiency of processes. In essence, it is designed to sustain the benefits acquired during the reengineering effort, so that the cleaning-up operation will not (by design or inadvertently) do away with any improvements brought about by BPR.

Role analysis refers to the careful study of what the process is about, what its contributions are to the value chain, and what (if any) improvements in efficiency and performance can or should be introduced.

SUMMARY

By now you must be tired of the level of detail that I have introduced into the text of this chapter. In all, the chapter can serve as an initial handbook for implementing cleaning-up operations. Overall, these localized changes are both focused and strategic. They offer the corporation the opportunity to look more closely into its affairs, and to reinvent itself through damage control.

NOTES

1.   James March and Roger Weissinger-Baylor (eds.), *Ambiguity and Command: Organizational Perspectives on Military Decision Making* (Marshfield, MA: Pitman Publishing Company, 1986).

2.   Philip Bromley, "Planning Systems in Large Organizations: A Garbage Can Approach with Applications to Defense PPBS," in March and Weissinger-Baylor, *op cit.*, pp. 120-139.

3.   *Ibid.*, pp. 121-122.

4.   Michael Cohen, James March, and Johan Olsen, "A Garbage Can Model of Organizational Choice," *Administrative Science Quarterly*, 17(1), 1972, pp. 1-25.

5.   J. March and J. Olsen, "Garbage Can Models of Decision Making in Organizations," in March and Weissinger-Baylor, *op. cit.*, pp. 11-35.

6.   *Ibid.*, p. 17.

7.   *Ibid.*

8.   I am not advocating that the garbage-can model is the best approach to the cleaning-up program. This type of model better describes the manner more appropriate to conduct localized changes. Other models may also be useful and should not be dismissed—providing that they satisfy the conditions of restoring balance and maintaining systemic and value chain integrity.

9.   The level of specificity of these subprograms is quite high, as they include specific activities. It was not my intention in this book to offer a precise, step-by-step manual for cleaning-up and restoration of balance. Therefore the activities/actions described in the subprograms are given in a somewhat generic manner, which then may be adapted to the unique and idiosyncratic characteristics of the individual corporation.

10.   Karl Weick, "Prepare Your Organization to Fight Fires," *Harvard Business Review*, May-June 1996, pp. 143-148.

11.   Paul Strebel, "Why Do Employees Resist Change?" *Harvard Business Review*, May-June 1996, pp. 81-92.

12.   The story of the acquisition is told in Laton McCartney, "Will Computer Associates' Manners Improve?" *Upside*, June 1996, pp. 64-84; also see the story of Computer Associates' rapid growth in 1995/6 in B. DePompa and C. Gillooly, "Right Time, Right Place," *Information Week*, May 6, 1996, pp. 14-15.

13.   See an account of Fel-Pro and other such companies in J. H. Green and S. Perman, "Doing Well by Doing Good," *Time*, May 20, 1996, pp. 42-43.

14.   Rick Delbridge, "Surviving JIT: Control and Resistance in a Japanese Transplant," *Journal of Management Studies*, 37(6), 1995, pp. 803-817.

15.   L. M. Shore, K. Barksdale, and T. H. Shore, "Managerial Perceptions of Employee Commitment to the Organization," *Academy of Management Journal*, 38(6), 1995, pp. 1593-1615.

16.   R. Ashkenas, D. Ulrich, T. Jick, and S. Kerr, *The Boundaryless Organization* (San Francisco: Jossey-Bass, 1995).

17. Although in this chapter I have used a more academic style to describe the changes and change models, I have done so to get the point across and to relate these change programs as much as possible to the current academic literature.

18. See an excellent discussion of this and related topics in P. Frost, V. Mitchell, and W. Nord, *Managerial Reality: Balancing Technique, Practice and Values,* 2nd ed. (New York: HarperCollins College Publishers, 1995), in particular, pp. 107-119.

19. G. Smith and J. Laderman, "Fixing Fidelity," *Business Week*, May 6, 1996, pp. 103-114.

20. An example of such managerial actions is found in James Collins and Jerry Porras, *Built to Last: Successful Habits of Visionary Companies* (New York: Harper Business, 1994).

21. There is an excellent article on shared values and targets: Christopher Bartlett and Sumantra Ghoshoal, "Changing the Role of Top Management: Beyond Strategy to Purpose," *Harvard Business Review*, November-December 1994, pp. 79-88.

22. Some discussion of this threat to systemic integrity is given in Michael Loh, *Re-Engineering at Work* (Brookfield, VT: Gower, 1995).

23. An excellent resource in this area is Jordan Lewis, *The Connected Corporation: How Leading Companies Win Through Customer-Supplier Alliances* (New York: Free Press, 1995).

24. Some titles and names of units have been modified to assure anonymity.

25. Kenichi Ohmare, *The Mind of the Strategist: Business Planning for Competitive Advantage* (New York:Penguin Books, 1982) p. 4.

26. Christopher Bartlett and Sumanthra Ghoshal, *Managing Across Borders* (Cambridge, MA: Harvard University Press, 1989).

27. Charles F. Knight, "Emerson Electric: Consistent Profits, Consistently," *Harvard Business Review*, January-February 1992, pp. 57-70.

28. *Ibid.*, p. 59.

29. Robert H. Schaffer and Harvey A. Thomson, "Successful Change Programs Begin with Results," *Harvard Business Review*, January-February 1992, pp. 80-89.

30. Stepwise change programs are currently the staple of business books that deal with organizational and corporate changes. See, for example, Gary Kissler, *The Change Riders: Managing the Power of Change* (Reading, MA: Addison-Wesley, 1991) and William Bridges, *Managing Transitions: Making the Most of Change* (Reading, MA: Addison-Wesley, 1991).

31. Lisa Watson and Thomas Tytula, "Process Improvement: Reengineering Spacelab Mission Requirements Flow," *Engineering Management Journal*, 8(1), 1996, pp. 21-26.

14

REFREEZING AND REINVENTING

REFREEZING

There is an overall agreement in the community of change researchers that when a change program is implemented in an organization, there is a need to "refreeze" it. The concept originated with Kurt Lewin and his work on social and organizational change. The idea is built around consolidation and the institutionalization of the change, so that it will be absorbed and adopted into existing frameworks of culture and behavior.[1]

The Role of Corporate Culture

Lisa Hoecklin recently summarized the role that culture plays in the strategic advantage of corporations.[2] She emphasized the importance of institutionalized norms, beliefs, behavior, and a shared system of meaning. Culture in the corporation has been defined as the context in which people make sense of the work environment, what it is, how it operates, and what it stands for. When such understanding and perceptions are widely shared by members of the organization, the cultural environment is formed, established, and becomes functional.

There is a vast literature on corporate culture, as I have mentioned throughout this book. When changes are introduced in the organization, some elements of the cultural context are shattered. Uncertainty, chaos, and a sense of loss and alienation tend to dislodge some beliefs and perceptions long held by members of the organization. Thus, when the reengineering effort swept through the company, it caused some, perhaps much, dysfunctional waves in the cultural context.

In order to make the changes/interventions introduced by the cleaning-up team "stick" and be incorporated into the culture, they must be institutionalized, or "frozen." This means that the changes must become an internal part of the routine activities, as well as part of the belief system of the corporation. Workers should be able to trust the changes, to understand their meaning and their contribution, and to adhere to the values that these changes are designed to sustain. Examples of such values are the return to stability and the revitalization of the company through localized curative interventions to counteract the negative effects of reengineering.

How to Refreeze?

Refreezing or institutionalizing the changes are usually done in two basic ways. First, changes are translated into solid structural frameworks. For example, the establishment of a liaison position is refrozen by making it part and parcel of the organizational chart, with clear lines of authority, functional lines, and links of communication and coordination clearly drawn in the chart. Second, changes are refrozen by connecting them to existing, new, or a combination (old and new) of procedures, rules, regulations, and norms of work processes, work flow, and work behavior. Organization scientists call this phenomenon "formalization of the company."[3]

As described in Chapter 8, this process of refreezing is closely linked to the process by which the champion/leader announces restoration of stability. It is a comprehensive effort to make the changes (interventions) a permanent fixture in the company, and make sure that everybody knows it. Co-optation of middle managers is also crucial to successful refreezing. If the workforce (including managers) perceives the interventions by the cleaning-up team as merely some temporary Band-Aid to lasting problems, the power of these interventions to bring back stability will be immensely curtailed. Therefore the battle is for the hearts and minds of the workforce as well as conducting the implementation of the interventions themselves. Stability is achieved when the interventions are institutionalized *and* are viewed as permanent solutions, not fads or some meager attempt by management to "plug some holes."

I must again reemphasize the importance of institutionalizing the interventions of the cleaning-up program. In the case of BPR, the institutionalization was doomed to failure by design, because reengineering was meant to re-create the organization, thus had no previous culture or design to "hang on to" and upon which to refreeze. Since much of BPR was carried out piecemeal, refreezing suddenly became a possibility, but few companies took advantage of it—to their consternation.

REINVENTING THE CORPORATION

Lately there have been many articles and books advocating reinvention of the corporation, or showing the "right" way to do it. What is "reinventing" the company? It seems to me that the question is one of degree—namely, how much change qualifies for invention? The main problem with BPR (albeit its greatest asset, according to its promoters) was that it was a program of *total* change, *total* redesign, obliteration—then rebuilding. So, what is reinvention?[4]

What Is Reinvention?

Reinvention is *not* a concept that is detached from the realities and present conditions of the corporation. It *is* a concept rooted in what the corporation is and what it desires to be. Hence the problem we encountered with BPR. Let me explain.

Reengineering or any other radical corporate change is based on the premise that there is a strategic vision generated by the CEO and his or her staff or consultants, and articulated through the design of a mission-like future duration. What follows, then, is the redirection of the corporation and the redesign of its resources.

As I have mentioned in this book, the main criticism by the promoters of reengineering or those who implemented it was the lack of vision or inability to articulate such vision. This argument was crucial to the promoters' basic stance that BPR is a total redesign following obliteration of what existed. Hence the key role played by the vision. Simply, if you destroy what you now have, you had better have an excellent, clear, and well-charted idea *and* a road map as to where you are heading.

I also suggested that if the tenets of strategic management are followed, there would be little need for radical change such as reengineering. This means that the popularity of BPR had something to do with the failure of strategic management to deliver successful change in today's beleaguered corporations.

Nevertheless, the element that both reengineering and strategic management share is that the corporation is bound by constraints of resources, abilities, competencies, and prior history. In the case of reengineering, the idea of starting totally anew totally disregards these constraints. In the case of strategic management, the tendency is to deemphasize their importance.

A classical case is that of the role that technology plays in determining the direction and abilities of the organization. John Kenneth Galbraith dealt with this topic in the 1960s in the context of national defense policy. He explained that a nation's policies are constraints (to the extent of being dictated) by the capabilities of its military technology—for example, the range of military aircraft. In the Second World War, the Japanese military devised an attack on Midway Island because they needed its airfields to be within striking distance of the American naval base in the Hawaiian Islands. Prior to that, in the same war, Nazi Germany occupied Holland only because its airforce needed the airfields for its aircraft attacking shipping in the North Sea.[5]

In the cases of both national policy and corporate strategy, such constraints as technology and other resources, capabilities, and competencies play an enormous role in determining where the organization is heading and how successful it will be in getting there. In the case of the corporation, it is easy to say: "totally redesign yourself by obliterating what you have." It is much harder to rebuild for a new vision. It is nearly impossible to do, as so many companies have realized in the mid-1990s. What so many have done was get rid of many resources and capabilities (downsizing) *without* the second phase—namely, to rebuild, redesign, and totally revamp their organization. Henry Lucas, a student of information technologies, has suggested in his new book that the design of organizations that we have had since the 1970s will continue to exist, with some modifications brought about by information technology and the new world of opportunities it provides.[6]

In the current controversy between those who believe that the new organizational designs of the 1990s and beyond are revolutionary and *totally* different from early eras, and those who believe as Lucas does, I take the view similar to Lucas'.

Those corporations that have undergone such change programs as quality improvements (TQM), efficiency improvements (downsizing), or selective redesign (BPR), have not necessarily revolutionized the way they are designed or operated. They are better equipped and better designed to cope with current (perhaps even future) conditions. But the basic tenets of work, working, and management have not *dramatically* changed. In particular, the imperatives of the impact and the role that resources (such as technology and skills) play on constraints in any business endeavor, *and* their interrelations to structure and processes have remained relatively unchanged.[7]

So my idea of reinvention is a joint effort that combines strategic direction (vision and its articulation) and the use of existing resources, capabilities, skills, technology, and competencies to create improvements along the entire spectrum of competencies, by utilizing as many available and feasible techniques and approaches as possible.

Reinventing the corporation is a concept that I fully discuss in another book.[8] Here it is sufficient to argue that reinvention is a process by which the corporation "makes do with what it has" and "uses what it has to advance its vision, goals and objectives by systemic leaps."[9] What this means is that the "vision" or strategic direction is articulated in light of the constraints of the existing resources—then *extended* to where the corporation wishes to go and how changes in resources, structure, processes, and capabilities will take it there.

Reinvention and Organizational Transformations

Business organizations, like biological beings, constantly reinvent themselves, albeit in small steps and in the form of continuous self-improvements. Organizational researchers have identified certain configurations that seem to be correlated with performance. These configurations are usually defined as "groups of firms sharing a common profile of organizational characteristics."[10] When certain structural configurations describe stable states of the corporation, thus allowing for comparison of these common traits with performance, the result is a typology. There are "types" of organizations that share similar characteristics, such as Miles and Snow's types—defender, protector, analyzer, and reactor.[11]

Research in organizations has not confirmed that such typological differences predict differences in performance across industries, markets, technologies, or time.[12] The consensus among researchers has lately been in favor of the hypothesis that only in the longer term and in periods of stability can such relationships between configuration and performance be verified.[13] Thus when periods of structural upheavals occur (as in the case of radical corporate change), the relationship between the way the company is structured and its performance cannot be empirically verified over a large number of companies, or conversely, in a short time period.

This is the basis for the confusion that exists today in the terminology used by scholars and managers alike. There is an interchangeable use of terms, such as "reinvention," for any (even minor) transformation or change that occurs in the company. For example, Sara Curtis (1996) described the strategic action of the Canadian newspaper company Thomson as reinvention.[14] In fact, Thomson merely grouped its newspapers into regional clusters to provide more centralized services. This was far from radical corporate change.

A similar definition was given by Polly LaBarre in the description of Electronic Data Systems (EDS).[15] LaBarre confused EDS' move to create strategic business units (SBUs) for the various services offered by the company—such as systems design, general consulting, and process reengineering—as reinvention.

Reinvention is creating a *new* set of characteristics that *change* the configuration of the corporation, so that its relationship with performance (measured over a stable and longer period that follows the reinvention) also changes. The motivation behind the reinvention process is that we assume that we know what such new relationships are going to be. In other words, that if we change configuration A to configuration B, the performance of the company will improve.

But managers who have been told this for several years are entitled to ask: How much do we know, and what criteria do I use to measure such relationship?

My view, expressed throughout this book, is that as organizational transformations, reconfigurations of the corporation are key to improved performance.[16] Dennis Slevin and Jeffrey Covin have studied 112 manufacturing companies and discovered that planned strategies were more related to sales growth in companies with mechanistic (rigid) structures, and emergent strategies more successful in organic structures (more flexible).[17] Such findings are not surprising and reinforce my point that reconfiguration which leads to periods of stability allow for a better fit with performance.

Not all reconfigurations are reinventions, and not every corporate change is reconfiguration. Managers need to understand the changes in their company from a systemic viewpoint, so that all relevant factors in the structure and processes of their company that affect performance are to be considered in any program of change. When continuous changes and stepwise reconfigurations fail to improve performance, then the time has come for reinvention, namely the shaking of the corporation. Reinvention radically transforms the configuration of structure and processes to the point where the company is transformed into a different type of organization altogether.[18] Reinvention is a radical occurrence in the life of the company. It is traumatic and requires a period of calm and recuperation for its results to be effectively measured.

Cleaning-Up and Reinvention

Under the definition above, the interventions brought about by the cleaning-up operation can be used to reinvent the corporation. The move to stability is not a move to stagnation. On the contrary, it allows the corporation to *regroup*, to carefully analyze its present and future course, and to initiate actions that will take it there.[19]

Reinvention is therefore a sum total of changes in the corporation, where the outcome is actually larger than the sum of the parts. The changes are both minor *and* major. They are scrupulously tied to the constraints facing the company, its ability to read its environment, and its ability to translate these into a cohesive program of changes. Hence my insistence on the systemic nature of the cleaning-up effort. *Every* planned change in the corporation must be viewed within the framework of reinvention.

Reinventing the corporation is an *on-going process of minor and major adjustments* that are strategically generated and that are guided by a determined and visionary leadership.

In summary, I am reminded of a well-written article by Andrew Bartmess and Keith Cerny, based on work done while attending the Harvard Business School.[20] They argue for a network of capabilities and say, for example, that if customers buy a product because it is the least expensive, the value the customers receive can be traced to efficient production, yet when a product is no longer marketable (because of obsolescence or replacement by another more attractive product), the efficient production line has little transferrable value to the corporation.

This is the key to what reinventing the corporation is meant to be and how the cleaning-up changes can be a part of it. It is the creation and the maintenance of interventions, all in light of an overall strategy that takes into account the current as well as the potential (albeit risky) assessment of what the value in the marketplace is likely to be ahead in the time horizon. There are no easy nor sudden ways to create a new, competitive, and successful corporation. TQM has not done it. BPR has not done it either. It is time to pause, regroup, regain stability, and continue to reinvent through what exists and what can be obtained, mastered, and achieved.

NOTES

1.   See, for example, John Kotter, "Leading Change: Why Transformation Efforts Fail," *Harvard Business Review*, March-April 1995, pp. 59-67.
2.   Lisa Hoecklin, *Managing Cultural Differences* (Reading, MA: Addison Wesley, 1995).
3.   See, for example, Paul Nystrom and William Starbuck, *Prescriptive Models of Organizations* (New York: North-Holland Publishing Co., 1977).
4.   Some illustrative publications are David Hurst, *Crisis and Renewal: Managing the Challenge of Organizational Change* (Boston: Harvard Business School Press, 1995); and Dwight Gertz and Joao Baptista, *Grow to be Great: Breaking the Downsizing Cycle* (New York: The Free Press, 1995).
5.   A more recent book that deals with this topic is: Roy Harmon, *Reinventing the Business: Preparing Today's Enterprise for Tomorrow's Technology* (New York: The Free Press, 1996).
6.   Henry Lucas, *The T-Form Organization: Using Technology to Design Organizations for the 21st Century* (San Francisco: Jossey-Bass 1996).
7.   There is a discussion of the relation between strategy and capabilities in Robert Hayes, G. Pisano, and D. Upton, *Strategic Operations: Competing Through Capabilities* (New York: The Free Press, 1996). The authors advocate a broader strategic approach, rather than imitating some other successful companies.
8.   Eliezer Geisler, "Balancing the Innovative Corporation: The Ultimate Recipe for Successful Corporate Management of the 21st Century," (manuscript in preparation).

9.   This is similar in some respect to the concept described in Adrian Slywotzky, *Value Migration: How to Think Several Moves Ahead of the Competition* (Boston: Harvard Business School Press, 1995).

10.   David Ketchen *et al.*, "Organizational Configurations and Performance: A Meta Analysis," *Academy of Management Journal*, 40(1), 1997, p. 224.

11.   Raymond Miles and C. Snow, *Organizational Strategy, Structure, and Process* (New York: McGraw Hill, 1978).

12.   D. Ketchen and C. Shook, "The Application of Cluster Analysis in Strategic Management Research: An Analysis and Critique," *Strategic Management Journal*, 17(2), 1996, pp. 441-458.

13.   S. Curtis, "Reinventing Thomson: Regional Clusters are the Key to a Shrinking Player's New Strategy," *Marketing*, 101(2), 1996, p. 13.

14.   See, for example, V. Choudhoury, "Stragegic Choices in the Development of Interorganizational Information Systems," *Information Systems Research*, 8(1), 1997, pp. 1-24. Also see R. Miles and C. Snow, "Organizations: New Concepts for New Forms," *California Management Review*, 78(3), 1986, pp. 62-73.

15.   Polly LaBarre, "Information Junction," *IW: The Management Magazine*, 245(2), 1996, pp. 26-7.

16.   See, for example, Norman Augustine, "Reshaping an Industry: Lockheed-Martin's Survival Story," *Harvard Business Review*, 75(3), 1997, pp. 69-82.

17.   Dennis Slevin and J. Covin, "Strategy Formation Patterns, Performance, and the Significance of Context," *Journal of Management*, 23(2), 1997, pp. 187-209.

18.   Some examples of such radical reconfigurations are Alan Pillington, *Transforming Moves: Renewal Against the Odds, 1981-1994* (Bristol, England: Bristol Academic Press, 1996); also John O'Looney, *Redesigning the Work of Human Services* (Westport, CT: Quorum Books, 1996).

19.   Two interesting books offer some challenging reading: John Sitonis and Beverly Golding, *Corporation on a Tightrope: Balancing Leadership, Governance, and Technology in an Age of Complexity* (New York: Oxford University Press, 1995); and William Rouse, *Start Where You Are* (San Francisco: Jossey-Bass, 1996). This second book discusses the preparatory effort before implementing a strategic approach.

20.   Andrew Bartmess and Keith Cerny, "Building Competitive Advantage through a Global Network of Capabilities," *California Management Review*, 35(2), 1993, pp. 21-36.

15

WHERE WE STAND

In the several months since I began to write this book, there have been some interesting developments. We have witnessed some exciting reversals of opinions on the topics of downsizing, reengineering, and radical restructuring of American corporations. In this chapter I will describe some of these developments and the contributions that this book brings to the current state of affairs, as well as to the understanding and better management of future trends.

Toward the end of his challenging book on work and organizations, the prolific British writer Charles Handy concluded: "Organizations are restructuring and rebalancing to stay alive. It is happening, let us be clear, out of self-interest and a survival instinct, not because there is some grand vision for society or even some new theory of management that has caught the imagination. We are stumbling backward into the future."[1] How befitting an epitaph to the decline of BPR and its manifestations in the form of downsizing.

Recently, there has begun a trend of management scholars who bemoan the negatives from reengineering and downsizing. Even those who initiated the movement and those who fiercely defended it are backing down. Here are some examples.

SOME RECENT DEVELOPMENTS

It was our fault, and our very great fault—
    and now we must turn it to use.
We have forty million reasons for failure,
    but not a single excuse,
So the more we work and the less we talk
The better results we shall get.
We have had an imperial lesson; it may
    mold us an Empire yet!
              Rudyard Kipling (1865-1936)
              "The Lesson"

In Kipling's words: We have many reasons for the failure of BPR, but not a single excuse. In his *mea culpa* treatise, Michael Hammer recently acknowledged: "I have now come to realize that I was wrong, that the radical character of reengineering, however important, and exciting, is not its most significant aspect. The key word in the definition of reengineering is 'process:' a complete end-to-end set of activities that together create value for a customer.[2] However, the lesson that Hammer has supposedly learned is only partially agreeable to closer examination. In the same few pages of the foreword to his book, Hammer writes: "For a world of process-centered organizations everything must be rethought: the kinds of work that people do, the jobs they hold, the skills they need. . . . Process-centered organizations demand the complete reinvention of the systems and disciplines of management." Here again is the reinvention of the corporation with a slight shift to a process-oriented focus.

Hammer has been joined by other recent critics of reengineering and downsizing. Warren Bennis, who has written widely on the topic of leadership, commented that restructuring and reengineering have "psychological malaise" which seems to counteract the positive contributions of the empowerment of managers.[3]

Several writers have expressed similar concerns in a series of articles in the business press. Most vocal are the following examples. Alex Markels and Matt Murray wrote in *The Wall Street Journal* that perhaps downsizing should be called dumbsizing.[4] They contend that companies continue to disregard warnings about the potential harmful effects of radical downsizing. Fred Bleakley emphasized Stephen Roach's reversal of opinion that he now believes it is "highly debatable" whether downsizing will indeed lead to increased productivity and other such benefits Roach had strongly advocated in the past.[5]

Down with Downsizing

The very few criticisms of downsizing are now becoming more of a generous sprinkle of reversals of opinion and some new ideas. Various industries have displayed their managers' displeasure. A growing number of restaurant managers have begun to "unsize," particularly in the ranks of middle managers.[6] In such disparate businesses as the music industry, telecommunications, consumer products, and health care, the debate continues on the damage from reengineering and downsizing.[7]

In the case of health care organizations, a study of 797 rural hospitals in the United States failed to show a relationship between downsizing and financial performance (measured by profitability and liquidity).[8] An excellent case study of a single hospital conducted by Seth Allcorn *et al.* has painfully documented the price people have paid for reengineering.[9] Similar voices are heard in other industries as well.[10]

Overall, the current literature reflects the shift from "why doesn't reengineering work?" to "what are the negative outcomes from reengineering?" Of all the nuances and components of BPR, *downsizing* seems to occupy a place of distinction among the dishonored and most criticized. The battle cry is "down with downsizing." Yet solutions are still very scarce, and those that are offered in the latest publications seem uninspiring and vague.

There are at least two problems with this trend to disparage downsizing. The first is in confusing the terms "reengineering" and "downsizing." Allcorn *et al.* made a clear distinction between the terms in their book on hospital downsizing. They concluded:

Restructuring and BPR are often discussed as part of downsizing, as is TQM, however, although they may all be employed concurrently or sequentially, they are each different from the others. Downsizing is an immediate response to declining profits by cutting labor costs, however, there is a growing recognition that a downsized organization also needs to reconsider its fundamental ways of doing business and thus enters the need for restructuring and reengineering (p. 5).

Precisely herein lies the problem. In practice, many managers who downsized believed they had reengineered. Conversely, when BPR was somewhat implemented and backfired in terms of lateral damage, many managers then blamed downsizing for the ills of their transformed organization.

The second problem is the fact that the emphasis on downsizing diverts attention from the damage associated with BPR in its many forms. In some respects we are now chasing the wrong culprit. As I explained in chapters four and six, BPR has yielded a plethora of consequences, and only a few of those are related directly to personnel cuts.

The paradoxical reality of the debate on downsizing and reengineering is emphasized in this book. In the new aphorisms of Hammer and others regarding the organization of the future, and their apostasy of reengineering—none of the aforementioned terms is inherently bad or invalid. Downsizing is not necessarily a reason for organizational trauma nor is it inherently forbidden. Restructuring is not necessarily inadvisable nor a source of lasting problems. As I have outlined in this book, these are all part of organizational change—in concept and in process. Organizations change, organically or by design. The manager's dilemma is how to exercise enough control over organizational change to ascertain its long-term success for the company's strategic survival.

Reinvention is NOT Reengineering

Charles Handy, the author of *The Age of Paradox*, has recently published a confused yet interesting collection of 35 essays.[11] In one essay entitled "What It Takes to Make a Manager," Handy wrote: "we shall increasingly see a distinction between 'business studies,' being the stock of common understanding, and 'management learning,' the art of helping individuals and organizations to shape their own futures and to make the most of their assets" (p. 193).

Handy's distinction parallels my contention that reinventing a corporation is a more complex and rare occurrence than reengineering or other "garden-variety" corporate change and transformation programs. Reinventing the corporation involves a major shifting of the business, in a combination of technology and structure. In other words, reinvented corporations change the way they do business, their dominant technology, as well as their structural design. Such reinventing phenomena drastically affect not only employees (who may be "downsized" due to the changing aspects of the business), but almost all the other stakeholders, particularly customers and suppliers.

Reinvented corporations are a rare phenomenon. Donald Frey reinvented Bell & Howell by transforming it from a manufacturing to an information company. Another example is Apple Computers. who announced in late December 1996 that upon its acquisition of Next Software Inc., it will name Steven Jobs to a top management position. Thus, Apple will be transformed by replacing its operating system with NeXt Graphics to challenge Microsoft's domination of the personal computers' world market. This reinvention affects Apple's customers (owners of the Macintosh computers) and its suppliers (such as Motorola, maker of its computer chips). In addition, in late 1996 Apple announced layoffs of almost 1,500 employees.

I bring this topic to further discussion at the closing of this book so as to revisit one of the problems in BPR as well as other recent change phenomena. American managers, academics, and consultants are mired in a cacophony of terms, most lacking satisfactory reasoning and conceptual designs. Michael Hammer is correct in pointing out that part of the problem with BPR was the misnomer of the term. Yet his scheme for the process-centered organization again leaves much to be desired in clearly defining the key operational terms, and in establishing the conceptual boundaries of the phenomenon.[12]

A Matter of Degree

A possible reason for the problems with definition and conceptual boundaries of key terms in corporate change phenomena may be the degree of change desired by the given program, and that which is achieved.

Recent developments and the recognition that managers are more than ever confused about what reengineering and other change programs mean lend credence to the view that terms represent different degrees of change. Although each change program differs from the other in several key aspects, all essentially describe corporate and organizational changes—but with different degrees of derived results as well as the means to accomplish them.

Regardless of the program currently in vogue (such as process-centered), all such programs boil down to corporate change efforts. Herein lies the power of this book.

STRENGTHS OF THIS BOOK

Notwithstanding the about-face of former advocates of BPR and their apologies, the damage from reengineering has occurred and is bound to haunt corporations worldwide.[13]

This book fulfills a triple function, which is the basis of its strengths and durability as a reference text for years to come. First, this book offers a doable way to repair the damage from reengineering (or any other radical corporate change), and to restore stability to the corporation. Second, this book offers a doable and practical process to assess and rebuild transformations. For example, organizations in the health care industry are currently undergoing massive restructuring, mergers, and consolidations.[14]

These trends are widespread and affect almost all the participants in the industry—from the stand-alone hospital to the corporate health care giants and healthcare maintenance organizations (HMOs). This book shows the way to recovering and regained stability.

The third function this book performs—and is perhaps its most powerful strength—is in providing the seminal approach to recovery from radical corporate change. Corporations will continue to be transformed as conditions so require. Cleaning-up after reengineering does not end with the discredited concept of BPR. On the contrary, the value of cleaning-up starts to grow in the aftermath, and is at its highest for the change programs that will follow in the future. This book offers a road map, a detailed and doable blueprint for repairing damage, bringing back stability, and healing the changed organization.

Clearly, the power and the value of this book will continue and grow as change programs are expected by corporations. Corporate change is way of life in organizations, and so is this book—now and in years to come.

NOTES

1. Charles Handy, *Gods of Management: The Changing Work of Organizations* (New York: Oxford University Press, 1995), p. 210.

2. Michael Hammer, *Beyond Reengineering: How the Process-Centered Organization is Changing Our Work and Our Lives* (New York: Harper-Business, 1996), p. xii, xiii.

3. Richard Hodgett, "A Conversation with Warner Bennis on Leadership in the Midst of Downsizing," *Organizational Dynamics*, 25(3), 1996, pp. 72-78.

4. Alex Markels and Matt, Murray, "Call It Dumbsizing: Why Some Companies Regret Cost-Cutting," *Wall Street Journal*, May 14, 1996, pp. A1.

5. Fred Bleakley, "Economist Finds Fleet Street Meaner than Wall Street," *The Wall Street Journal*, May 20, 1996, p. B6D. Bleakley also told the story that a journalist with the British Broadcasting Corporation insisted on inquiring whether Roach wished to apologize for all the hardship his views on reengineering and downsizing had brought upon those workers hurt by corporate cuts.

6. Steve Brooks, "Downsizing's Comeuppance (Backlash) to Downsizing," *Restaurant Business*, 95(2), 1996, pp. 80-81.

7. See Frank Calamita, "Reflections on the Downsizing Debate," *HR Focus*, 73(3), 1996, pp. 9-10; also see Brooke Tunstall, "The Downsizing of AT&T: Is There a Better Way?" *Telecommunications*, 30(2), 1996, pp. 40-46; Stephen Mick and Christopher Wise, "Downsizing and Financial Performance in Rural Hospitals," *Health Care Management Review*, 21(2), 1996, pp. 16-25; and J. Stanton, "Downsizing Comes Back to Haunt a Brand," *Brandweek*, 37(3), 1996, p. 40.

8. Mick and Wise, *op. cit.*

9. Seth Allcorn, H. Baum, M. Diamond, and H. Stein, *The Human Cost of a Management Failure: Organizational Downsizing at General Hospital* (Westport, CT: Quorum Books, 1996).

10. See, for example, Gus Welty, "Re-engineering May Need Rethinking," *Railway Age*, 197(4), 1996, p. 12; also see A. Halachmi, "Business Process Reengineering in the Public

Sector: Trying to Get Another Frog to Fly?" *National Productivity Review*, 15, Summer 1996, pp. 9-18; and Mark Klein, "The Most Fatal Reengineering Mistakes," *Information Strategy: The Executive Journal*, 10(4), 1994, pp. 21-28.

11.   Charles Handy, *Beyond Uncertainty: The Changing World of Organizations* (Boston: Harvard Business School Press, 1996).

12.   Hammer, *Beyond Reengineering, op cit.*

13.   See, for example, David Gordon, *Fast and Mean: The Corporate Squeeze of Working Americans and the Myth of Managerial Downsizing* (New York: Martin Kessler Books, 1996); and Alan Downs, *Corporate Executions: The Ugly Truth About Layoffs—How Corporate Greed is Shattering Lives, Companies, and Communities* (New York: Amacom, 1995).

14.   See, for example, S. Shortell, R. Gillies, D. Anderson, K. Erickson, and J. Mitchell, *Remaking Health Care in America: Building Organized Delivery Systems* (San Francisco: Jossey-Bass, 1996) and Walter Zelman, *The Changing Health Care Marketplace* (San Francisco: Jossey-Bass, 1996).

16

WHAT THE FUTURE HOLDS

In a reflective piece in the *Chicago Tribune*, senior writer R. C. Longworth argued that the economic hardships of U.S. industrial transformation have become "a crisis of spirit."[1] He quotes some statistics that I have used in this book about workers who were downsized and the ripple effect of their woes in the remainder of the economy.

There is clearly a new, or perhaps more precisely a modified, structure that businesses are acquiring, and certainly modified practices they have adopted. Disregarding for a moment the sociological and political frameworks for analysis (as valid as they may be), the reality in the workforce is that the 1990s have produced a plethora of radical (to some even earthshaking) developments. These resulted in layoffs, reduced economic benefits, and a feeling shared by millions of uncertainty and fear of future events. These sentiments (as Longworth reported) can even be found among the highly trained "new technological aristocracy," who supposedly have nothing to fear and are the leading marching band of the new industrial reality.

Reengineering has contributed to these sentiments. Moreover, the general belief that it failed to fulfill its promises reinforces the need to clean up and to restore stability and balance in corporate America.

The future holds a mix of a high-speed race peppered by efforts to stabilize and to provide balance and reason. It is impossible to stop the contributions that technological advances and improvements in management philosophy and skills have added to our knowledge pool. The mere weight of inertia will propel corporations forward, fueled by movements that are generated by technological innovations and our managerial skills. These propellants are too numerous and compact to be overlooked or ignored. Like a Roman legion or a heavy truck they roll down the way almost unstoppable.[2]

Significant course adjustments and the maintenance of a sense of balance are essential to a company's success in this environment. We cannot turn the clock back, but we can adjust our direction.

Business corporations need a balanced approach within such compelling progress and heightened competition. The interplay between innovation and stability are the key measures of future success. Those who will be able to best achieve such a balancing act will survive.

NOTES

1.   R. C. Longworth, "The Dream, in Pieces," *Chicago Tribune Magazine*, April 28, 1996, Section 10, pp. 15-19.

2.   See, for example, G. Brutton, J. Key Keels, and C. Shook, "Downsizing the Firm: Answering the Strategic Questions," *Academy of Management Executive*, 10(2), 1996, pp. 38-45. In this article the authors make a point similar to what I have argued in Chapter 15. They say: "Done strategically, even modest cuts have positive impact." They also contended: "We do not advocate downsizing as a universally good practice" (p. 44).

EPILOGUE

Reengineering was introduced in the early 1990s with a promise of a radical transformation of American business. In this book I have shown that this promise was impossible to keep. By using BPR's very own rationale and key assumptions, this book unveiled the infeasibility of the reengineering approach—as devised by its promoters.

Contrary to criticism from BPR's creators and supporters, senior managers of American corporations do *not* lack vision nor the will to adopt radical change programs, which they have done with much hope and energy since the early 1980s. What we do have today is a crisis of overexposure to change programs and unfulfilled promises. This is a crisis of management that has overflowed to the general population with feelings of uncertainty and uneasiness regarding the future.

This book has proposed a program to clean up the damages from reengineering. Moreover, it also provides senior mangers with an opportunity to reinvent their corporations, as they build upon the cleaning-up change activities and focused interventions.

This book promotes a move toward balance and stability, as prerequisites to any further redirection of the company. Instead of a one-time radical transformation, this book advocates a rolling, continuous reinvention and redirection.

Today American corporations are more efficient and more adaptable to fluctuations in their environment. But are they better positioned in the global business arena? Clearly, since the 1970s, these corporations and their management have learned some valuable lessons. One lesson that this book has emphasized is that the changing business environment of the 1980s does not necessarily obligate the corporation to engage in total redesign and overhauling—as proposed by reengineering. This is tacit overkill, overreaction, and is bound to fail.

Balance, innovativeness, and strategic application of resources and competencies are at the heart of the successful corporations as we rapidly approach the next century. Cleaning-up after reengineering will open the door to a more balanced approach, and to a more applied as well as *realistic* reinvention of the corporation. With faith in the future and in the capabilities of corporate America, senior managers can bring their organizations back to stability and to a rolling reinvention following their activities in cleaning-up after reengineering.

About the Author

ELIEZER GEISLER is Professor of Management in the College of Business and Economics, University of Wisconsin-Whitewater. A past chair of the College of Innovation Management and Entrepreneurship of INFORMS, Dr. Geisler is associate editor of the *IEEE Transactions on Engineering Management* and was the editor of the Special Issues Series on managing technology in health care for the *International Journal of Technology Management*. He is founder and editor of the forthcoming *Journal of Management of Medical Technology*. Dr. Geisler is author of two previous books and more than 60 articles in academic journals.